eResumes

eResumes

Everything You Need to Know About Using Electronic Resumes to Tap into Today's Job Market

Susan Britton Whitcomb
Pat Kendall

McGraw-Hill

New York • Chicago • San Francisco • Lisbon • London
Madrid • Mexico City • Milan • New Delhi • San Juan
Seoul • Singapore • Sydney • Toronto

McGraw-Hill

*A Division of The **McGraw·Hill** Companies*

1 2 3 4 5 6 7 8 9 0   QPD/QPD 0 9 8 7 6 5 4 3 2 1

ISBN 0-07-136399-8

Printed and bound by Quebecor/Dubuque.

McGraw-Hill books are available at special quantity discounts to use as premiums and sales promotions, or for use in corporate training programs. For more information, please write to the Director of Special Sales, Professional Publishing, McGraw-Hill, Two Penn Plaza, New York, NY 10121-2298. Or contact your local bookstore.

 This book is printed on recycled, acid-free paper containing a minimum of 50% recycled, de-inked fiber.

Dedication

In honor of our families ... our greatest treasure

Contents

Preface

Whether it's a pink slip, golden opportunity, or simply greener pastures that put you into job-search mode, getting your resume in order will probably be at the top of your "to-do" list. Resumes always have been—and will continue to be—the requisite passport to new employment. Nearly 60 million Americans work in business or professional jobs for which they almost certainly had to submit a resume to be hired. And those who changed jobs in the past few years were likely faced with a new compulsory requirement—the submission of resumes in an electronic format. To the technically inclined, this was a walk in the park. For many others, it was a painful journey. We know, because we've talked with hundreds of you who have expressed frustration over having to learn the new rules and technology associated with the online job-search game.

Why We Wrote This Book

As authors of prior books on resumes and online job search, we know that resources for electronic resumes are, at best, lacking. Online information is available, but it barely skims the surface and typically ends with the advice: "Buy a book." However, the few books about electronic resumes that do exist often contain erroneous information or focus only on one type of electronic format, such as the ASCII resume. As this book goes to press, there is no other resource that contains all of the information contained here, including

- *A comprehensive presentation of more than a half dozen types of eResumes*

- *An important review of resume writing strategies for effective content and keywords*

- *Simple steps with helpful visual aids to get your resume "email ready"*

- *Insider tips for posting your resume to sites like Monster.com*

- *A candid analysis of fee-based and free Web resume builders, career Web site posting opportunities, and resume distribution services*

- *The "Top 10" list of rules for designing Web resumes, common faux pas, and other pitfalls*

- *Easy-to-follow how-to's for creating a resume Web page (without having to learn HTML)*

- *Some of the best-looking design templates seen anywhere for Web page resumes and portfolios (several of which can be downloaded at our www.eResumeIQ.com site)*

How This Book Is Organized

The first half of *eResumes: How to Write, Design & Deliver Your Resume Online* focuses on electronic resumes that can be emailed to employers or pasted into career Web sites. The second half of the book addresses electronic resumes in their incarnation as Web pages or multipage Web sites.

Chapter 1 touches briefly on the trends in Internet recruiting and why eResumes have become so popular. We explain who can benefit from an eResume and give examples of how and when to use one. The end of the chapter has helpful at-a-glance tables that outline seven different types of eResumes—ASCII, formatted, PDF, posted, RTF, Web resume, and ePortfolio. In each table, you'll find that we clarify potentially confusing terminology, as well as outline the pros and cons of each type. Samples are included for all seven genres.

Chapter 2 is a primer in resume development. You'll be introduced to the ROI strategy for eResume writing—ROI stands for *Readable, Other-focused,* and *Impact-oriented,* which will give you a valuable template for laying out and penning an impressive resume. We'll touch on the importance of thinking like an advertising copywriter and not a biographer when it comes to writing about yourself. And, of course, keywords—the linchpin of an eResume—will be covered. You'll learn the four types of keyword categories, the best places to find keywords, how to determine the keywords for your industry, and how to take keywords a step further than your competition. The chapter ends with keyworded resume examples for four different career professionals (new graduate, mid-career, transitioner, and executive).

Chapter 3 explains ASCII (American Standard Code for Information Interchange) in laymen's terms, then walks you through the steps for a glitch-proof conversion from your formatted MS Word resume to a text-only ASCII resume. We explain which file format works best for emailing resumes or pasting resumes at Web sites (and why using the same file format for both can create problems). Our "10 Tips for ASCII Cleanup" will ensure that you deliver one of the best-looking resumes a recruiter or employer will see. Screen captures are included to help you through the technical steps, and before-and-after examples will give you a target for your end product.

Chapter 4 takes you through the process of pasting your resume into eforms or resume builders, which are common at career Web sites. We've also included a list of the "Top Five Faux Pas" job seekers make when using resume builders, as listed by Monster.com's current resume expert. You'll get a glimpse of some proprietary applicant-tracking software used by recruiters, which will help you understand what happens to your posted resume *after* you click "submit." With respect to emailing resumes, we'll cover the differences in popular email programs and how to format your resume for the lowest common denominator (doing so will make it readable by the greatest number of people). Our "Tips for Writing Tantalizing Titles" will give you insight into recruiters' preferences and pet peeves with respect to the "subject line" on emails.

Chapter 5 discusses the controversial practice of sending your resume as an attachment. We'll look at the drawbacks and benefits, and reveal the most important criteria for sending an attachment. Our tips will help ensure that you use the right file format, name your resume attachment correctly, and send a virus-free file. eLetters are discussed and samples are provided.

Turning to Chapter 6, you'll explore the new gold standard in resumes—Web resumes and portfolios. The six unique advantages to these Web-based models are explained, followed by descriptions of how every breed of "career activist" (new grad to exec, artist to techie, full-time employee to freelancer) can use these tools. Examples of Web resumes for multiple professions help bring to life the effectiveness of these tools.

Job seekers have a range of options available to them when it comes to creating a Web-based resume. In Chapter 7, we'll discuss the options of using a professional Web page designer, doing it yourself, or using an online "click-and-build" service (including a comparison of some of the more popular fee-based and free services on the Web).

In Chapter 8, we pinpoint the most common design blunders in Web resumes, along with the design guidelines for fashioning your own online resume. Our helpful Web resume effectiveness checklist will ensure that you've played by the "new medium" rules for typography, color, style, functionality, hyperlinks, copy, and professionalism.

Chapter 9 unravels the technical aspects of Web resume creation. You'll learn about the components of a Web page in simple, understandable terms and, near the end of this chapter, have a chance to create your own resume using Netscape Composer (a free download from netscape.com). For those who want to soup up their resume with flash animation, streaming video, or other high-tech wizardry, you'll find additional information in sidebars and resources at the close of the chapter.

Chapter 10 explains delivery options (and privacy precautions) you can take to promote your eResume. We have reviewed the resume posting options at top career sites, including the recommended format to submit resumes and a rating of the quality of resume advice. For posting options beyond major career sites, we provide tips on how to find niche sites, regional sites, and company sites (along with a list of some of our favorite niche and regional sites). We'll also fill you in on the difficult task of finding email addresses on the Net. Resume distribution services are also reviewed and recommended. For those with a Web resume or portfolio, you'll learn about registering with search engines, including keywording your meta tags, page title, filename, and content.

And, finally, at the end of the book is a gallery of Web resume and portfolio examples that will no doubt give inspiration to your writing and creativity. Whether you consider yourself to be an active or confidential job seeker, high-tech or low-tech, experienced or just starting out, we're confident there is valuable information here that will help you negotiate the maze of Internet job searching and advance your career. Let's get started!

Acknowledgments

This book is based on the collective insights and experiences of a number of industry experts who were generous in sharing their time and knowledge. At the forefront of our thank-you list is our advisor: Kevin Skarritt, COO and Designer, AcornCreative.com. Kevin is the creative genius behind some stunning Web sites, and his input on resume Web site design, functionality, and technical issues was vital to the development and finalization of several chapters.

The vastness of the World Wide Web can make researching an Internet-based subject daunting. As Mark Demaree (one of our industry experts) put it, "Going online is like taking a drink from a fire hose." The following experts helped us absorb a massive amount of information on technology and industry trends:

Brian Alden, CEO, Resumezapper.com

Dale Carpenter, Regional Research Director, Manchester Inc.

Gerry Crispin, Author and Cofounder, careerXroads.com

Mark Demaree, Vice President, Top Echelon Network, Inc.

Neil Fox, CIO, BrilliantPeople.com/Management Recruiters International

Wayne Gonyea, President, ResumeXPRESS.com

Mark Graeber, National Account Manager, Management Recruiters International

Brent Harris, President, Networker Career Services/CareerCatalyst.com

Bret Hollander, President, NetRecruiter.net

Kim Isaacs, Monster.com Resume Expert and President of ResumePower.com

Peter Newfield, Managing Partner, YourMissingLink.com

Dave Opton, President, ExecuNet.com

Karen Osofsky, Chief Marketing Officer, TiburonGroup.com

John Sumser, President, Interbiznet.com

Dianna Thompson, President, ResumeBlaster.com

Bill Vick, CEO, Recruiters Online Network

Dr. Wendell Williams, Managing Director,
ScientificSelection.com

We wish to acknowledge Scott Amerman, Editing Supervisor, Clare Stanley, Production Manager, and the rest of the editorial and production team at McGraw-Hill for adding their special touch to our copy and artwork. Special thanks are owed to Yedida Soloff, Associate Editor at McGraw-Hill, who went to bat for us as this book evolved from its original concept.

On a personal note, Pat would like to acknowledge her assistant, Nathan Newman, whose organizational talents, sense of humor, and willingness to assume the role of guinea pig made all the difference.

Part 1

A Primer on eResumes and eMail Delivery

Chapter 1
The Many Faces of an eResume

Are you an Internet veteran or an Internet newbie? You may categorize yourself as a novice, just beginning to use the World Wide Web. Or you may describe yourself as a seasoned Internet user with a firm grasp of HTML, FTP, ASCII, JavaScript, or a popular Web page development program such as FrontPage or Dreamweaver. Some of you are excited about the new possibilities that the online world offers, while others are being dragged "kicking and screaming" into Cyberspace. Whether or not you understand the Web's alphabet-soup acronyms, you are probably resigned to the fact that this Internet phenomenon is not going to go away . . . and now is the time to gain some mastery of the World Wide Web and the electronic job market.

As veterans of the online job-search industry, we continually encounter job seekers—from Web experts to Web novices, from college grads to dot-com executives—who have questions about the do's and don'ts of developing and using eResumes. For example, take a look at these inquiries, which are typical of those we get at our collective Web sites:

- *How do I choose the right electronic format? (Chapter 1)*

- *How do I email my resume to an employer so it doesn't end up looking like it went through a meat grinder? (Chapter 4)*

- *What's the difference between text only and text with line breaks? (Chapter 3)*

- *Why can't I just send an attachment? (Chapter 5)*

- *Do those resume blasting services really work? (Chapter 10)*

- *What's the difference between a Web resume and a Web portfolio? (Chapter 6)*

- *Should I include a photograph on a Web resume? (Chapter 9)*

- *I used a really cool font for my Web resume, but it isn't showing up right on other computers. Does it matter what font I use? (Chapter 8)*

- *Where do I put keywords, and which keywords should I use? (Chapter 2)*

- *I used one of those free services for my Web resume. Is there some way I can remove the advertising? (Chapter 7)*

- *Do I have to know HTML to create a Web resume? (Chapter 9)*

- *I want to use the Internet for my job search, but I'm concerned about privacy. What should I do? (Chapter 10)*

This book, *eResumes: How to Write, Design & Deliver Your Resume Online*, addresses the above issues and more in detail. But first, let's get a firmer handle on what, exactly, an eResume is.

What Is an eResume?

The term is used broadly for a number of resume e-incarnations, including the following:

- **Text resume.** *In its simplest form, an eResume is an unformatted, text-only version of your traditional resume that can be pasted into the body of an email message. This basic tool allows you to get your credentials into the hands of potential employers, recruiters, and networking contacts in an instant. Though not terribly eye-appealing, its frugal format has several redeemable qualities—it is easily transportable, compatible with all systems, and guaranteed to be free of computer viruses as long as it is pasted into the email message and not sent as an attachment.*

- **Web resume.** *In its next stage, an eResume is a traditional resume turned into a Web page. Web resumes incorporate some (or all) of these elements: design and color to enhance your professional image, an email link to give employers easy access to communicate with you, a downloadable text-only version (or other format) to satisfy possible resume database requirements, and hyperlinks to samples of your work or other documents that support your candidacy. In this form, eResumes are the answer to "ugly" text resumes, and more—they're attractive, compatible with virtually every computer system, virus-free, accessible 24 hours a day, and easily modified. As an added bonus, you'll impress potential employers with your technical IQ.*

- **Web portfolio.** *In its most advanced form, the eResume evolves into an online portfolio—a full-fledged Web site with an internal navigation system and a consistent design theme. Content is comprehensive and organized into clickable, bite-sized pieces that can include a resume, reference letters, a philosophy statement, representative projects, work samples, technology skills, or other special qualifications. Audio and* *video files can be used to give potential employers a sample of your verbal or presentation skills, as well as a preview of how you might answer a difficult interview question. Like Web resumes, Web-based portfolios are flexible with respect to the visibility factor. In other words, they can be promoted aggressively through URL references and search engine registration (enabling e-recruiters to find you via Boolean queries) or they can be posted in secure databases or hosted privately, giving you control over who can access your credentials.*

It's clear that there are many varieties of eResumes. Regardless of format or features, however, they certainly share one common characteristic: All resumes (e or otherwise) are marketing pieces.

Your resume is part advertising, part business communication. It must sell the benefit, or return on investment (ROI), that employers will receive by hiring you. It must communicate hard skills and soft skills—experience and "fit." Not only is your resume the marketing piece that makes that all-important first impression on employers, but in the e-recruiting world it can also have a long-lasting impact as employers store (for extended time periods), keyword search, and use complex algorithms to match databased resumes to job openings.

Who Needs an eResume?

It's nearly impossible to conduct a job search these days without some type of eResume—whether plain-text, formatted, or Web-based. In fact, it's a safe assertion that the only job seekers who won't need an eResume are those who want to work for an employer that does *not* own a computer.

Can you name five potential employers that don't own computers? If you can, you don't need this book, but you'll miss out on great advice about writing killer keyword content—applicable to both online and offline resumes—resume samples for a number of professions, designs that will give you inspiration for your resume, and insider tips from veteran job-search experts!

The reality is this: Virtually all employers have computers and most have Internet access. Gerry Crispin and Mark Mehler (CareerXRoads.com)—who annually conduct more than 100 e-recruiting workshops for major corporations such as AT&T, Deloitte & Touche, GE, and General Mills—estimate that 80 percent of Fortune 500 companies post jobs on their own Web sites. Following suit are perhaps a million more companies, both small and large, that have expanded their Web sites to include employment opportunities and recruiting centers. Many of these sites are fitted with sophisticated eforms that collect applicant biographical data, then email job announcements to viable candidates via "push" technology.

Interbiznet.com's *2001 Electronic Recruiting Index* offers more statistical incentives to take your search online. John Sumser, president of Interbiznet, reports "We estimate that there are about 100,000,000 resumes and credentials documents pocketed around the Web. Factoring for the certain duplication of some documents, there are likely more than 20,000,000 unique resumes on the open World Wide Web." This means that recruiters can forgo the costly fees charged by career portals and hunt down resumes on the Web by tapping into virtual communities or by using high-powered search engines, such as the popular AltaVista.com.

And speaking of career portals, major players such as Monster.com and Headhunter.net entice millions of job seekers with volumes of free career advice. These sites captured much of the $500 million that recruiters spent last year to attract online job seekers. Millions of job postings—representing virtually every profession imaginable—can be found on the Web, from accounting clerks to auto mechanics, nurses to nannies, and Zydeco musicians to zoologists. (Not surprisingly, the correct answer to this page's eResumeIQ Quiz is "All of the above." All of these positions were available on Flip-Dog.com's Web site as this book went to press.)

When Do You Use an eResume?

Given the Internet-driven recruiting trends, you'll need an eResume to paste into online forms, submit to resume databases, post at career portals, or host in a private or public Web site. Even if you're keeping

---

eResumeIQ Quiz

Which of the following job titles is recruited for on the Web?

- Chicken Salesperson
- Aesthetician
- Sleep Technologist
- Pizza Maker
- Sculpture Instructor
- All of the above

a low profile in your job search, it's a safe bet that, at the very least, you'll be asked to email your resume to a networking contact or recruiter.

You can take advantage of an eResume whether you're offline or online. Consider these scenarios:

- *No access to a computer. Jeremy H. is a successful general manager who had no computer at home. During a period of unemployment, it took two to four days for his "snail-mail" resume to arrive on a potential employer's desk, causing him to miss out on some opportunities. Jeremy solved this problem by hiring a service to create his Web resume. He reported, "I telephoned a networking contact who wanted to give my resume to her Board of Directors that same night. With my resume on the Internet, all I had to do was give her the Web site address. She was able to print my resume immediately and give it to the Board a few hours later. Without the Web resume, I would have missed that window of opportunity."*

- *Wary of using her employer's computer for job search. Tara S. was in a situation similar to Jeremy's, except that she was gainfully (though unhappily) employed. Careful not to spend her boss's nickel to search for her new job, she spent lunch hours calling networking contacts and recruiters on her cell phone. Tara used a Web resume that included a downloadable text version for recruiters' database needs. The eResume helped her search for new work and hold down her current job, not to mention resist the temptation to appropriate her employer's computer and email system for personal use.*

- *Talent that couldn't be conveyed on paper. Lara M. designed upscale homes as an independent draftsperson. Hindered by the lack of a degree, she knew a paper resume wouldn't do her justice when it came time to transition from freelancer to full-time employee. An online Web folio showcased the quality of her work (without her having to carry a cumbersome portfolio from firm to firm) and gave her the confidence she needed to compete with credentialed professionals.*

- *Lend me your ear. Harrison G. is a voice-over artist who also found that mere words weren't enough to convey his broadcasting talents. A Web portfolio, complete with streaming audio and video, was just the ticket. Employers had immediate access to his skills, saving Harrison the hassle of rushing across town to deliver demo tapes.*

- *Long-distance job search. Lanny M. was moving from one side of the country to the other. His text eResume was the lone format acceptable to resume distribution services.*

("Distribution" or "blasting" is the online equivalent of a direct-mail campaign.) With this technology, Lanny was able to target employers and recruiters by industry and telephone area code in less than an hour. Without the Internet, it would have taken weeks or months to research and get in touch with those contacts.

- ***Just learning to use email.*** *Zay G. is a nursing case manager with more than 25 years of healthcare experience. From the "old school," Zay was just learning to use email, yet continued to fax her resume to employers even when job postings mentioned a preference for emailed resumes. Zay began using a text-only "pasteable" resume and found emailing to be a "much easier, faster, and safer" method of sending her resume.*

- ***Anxious to get the word out.*** *With no qualms about maintaining confidentiality, Chris J. was prolifically posting resumes at major career sites. Her text resume submitted at BrilliantPeople.com, the Web site for Management Recruiters International, was seen by just the right recruiter, which led to her next job as an operations manager.*

- ***Totally tech savvy.*** *Tony P., a high-tech marketing executive with an interest in dot-com firms, wanted to make sure his resume portrayed the right image. A Web portfolio was the perfect stage for presenting significant accomplishments via hyperlinks to pages with graphs, recommendation letters, and other documentation that supported his candidacy. Tony noted, "My recruiter and the venture capital firms were very impressed!"*

How Hard Is It to Create an eResume?

If you can create a document using MS Word or WordPerfect, you can create a plain-text resume or a Web resume. It's a matter of just a few clicks to take your resume from a formatted file to a plain-text file. Now that there are Web-enabled, cut-and-paste tools that don't require the application of HTML coding you can also create a Web page using Word or WordPerfect. Of course, you can also create a Web resume using Web site design software, such as Macromedia's Dreamweaver, Microsoft's Frontpage, or Netscape's Composer.

Types of eResumes

The parallel between product marketing and career marketing was touched on earlier. In the corporate world, marketing executives know that a single product cannot be all things to all people. Beverage behemoth PepsiCo Inc. is a classic example. When researchers learned that consumers wanted more variety in their beverages, PepsiCo jumped into the profitable bottled water market, snatched up the maker of Gatorade, and aggressively pushed new product development.

In the business of marketing your career online, it is nearly impossible to have one resume format (product) that fits every hiring manager's needs. Over the past few years, the variety of computer systems, database requirements, and recruiting protocols have spawned a number of eResume file formats and delivery methods. In the tables that follow, we've listed the most common types of eResumes:

- *ASCII, or Text, Resume*
- *Formatted Resume*
- *PDF Resume*
- *Posted Resume*
- *RTF Resume*
- *Web Resume*
- *Web Portfolio*

Following each definition, you'll find a list of alternative terms (eResume vernacular has yet to be standardized!), the format's pros and cons, and an outline of when to use each type. Figures 1-1 through 1-10 illustrate each type of eResume.

ASCII, or Text, Resume

This simple and functional format is the most common type of eResume because it's easy to create and compatible with all systems. Table 1-1 outlines its many benefits, while Figure 1-1 displays the format of an ASCII resume.

Table 1-1 Profile of an ASCII Text Resume

ASCII, or Text, Resume	
Definition	Resume stripped of all formatting enhancements that can be pasted into email messages or Web site eforms. Its generic format makes it compatible with all computer systems. Content is typically the same as a traditional resume or abbreviated slightly.
File Extension	• .txt (text)
Sometimes Referred to as	• ASCII Text Resume • Simple-Text Resume • Emailable Resume • Text-Only Resume • eResume or Electronic Resume • Text Resume with Line Breaks • Pasteable Resume • Text Resume without Line Breaks • Plain-Text Resume • Unformatted Resume
Advantages	• Preferred format for submitting resumes electronically • Universally readable by any application (email, word processor, text editor, presentation, browser programs) • Can be copied and pasted easily into different programs (especially applicant-tracking database programs and human resources information systems) • Cannot contain a computer virus • May be delivered in seconds to an employer • Opens quickly • Small file size requires little disk storage space • Provides a cleaner, more accurate file than resumes that have been scanned • Can be easily searched • Eliminates need to print, photocopy, mail, or fax a traditional resume
Limitations	• Does not support any formatting enhancements (bold, italic, tabs) • Adheres to recipient's default font settings, preventing you from controlling the "look and feel" of the document after it has left your computer • Plain-looking and often difficult to read, especially in comparison to a formatted or traditional print resume • Loses original line breaks when recipient forwards on to others, further degrading its appearance • One-dimensional—cannot incorporate graphics, images, audio, or video
When to Use	• To respond to job postings that state "email your resume to . . ."; also, when an online "apply here" button opens your email program • When using resume builders or eforms at company or career Web sites • To supply a resume to Internet resume-distribution services • To make cold contacts with employers or recruiters • To solve system disparities (Mac vs. IBM, WordPerfect vs. Word)

```
HOWARD BRANELL
55 Bayview Drive
Miami, Florida 54321
Cellular: (554) 554-4545
hbranell@mediaone.net

QUALIFICATIONS
~ ~ ~ ~ ~ ~ ~ ~ ~ ~ ~ ~ ~ ~ ~ ~ ~ ~ ~ ~ ~ ~ ~ ~

Top-performing manager with 7-year history of exceeding quarterly and annual sales goals. Fast-tracked
through sales, sales management, and operations management positions. Highlights:

* Sales Record: Set regional sales records with nation's leading leasing company. Ranked nationally in top 1%
of sales associates for international rental company. Secured first-time business with major contractors and
developers, such as Ball & Bandy, Cranch & Moats, C.A. Rawlings, and more.

* Management: In first branch management position, more than doubled sales in less than 1 year. Worked
closely with corporate team on acquisition and conversion of 20 stores. Strengths in budgeting, sales
projections, marketing strategy, operations, IT conversions, vendor negotiations, and employee training.

* Trades & Project Experience: Thorough knowledge of general contracting. Basic experience in estimating,
scheduling, purchasing / materials management, and field supervision.


EDUCATION
~ ~ ~ ~ ~ ~ ~ ~ ~ ~ ~ ~ ~ ~ ~ ~ ~ ~ ~ ~ ~ ~ ~

MBA - University of Florida, Miami
BS, Marketing - University of Texas, Austin

PROFESSIONAL EXPERIENCE
~ ~ ~ ~ ~ ~ ~ ~ ~ ~ ~ ~ ~ ~ ~ ~ ~ ~ ~ ~ ~ ~ ~ ~

PREMIERE CONSTRUCTION, Miami, Florida
1998-Present

Branch Manager (10/99-Present): Manage operations for newly acquired store with 24 employees and $12
million fleet. Lead and develop sales associates and production staff. Manage $3.2 million budget.

* In less than one year, increased sales from $2.0 million to $4.7 million, doubled fleet value, and ranked in
top 5 among 75 regional stores for productivity.

* Promoted from sales manager, increasing store sales 150% and improving its ranking from #32 to #12.

BUILDERS, INC., Tampa Bay, Florida
1996-1998

Sales Representative: Assigned to underperforming store with goal of jump-starting lagging sales.

* Added 100+ accounts in just 9 months, generating record 325% annual sales increase.

TRAVEL, LANGUAGE, INTERESTS
~ ~ ~ ~ ~ ~ ~ ~ ~ ~ ~ ~ ~ ~ ~ ~ ~ ~ ~ ~ ~ ~ ~

Extensive travel (logged more than 100,000 miles in past 2 years) - visited Australia (for 2000 Olympics), the
Bahamas, Canada, England, Mexico, Wales, as well as nearly 40 states. Fluent Spanish skills. Enjoy hot-air
ballooning, weight training, biking, scuba diving, and family activities. Member, Builders' Industry Alliance.
```

Figure 1-1 ASCII (plain-text) resume—the mainstay of an electronic job search. Formatting enhancements are minimal; characters are limited to those found on the keyboard.

Formatted Resume

A formatted resume is, in the majority of cases, delivered as an email attachment. Table 1-2 outlines its features and drawbacks; Figure 1-2 displays a resume formatted in MS Word. The popularity of attachments seems to ebb and flow with the presence or absence of high-profile viruses. Despite the liabilities associated with attachments (especially MS Word documents, where hackers love to hide viruses), many hiring managers still request a formatted resume because it provides the convenience of an electronic format and the familiarity of a traditional resume layout.

Table 1-2 Profile of a Formatted Resume

Formatted Resume	
Definition	A resume created in a word processing program (MS Word, Corel WordPerfect) that contains formatting enhancements, such as bold, italic, indented text, columns, fonts, graphic lines, and so on. Formatted resumes are sent as an attachment to an email. Content is the same as a traditional resume.
File Extension	• .doc (for MS Word documents) • .wpd (for Corel WordPerfect documents) • .rtf (for Rich Text Format documents—both MS Word and Corel WordPerfect programs can save to the Microsoft RTF format. See separate entry for RTF resumes later in this chapter for more information.)
Also Referred to as	• Doc File • MS Word Resume • Resume Attachment • Resume in Word Processor Format • RTF, or Rich Text Format (see RTF resumes, Table 1-5) • Word-Processed Resume
Advantages	• Retains formatting enhancements • Easy to read, which enhances reader comprehension • Provides a close visual match to a traditional paper resume • Can be forwarded from a recruiter to a client company when prepared with a common word processing program such as MS Word
Limitations	• May be deleted or unopened due to concerns about computer viruses • Requires an additional step on the part of the recipient to open, download, or print the file • Depending on file format, may be incompatible with recipient's system • Content can be altered, unless a password is established when saving (in the Save function, click Tools, General Options, and enter a password in the Password to Modify box) • May not retain exact formatting due to differences in recipient's printer, software release, or default settings (margins or page breaks may change, bullets may morph into a different character, and so on) • In many instances, cannot be attached to an automated resume-builder or other eforms found at Web sites
When to Use	• When employer specifies that an attachment is acceptable • When employer requests a "formatted" resume or any of the alternative names listed above. • In combination with an emailable (pasteable) resume

ELIZABETH BRADFORD

One Playa Way ▪ San Diego, CA 95678
(555) 555-5555 ▪ ebradford@worker.net

GOAL	Provide managerial expertise in the areas of Project Management, Operations Management, Human Resources Development, or Organizational Development.
EDUCATION	**Masters Degree in Management**—National University, San Diego, California 2000 **Bachelor of Arts Degree**—California State University, San Jose 1993

STRENGTHS, SKILLS, AND KNOWLEDGE

Project Management
- Project Lifecycle Management
- Process Improvement
- HRD, OD Initiatives

Operations Management
- Production, Assembly
- Shipping, Distribution
- Warehousing, Inventory

Human Resources
- Diversity Issues
- Performance Management
- Benefits Development, Administration

Organizational Development
- Management Development
- Organizational / Business Systems
- Growth / Change Initiatives

CAREER EXPERIENCE

Plastics Plus, San Diego, California   1993-Present

Manager—Production & Distribution (1994-Present)

HIGHLIGHTS
Corporate management team member, involved in planning and managing systems to sustain aggressive growth (20% annually). Manage production, assembly, packaging, warehousing, and shipping. Plan and control $620,000 operating budget. Direct a 10-member staff. Coordinate operations and communicate daily with team leaders from product development, marketing, telemarketing, sales, and customer service. Assist with organizational development and human resource development initiatives.

ORGANIZATIONAL DEVELOPMENT
- Created organizational structure during startup phase—company earned a place on the San Diego Sentinel's list of Top 100 Fastest-Growing Companies.
- Consulted Customer Service Department on performance management processes—designed systems that increased communications and boosted order-processing efficiency 20%.

PROJECT MANAGEMENT
- Designed and implemented special projects, focusing on organizational development, team building, time-and-motion efficiencies, and production enhancements.
- Guided full project lifecycle for $400,000 packaging-equipment upgrade, delivering project on schedule and 6% under budget.

OPERATIONS MANAGEMENT
- Accommodated a 40% increase in production volume without additional FTEs—achieved increases through cross-training and restructuring of departmental processes.
- Cut expenses $352,000 through process improvement and training initiatives.
- Improved workplace safety and ergonomics at negligible cost to company.

HUMAN RESOURCES
- Authored company's first employee manual—established and clarified corporate policies, performance expectations, and employee benefits.
- Maintained turnover at less than 1%, managing a culturally diverse workforce.

CUSTOMER SERVICE
- Promoted from customer service representative—serviced national and international customers such as PlayPlastics, LifeGear, and Gitone.

Figure 1-2   Formatted resume prepared in MS Word and delivered as an email attachment.

PDF Resume

The PDF resume gives recruiters a digital image, or photograph, of your entire resume—searchable, no less. Table 1-3 highlights the advantages and limitations of PDF, and Figure 1-3 shows how a resume appears in PDF.

Table 1-3 Profile of a PDF Resume

	PDF Resume
Definition	A resume saved in PDF (Adobe Corporation's Portable Document Format) that can be posted on the Web, emailed, viewed, printed, searched, or saved using any type of computer. Readable only if recipient has a PDF viewer (e.g., Acrobat Reader, which is a free, widely distributed download from Adobe.com).
File Extension	• .pdf
Associated Terms	• Acrobat File • Digital Imaging • PDF Document • PDF Format • Printable Format • Printer-Friendly Format
Advantages	• Compatible with all systems • Uses digital imaging and printer-style output that retains resume formatting • Easy to read, which enhances reader comprehension • Provides the nearest visual equivalent to a traditional paper resume • Free of viruses • Cannot be altered easily
Limitations	• Job seekers must have PDF Writer software (or pay someone to convert the resume to a PDF file). • Recipients must download Adobe Acrobat Reader or PDF viewer. • Current search functions are limited to just one keyword at a time. • Though growing in popularity, some employers are not familiar with PDF. • Larger "footprint" (or file size) requires more disk space. • Requires an additional step on the recipient's part to open, view, or print. • Graphics may blur slightly when printed, depending on viewer's print settings.
When to Use	• When employer specifies that PDF is acceptable • In combination with an emailable (pasteable) resume • As an optional download on a Web resume

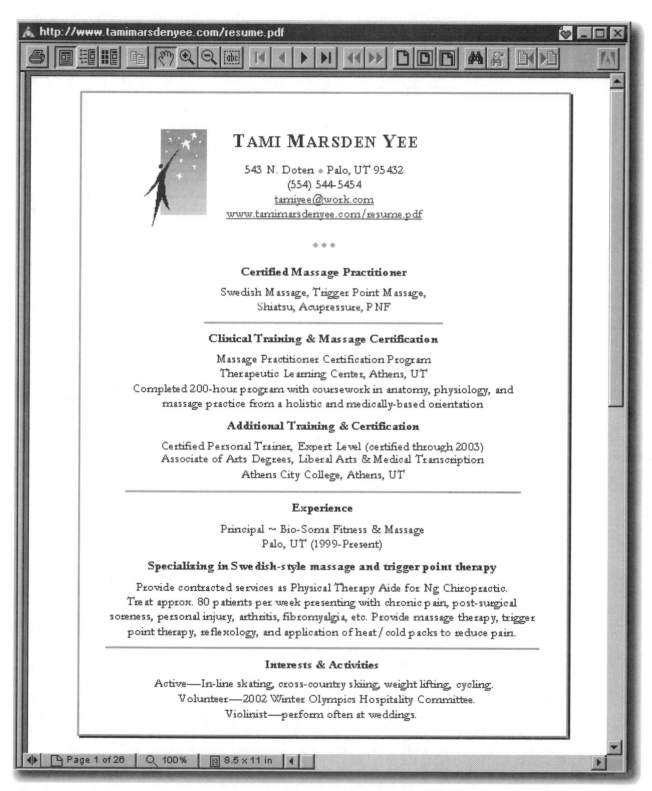

Figure 1-3 PDF resume—is formattable, portable, searchable, and virus-free.

Posted Resume

There's potential for confusion with the term *posted resume* because there are so many options associated with it (we will cover this topic in Chapters 4 and 10). For purposes of discussion, we'll limit the definition of a *posted resume* to "a text resume stored in an online database that hiring professionals can search (whether for free or for a fee)." Subsequent access to the resume by the job seeker, if possible, is via the site's navigational system; no personal URL (or direct route to the Web page) is supplied to the job seeker.

Some sites on the Web—America Online, Yahoo.com, Geocities.com—will take your posted text resume and convert it to an HTML document with its own URL that the general public can

Table 1-4 Posted Resume

	Posted Resume
Definition	Resume submitted to a Web site, then saved in a searchable database. The Web site may be a career site (e.g., Monster.com, FlipDog.com, BrilliantPeople.com) or a corporate site (e.g., General Motors, Intel, McGraw-Hill). Career sites typically provide job seekers with password-protected access to the posted resume in order to make changes, facilitate pasting into email in response to job postings, or delete when the time comes. A posted resume typically appears in text-only format.
Filename	• Database record generated by Web site
Associated Terms	• Internet Resume • My Online Resume • Resume Builder • Web-based Resume
Advantages	• When used at career portals—gives you exposure to a large recruiting audience • When used at corporate Web sites—gives your application longevity, with many databases holding resume records for 6 months, 12 months, or indefinitely • Automatically puts your hat in the ring for positions you may otherwise not have known about • Is easily searched for keywords when prepared according to Web site recommendations
Limitations	• When posted to a fee-based site (e.g., Monster.com), is searchable only by employers and recruiters with paid subscriptions • Does not allow you full control over the "look and feel" of your resume • Frequently displayed as text-only, making it plain-looking and difficult to read • In some cases, forces candidates to use a rigid, predefined resume format, preventing you from camouflaging career weaknesses (job-hopping, no prior industry experience, etc.) • May compromise a confidential job search, despite the site's claims about security • May stay on line indefinitely . . . long after your job search is over
When to Use	• At career portals that offer a "post your resume" service • At niche sites, such as an industry-specific job sites (e.g., http://www.pharmaceuticalrepjobs.com for pharmaceutical reps) or industry association sites (e.g., http://www.association-jobs.com) • At corporate Web sites when the goal is to target specific companies

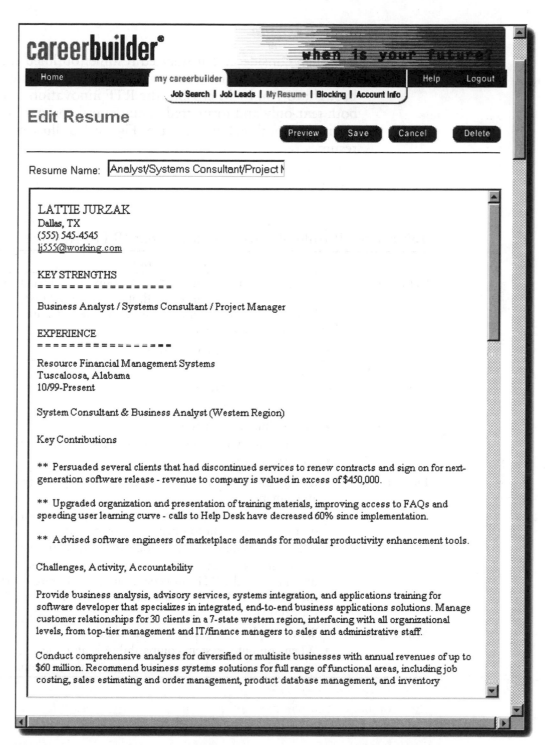

Figure 1-4   Posted ASCII resume as it appears at www.CareerBuilder.com.

access. When this is the case, the resume falls into the category of a Web resume (albeit a very basic one in most cases, with constraints on personalizing the design, typography, or hyperlinks). Posted resumes are summarized in Table 1-4, with an example shown in Figure 1-4.

RTF Resume

Although considered a formatted resume (outlined earlier), the RTF resume warrants its own category because of its unique features. Brought to you by Microsoft, the RTF innovation offers the best of both text-only and formatted documents—compatibility and readability—as outlined in Table 1-5. Figure 1-5 illustrates an RTF resume.

Table 1-5 Profile of a Rich Text Format (RTF) Resume

	RTF Resume
Definition	Resume in ASCII format but "marked up" with formatting codes, allowing the recipient to see bold, italic, indented text, and other style enhancements. Its text-only foundation makes it immune to viruses (with the exception noted below).
File Extension	• .rtf (Microsoft Rich Text Format)
Associated Terms	• Formatted Resume • Printer-Friendly Format • Rich Text Format
Advantages	• Compatible with all systems • Easy to read, which enhances reader comprehension • Free of viruses
Limitations	• It may still be viewed as "virus capable" since it arrives as an attachment. • Because it comes as an attachment, it requires an additional step on the part of the recipient to open, view, or print. • File type (rtf) may not be familiar to some recruiters or employers. • Although not common, the file can contain a virus caused by a disruption in the RTF conversion process (despite its .rtf extension, the file remains a .doc file where macro viruses can "hide"—see Chapter 5 for details).
When to Use	• When employer requests a formatted document • When computer system compatibility is an issue • In combination with an emailable (pasteable) resume

Emily Olivia Wymore

Box 3, Mills, NH 51111   jaynajw@isp.net
(555) 544-4343   www.jjw.com/folio

CREATIVE MANAGEMENT ■ MARKETING ■ PUBLIC RELATIONS

PROFESSIONAL HISTORY

Director of Public Relations — STG Advertising   1996-Present
Executive Director — Regional Arts Council   1992-1996
Executive Producer — KMTP-TV, Channel 17   1985-1992

SKILLS & ACCOMPLISHMENTS

Ability to analyze, facilitate, plan (budgets, logistics, timelines)...

■ **Special Events:** Orchestrated large-scale events, including successful grand opening of Zen's MicroBrewery ($80k budget), promotions for MB Mercedes that yielded record sales, as well as corporate sales meetings and other events.

■ **Broadcast Operations:** Instrumental in startup of PBS affiliate (Channel 17). Participated in programming decisions; produced forum shows.

■ **Fund Development:** Organized several county arts agencies to collaborate in lobbying for increased funds at the local and state levels.

■ **Organizational Development:** Co-founded the New England Assembly of Art Agencies, an organization that provides technical assistance and lobbying support for arts associations throughout New Hampshire, Vermont, and Maine.

Ability to communicate, market, promote, persuade...

■ **Media Coverage:** Enlisted favorable press for products, businesses, political candidates, and individuals. Secured *New Hampshire News* front-page stories.

■ **On-Air Talent:** Hosted television public affairs program.

■ **Network:** Solid contacts in business, the arts, government, and the media.

Ability to conceptualize, create, design...

■ **Print Ads:** Cast and coordinate technical and creative talent; serve as prop stylist, colorist, and trend advisor.

■ **Corporate Image Enhancements:** Experienced in business and retail interior design, seasonal décor, and floral design.

■ **New Products:** Assembled leisure travel packages that featured unique environmental, spiritual, and adventure themes.

Figure 1-5   RTF resume. Appearance can be identical to MS Word documents.

Web Resume

Web resumes offer notable advantages over other types of eResumes, and they are becoming very popular. Some recruiting experts estimate that there are several times more Web resumes than there are text resumes in the bulging databases of sites such as Monster.com, HotJobs.com, and Headhunter.net. Table 1-6 outlines the advantages of Web resumes, and Figure 1-6 displays a Web resume.

Table 1-6   Profile of a Web Resume

Web Resume	
Definition	A resume that resides permanently on the World Wide Web with its own URL (Web address). In its most basic form, all content is contained within a single Web page. In its enhanced form, hyperlinks provide viewers with immediate (online) access to supporting documents.
File Extension	• .html (HyperText Markup Language) • .htm (HyperText Markup) • .xml or .xhtml (eXtensible Markup Language)
Also Known as	• eResume/Electronic Resume • HTML Resume • Internet Resume • Online Resume • Resume Web Page
Advantages	• Accessible 24 hours a day, 7 days a week • Compatible with different computer systems • Can include other formats, including downloadable text, PDF, or MS Word resumes • May incorporate Flash animation and other advanced technology • Unique potential for hyperlinks, photographs, graphics, audio files, or video clips • Formatted appearance can emulate the "look" of a traditional print resume, but with more interactivity • More visually appealing due to expanded layout, color, and typography options • May eliminate need to photocopy, mail, fax, or email a resume
Limitations	• Requires viewers to have Internet access • May require a long, unwieldy URL (e.g., http://www.itjobs.com/cgi-bin/person-show?P_PINDEX=Q44238ZDF) when created with a click-and-build service • Appearance can vary when viewed with different browsers • For those who register their resume with search engines for an aggressive job search—the URL may not be found by all search engines, depending on how keywords are used in title bars and text • Can make a poor impression on employers if not designed well
When to Use	• As an online career-marketing tool for active job seekers, passive job seekers, consultants, independent contractors, or freelancers • In place of a traditional print resume • When access to emailing or faxing a resume is difficult • When cyber-savvy image is critical • When compatibility is a problem

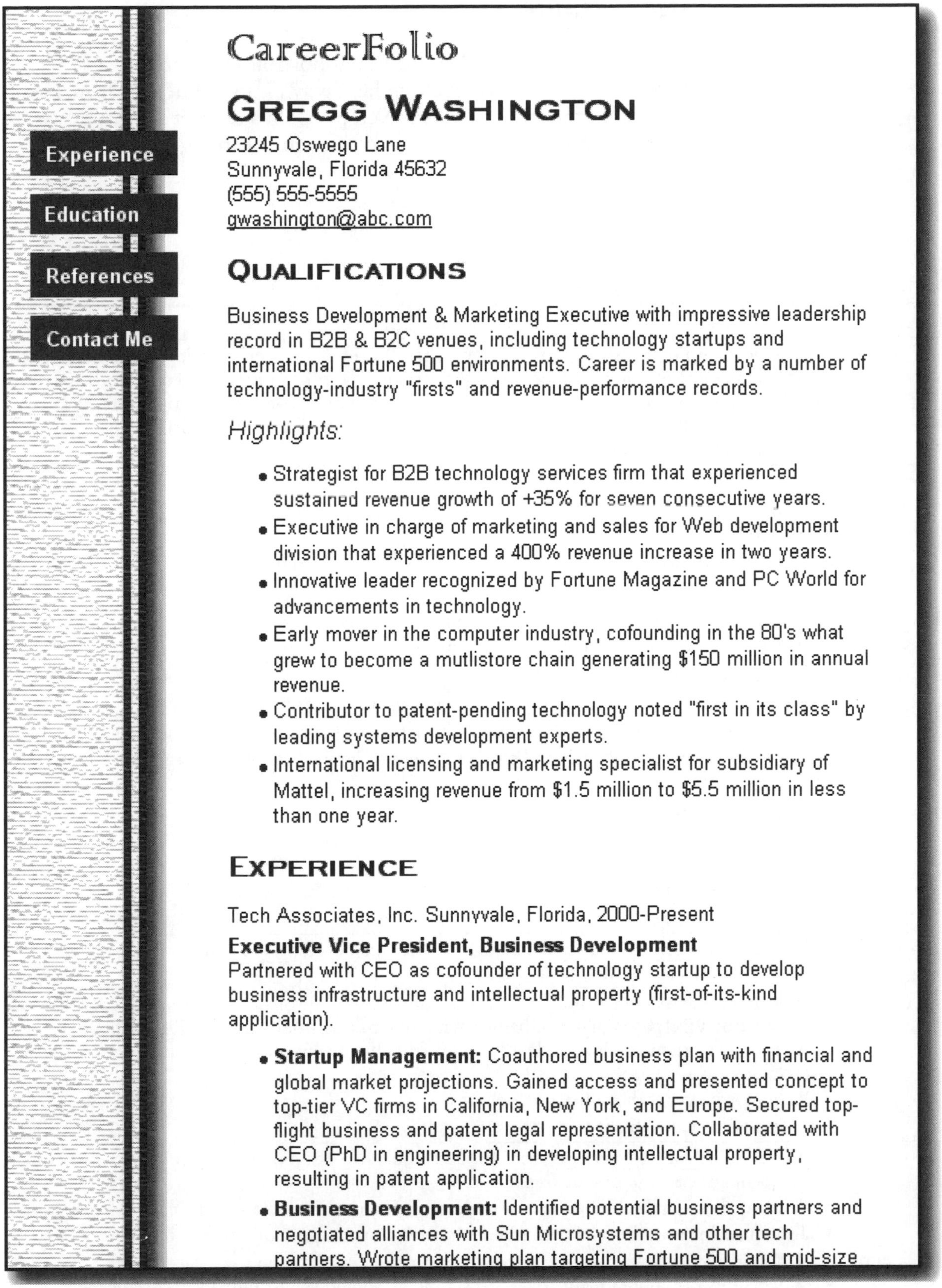

CareerFolio

GREGG WASHINGTON

23245 Oswego Lane
Sunnyvale, Florida 45632
(555) 555-5555
gwashington@abc.com

QUALIFICATIONS

Business Development & Marketing Executive with impressive leadership record in B2B & B2C venues, including technology startups and international Fortune 500 environments. Career is marked by a number of technology-industry "firsts" and revenue-performance records.

Highlights:

- Strategist for B2B technology services firm that experienced sustained revenue growth of +35% for seven consecutive years.
- Executive in charge of marketing and sales for Web development division that experienced a 400% revenue increase in two years.
- Innovative leader recognized by Fortune Magazine and PC World for advancements in technology.
- Early mover in the computer industry, cofounding in the 80's what grew to become a mutlistore chain generating $150 million in annual revenue.
- Contributor to patent-pending technology noted "first in its class" by leading systems development experts.
- International licensing and marketing specialist for subsidiary of Mattel, increasing revenue from $1.5 million to $5.5 million in less than one year.

EXPERIENCE

Tech Associates, Inc. Sunnyvale, Florida, 2000-Present
Executive Vice President, Business Development
Partnered with CEO as cofounder of technology startup to develop business infrastructure and intellectual property (first-of-its-kind application).

- **Startup Management:** Coauthored business plan with financial and global market projections. Gained access and presented concept to top-tier VC firms in California, New York, and Europe. Secured top-flight business and patent legal representation. Collaborated with CEO (PhD in engineering) in developing intellectual property, resulting in patent application.
- **Business Development:** Identified potential business partners and negotiated alliances with Sun Microsystems and other tech partners. Wrote marketing plan targeting Fortune 500 and mid-size

Figure 1-6 Web resume. Hyperlinks at left transport readers to categories on the resume Web page.

The sidebar navigation buttons read: **Experience**, **Education**, **References**, **Contact Me**

Web Portfolio

An improvement over the traditional portfolio delivered in a binder, Web portfolios are also making headway as an online career marketing tool. In the strictest sense, Web portfolios are not just an expanded resume, but a "diversified" document that goes beyond the

Table 1-7   Profile of a Web Portfolio

Web Portfolios	
Definition	Online portfolio that resides permanently on the World Wide Web with its own URL (Web address). Useful for landing a new job, an internal promotion, or a consulting contract position, Web portfolios provide hiring managers with a three-dimensional picture of a candidate's qualifications. Web site layout and navigation of an online portfolio is comparable to that of a small commercial Web site.
Also Known as	• Career Portfolio • eFolio • ePortfolio • Online Portfolio • Resume Web site
File Extension	• Multiple .html files contained in one domain name ending in any extension available on the Internet (common extensions include .com, .edu, and .net)
Advantages	• Versatile career marketing tool • Easily expanded, contracted, refocused, or revised • Gives employers a more-than-mere-words picture of your candidacy • Enables employers to "click and choose" pages of interest (via home page navigation system) • Almost unlimited content • Continually evolves with career, giving employers reason to revisit the site • Free of viruses • Can be found via Boolean searches (unless posted in a confidential database) • Implies technology know-how on the candidate's part
Limitations	• Requires job seeker to have knowledge of Web site development software or pay for professional Web site design services • May require fees to update • Printing of Web pages may not be practical, due to potential "text loss" on right side when pages are printed (include a "printer-friendly" version to counter problems with cropping) • Requires viewer to have Internet access • May not be accessible if Internet server is down
When to Use	• As an online career-marketing tool for active job seekers, passive job seekers, consultants, independent contractors, or freelancers • When distance, scheduling, or cost make it impractical to use a traditional portfolio • To deliver information that can't be included in a print portfolio (e.g., audio, video, interactive content) • When supporting documents or work samples (beyond the resume itself) are needed • When the need or ability to project "style" is critical

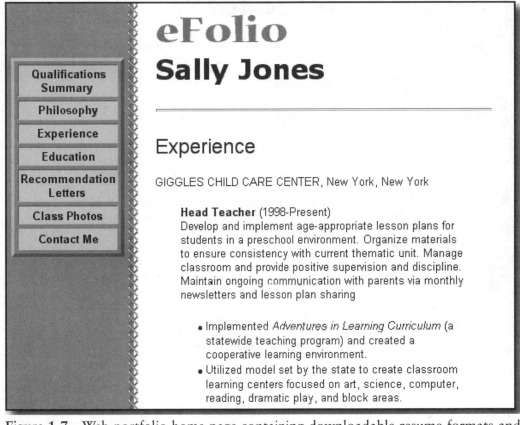

Figure 1-7   Web portfolio home page containing downloadable resume formats and navigation system to philosophy, class photos, and more.

confines of a single Web page and provides instant access to work samples or artifacts, philosophy statements, representative accomplishments, project details, mentor-mentee relationships, educational background, and the like. Of course, a chronological or functional resume can (and should) also be included as one of the pages in your Web portfolio. See Table 1-7 for more details and the illustrations in Figures 1-7 through 1-10 for an example of a Web portfolio.

Figure 1-8   Web Portfolio experience page.

Figure 1-9   Web Portfolio education page.

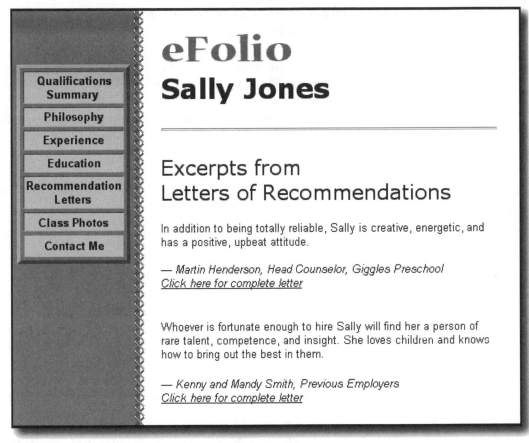

eFolio
Sally Jones

Excerpts from Letters of Recommendations

In addition to being totally reliable, Sally is creative, energetic, and has a positive, upbeat attitude.

— *Martin Henderson, Head Counselor, Giggles Preschool*
Click here for complete letter

Whoever is fortunate enough to hire Sally will find her a person of rare talent, competence, and insight. She loves children and knows how to bring out the best in them.

— *Kenny and Mandy Smith, Previous Employers*
Click here for complete letter

Navigation buttons: Qualifications Summary · Philosophy · Experience · Education · Recommendation Letters · Class Photos · Contact Me

Figure 1-10   Web Portfolio recommendation letter page.

What About Scannable Resumes?

You may be wondering why we have not mentioned scannable resumes in this chapter. It's a common misconception that a scannable resume is an eResume. It is not. A scannable resume can become an eResume, but only after some work on the part of the employer. When a resume is sent by surface mail, someone must scan the resume using OCR (optical character recognition) technology. When sent by fax, the resume may be scanned manually or it can be routed and scanned automatically into an applicant-tracking

U
TIP

Hotel Kinko's

For those with no computer at home, take up e-residence at Kinko's (your local library also has Internet access and is less expensive). Kinko's computers offer the benefit of current software programs to word process or convert your resume. Wherever you choose, you can log on to the Internet, set up a free email account, search job postings, build your Web resume, research companies, and more.

system. Once past the OCR process, the scanned resume graduates to an eResume and takes on the attributes of an ASCII resume.

When given an option between faxing and emailing, always choose the latter. Mark Graeber, a national account manager with Management Recruiters International at its Fresno office, confirms the preference for email. "Scanning is time consuming—something I hope we never go back to. I'd beg someone to go to Kinko's first and email me their resume instead of faxing."

On the off chance a potential employer asks for a scannable resume, refer to these do's and don'ts:

Do's

- *When choosing a font, use a standard typeface that ensures letters do not touch one another. Sans serif fonts such as Arial and Helvetica are good choices, as are the serif fonts Times and Courier. In Figure 1-11* John Sterling Deere *is in a serif font, and* 555 Sunnyside *is in a sans serif font. A serif is a fine line, usually horizontal, finishing off a letter. Faxing can cause the text to shrink and distort, so start with a point size of 10 for sans serif fonts and 11 for serif fonts.*

- *List your name on the top line and use a separate line for address, phone number(s), fax, and email; if your resume goes to two pages, place your name and telephone on separate lines at the top of the second page.*

- *Set margins to one inch on top, bottom, left, and right (lesser margins may cause text to creep into the scanner's "unviewable" areas).*

- *Use a ragged right margin. Body text should be flush left or indented only slightly under category headings (no more than 0.5 inch).*

- *Be detailed about your job experience (but concise); avoid abstract nouns and focus on tangible, concrete nouns. Don't say "computer literate" when you could say "MS Office (Word, Excel, PowerPoint, Access), Dreamweaver, Photoshop, Act!, MSIE, Netscape Navigator."*

- *Use common headings such as Objective, Summary, Summary of Qualifications, Accomplishments, Experience, Strengths, Education, Professional Affiliations, Publications, Certifications, Honors, Personal, Miscellaneous, etc. Less familiar category headings, such as Mission or Know-How, may throw off resume tracking systems that scan resumes to provide automated categorization of skills.*

- *Clearly indicate your job target (for systems that may be dependent on an operator to input your skills classification).*

If you are interested in a variety of positions, list the possibilities and separate them with slashes (add an extra space before and after the slash to be sure no characters touch), for instance, "Administrative Manager / Administrator / Business Administrator / Business Manager."

- *Include a keyword-based summary at the beginning of the resume or a keyword list at the end of the resume. Doing so gives employers the option of cutting and pasting it into a keyword summary tab in their tracking software.*

- *For cleanest delivery, fax the resume directly from your computer using fax software such as WinFax Pro. The next best option is to mail an unfolded, laser-printed original on crisp white paper. Least attractive is faxing an original or copy on a standalone fax machine—this method increases the risk that characters will be blurred or distorted.*

Don'ts

- *Avoid decorative or recycled papers (a speck in the paper can cause the software to interpret an "O" as an "8" or an "i" as an "l").*

- *Eliminate graphics, industry icons, borders, columns, or a landscape (paper turned sideways) presentation.*

- *Avoid unusual bullets (most scanners can read a solid round bullet and asterisk).*

- *Don't condense spacing between letters.*

- *Don't hyphenate words at the end of a line.*

- *Don't print on both sides of the paper.*

- *Don't staple pages together.*

Figure 1-11 illustrates a scannable resume.

JOHN STERLING DEERE

555 Sunnyside
Sun City, ID 55432
(555) 543-4342
johndeere@yahoo.com

OBJECTIVE

Honors graduate pursuing investment banking opportunities where competencies in technical finance, accounting, computers, and business will be of value.

EDUCATION

B.S., Business Administration with Concentration in Finance (May 2000)

Idaho State University, Boise (ISU) – Selected from competitive candidate list for business school's first honors program. Earned 3.95 GPA. Program features:

- **Advanced finance course work** – Financial management, business forecasting, securities analysis, portfolio management, quantitative analysis, and valuation in a global environment.

- **Preparation of thesis** – Empirical study of implied versus historical volatility in option pricing of Internet stocks (findings to be presented for publication in financial journal).

- **Certification** – Pursuing Chartered Financial Analyst Certification. Preparing for Level I Exam with studies in accounting, finance, economics, and ethics.

KNOWLEDGE BASE, EXPERIENCE

- **Portfolio Management** – Outperformed S&P 500 in managing stock portfolio for ISU School of Business. Experience developed skills in fundamental and technical analyses of securities markets, as well as managing and hedging risk.

- **Mathematics** – Knowledge of mathematical models, probability distributions, sampling statistics, regression analysis, analysis of variance, and principal components.

- **Trading Operations** – Familiar with debt / equity instruments, swaps, options, futures, bond pricing, present value, duration, and convexity. Online trader. Avid reader of investment publications (Investors Business Daily, Forbes, Smart Money).

- **Entrepreneurial Finance** – Studied venture capital markets, deal structuring, business forecasting, financial planning, valuations, public offerings, and harvesting methods.

COMPUTER APPLICATIONS

Advanced skills in MS Excel, Access, Word, and PowerPoint, as well as Internet research and use of browsers (Netscape, IE); knowledge of database applications and proprietary banking software. Invited as teaching assistant for ISU computer labs.

EMPLOYMENT EXPERIENCE

Western Bank, Boise, ID
1996-Present

Credit Analyst, Commercial Credit Center (4/99-Present)

Promoted from senior customer service representative, where responsibilities included training new employees and promoting bank products. Ranked in top 20% among 260 employees for overall sales volume. Analyze financial statements and present lending recommendations for middle-market clients (agricultural, commercial accounts).

Figure 1-11   Scannable resume.

Checklist to Choose the Right Format

In choosing the right format, remember that a one-size-fits-all product won't work. More than likely, you'll need a couple of file formats. Because of compatibility and convenience, we recommend both an emailable/plain-text version and a Web resume. Table 1-8 will help you decide which formats will best support your job search.

Familiarize yourself with the many faces of an eResume; then we'll look at the strategy behind writing one. On the Internet, content is king and keywords are critical. In Chapter 2, we'll teach you how to write and "keyword optimize" your resume for maximum success.

Table 1-8   Checklist to Choose the Right Format

	ASCII or Plain-Text Emailable Resume*	Formatted or RTF Resume Attachment**	Posted Resume	PDF Resume	Web Resume or Portfolio***
Situations					
Employer requests emailed resume.	U				
Employer requests formatted resume (or specifies a Word doc, RTF file, or WordPerfect file).		U			
Employer requests printer-friendly or PDF file.				U	
You want your resume to receive broad exposure.			U		U
You plan to use a resume distribution service.	U				
You need to resolve compatibility issues between computer systems.	U				U
You need to keep your job search confidential or private.					U
Appearance and design are critical to your image.	U			U	U
Type of job seeker					
Active job seekers	U	U	U		U
Passive job seekers	U				U
Freelancers/1099-ers					U
Contract or temporary workers					U
Those without Internet access					U

*In situations where an emailable resume is the format of choice, you can still make reference to your Web resume by including its URL on the text resume.

**When sending an attachment, we recommend also sending a plain-text resume pasted into the email message. Doing so will cover your bases should the attachment be unreadable for any reason.

***Web resumes and Web portfolios are combined as one in this table. In terms of development, it's easiest to start off with a simple one-page Web resume. If you're developing a Web portfolio, include a resume as one page of the site.

Chapter 2

eResume Writing 101: An ROI Formula for Content and Keywords

One tiny word had been left out of Ellen Hanson's resume. Unfortunately, this three-letter omission (*fab,* short for fabrication) was on her potential employers' "must have" keyword list. The oversight stalled Ellen's job search, excluding her from the interview she wanted with a high-tech manufacturer in Oregon's "Silicon Forest."

Ellen put a great deal of effort into writing her resume, but she made a classic error. She took it for granted that employers would read between the lines, interpret the facts, and comprehend the sum total of her experience . . . a costly assumption.

What Ellen and many other job seekers fail to understand is that today's hiring managers use computer technology to find and process candidates. Gone are the days when a hiring manager would read your paper resume and say, "This person looks perfect for the job." Now, a computer does the initial screening of your resume and "decides" whether you fit the bill.

Virtually all large corporations have sophisticated database software that enables them to store, search, and rank ASCII and scanned resumes. With the proliferation of Web-based recruiting applications, even the smallest companies can now afford this technology. The process of finding candidates is similar to using an Internet search engine to research information on the Web. With the help of a special computer application, hiring managers type in a string of keywords that relate to an open position. The computer then searches a database for resumes containing those words. Resumes with the most relevant matches appear at the top of the list (which gives them high priority). Resumes with fewer matches appear at the bottom of the list. Resumes without the right keywords won't appear at all.

This technology has some sobering repercussions for job seekers, including these scenarios:

- *Emailed resumes. When emailing an ASCII resume to a hiring manager, there's a strong possibility that it will not be printed and read. Instead, it may get only a cursory review (if you're lucky) before it's transferred to a resume database for future searches. Without the right keywords, it may never be seen again.*

- *Posted resumes. Without a doubt, a resume posted at a career site such as Monster.com will be warehoused in a searchable database. Here, paid subscribers search resumes using keywords. Again, the right keywords will determine whether your resume is "lost" or "found."*

- *Web resumes. When submitting a Web resume or portfolio URL to a search engine such as AltaVista.com, certain information (page titles, meta tags, home page content, and so on), will be indexed by the search engine. You've undoubtedly got the picture by now—wrong keywords, no contact with employers.*

Because of this, job seekers must build their resumes around keywords—from basic "assumed" skills to advanced technical skills. This chapter will explain how to find and sift through keywords, as well as incorporate and optimize them in your resume. To ensure that you build on a good foundation, we'll first review the principles of what constitutes a great resume using the ROI formula. We'll also expose one of the biggest "sins of omission" made by online job seekers (one that can be easily corrected). In our discussion, we'll focus on the genre of ASCII plain-text resumes. For those who are creating a Web resume, refer to the organization and design tips in Chapter 8 and the meta tag tips in Chapter 10 (Table 10-6). Our instructions for researching keywords later in this chapter (specifically Table 2-2) are relevant to both plain-text and Web resumes.

ROI Resumes

In business, the term *ROI* stands for return on investment. In its simplest form, it compares a company's earnings to its expenses. Many investors regard ROI as the most important financial indicator of a company because it shows how well management has used the company's resources.

We encourage job seekers to embrace an ROI mentality when it comes to the search process. In other words, you should understand the business considerations that a company makes in a hiring decision. The employer must make an investment (wages, benefits, training) in you and expects a return on that investment. The return can typically be measured in tangible, number-driven terms, such as an increase in productivity, a reduction in costs, or the resolution of a long-standing problem.

In addition to remembering the ROI business definition, we'd also like for you to adopt a resume writing definition for the term. Doing so will reveal the secret to writing a winning eResume. In short, an ROI resume is . . .

- *Readable*
- *Other-Focused*
- *Impact-Oriented*

Let's explore each term in detail.

Readable

In software development, *readability* refers to how easily a programmer can read and understand the source code. In eResumes, the term reflects how easily a hiring professional can read and comprehend your qualifications. Readability is critical to a good first impression, which is why we've made it the first ingredient in our ROI resume formula. Of course, when searched initially by computers, readability isn't an issue—computers don't discriminate; they only search for keywords. However, once your resume is unearthed from a pile of databased resumes, it will be read by humans. At this point, it's essential that the document you have delivered is organized, squeaky clean, and inviting to read.

ORGANIZATION

Mother always said, "A place for everything and everything in its place." And so it goes with resumes. For starters, your name and contact information should appear at the top in this order:

Name
Address*
City, State Zip*
Telephone*
Alternative Telephone*
Email
Web URL

The order of categories on your resume will depend on your background and level of experience. In general, consider the following hierarchies as guidelines for organizing your resume. (Sample resumes for each of these categories can be found at the end of this chapter, Figures 2-3 through 2-6).

*Items with an * may be omitted if conducting a confidential search.

New Grads

Objective

Education

Knowledge & Skill Set (based on course work)

Internships

Experience (move this up higher if relevant and strong)

Affiliations & Activities

Keyword Summary

Mid-Career Professionals

Goal

Strengths

Accomplishments

Experience

Education

Affiliations & Activities

Keyword Summary

Career Transitioners

Target

Skills & Accomplishments

Employment Summary

Affiliations & Activities

Keyword Summary

Executives

Qualifications Summary

Experience & Accomplishments (detailed)

Education

Patents, Publications, Presentations

Keyword Summary

Of course, not all of these categories will be used in every situation, and some situations will call for different categories. There are probably as many combinations of headings as there are job seekers—so be flexible and creative in determining what will work best for you. (Although you'll find a good deal of advice and many samples here, the scope of this book doesn't allow us to cover special resume writing issues, such as how to downplay being "overqualified" or camouflage a history of job hopping. For a more in-depth look at the subject of resume writing, we recommend *Resume Magic* by Susan Britton Whitcomb, JIST Works, Inc., Indianapolis, 1999. At 595 pages, it's one of the most comprehensive resources on the subject.)

Squeaky Clean

"Clean" resumes are free of typos, uniform in formatting, and consistent in grammar usage. For instance, did you run a spelling and grammar check on the document? Has an eagle-eyed friend of yours also reviewed the document for any little hiccups? Regarding uniformity, is there the same amount of space between every category heading and between every title? If one bulleted heading uses a colon, do all the headings have colons? Have you used commas, semicolons, colons, and dashes in the same manner throughout the document? If these details seem inconsequential to you, think again. In researching an earlier book on resume writing, Susan conducted a "resume preferences" survey of top U.S. employers. Eighty-two percent of human resources professionals agreed that typos and poor organization would eliminate an otherwise qualified candidate. Details count. Be meticulous! Your livelihood depends on it.

Inviting to Read

This is especially challenging when dealing with ASCII text, since you're limited to one font (no bolding or formatting) and a few characters to add visual appeal. In essence, your only design tools are a handful of keyboard symbols (~, #, =), the space bar, and the enter key. (See Chapter 3 for a thorough explanation of ASCII characters, conversion processes, and resume formatting.) Nonetheless, you'll need to use these to the best of your ability to give the resume balance, plenty of white space, and some semblance of pattern. The resumes at the end of this chapter demonstrate these concepts.

Other-Focused

The second element of ROI resumes deals with the person on the other end of your resume—the employer! All too often, job seekers approach resume writing from the perspective of a biographer instead of a copywriter. Yes, employers are interested in your work history, but they're not inclined to read protracted details about every facet of your life. Be assured that your resume will be more effective if you adopt a copywriter's strategy. In advertising, copywriters first determine a product's features, then translate those features into benefits. Here's an important concept espoused by Madison Avenue advertising wizards:

Advertising Model

Features attract the interest of buyers, while *benefits* motivate them to buy.

Your resume should do the same. We don't mean to diminish you to human chattel, nor do we expect you to paste a catchy tag line at the end of your resume (e.g., "John Doe—your single source for accounting, at a price you can afford" . . . ack!). The parallel in resume writing is more subtle, as noted here:

Resume Writing Model

Keywords attract the attention of computers, while your *record of impacts* persuades hiring managers to "buy."

To identify the features in your background, consider details such as occupational skills, degrees, certifications, or your number of years in the trenches. All of these items are features, which is how keywords tie in to your resume.

Features = Keywords

In the copywriting–resume writing analogy, product features are keywords. Determining those features, or keywords, will require some research on your part. (Don't worry—the Internet has made research less tedious than it was a decade or so ago.) We'll get to research techniques a bit later in the chapter. Before we do, we'll explain the final building block of an ROI resume.

Impact-Oriented

In the advertising model, we learned that features (keywords) attract interest, but benefits clinch the deal. The equivalent to benefits in resume writing is clear:

Benefits = Impacts

Impacts are synonymous with accomplishments, results, and contributions. To "clinch the deal," you must present a strong record of impacts. This, more than anything else, will set you apart from your competition in a human being's eyes. And what impacts might motivate an employer to decide to open his or her wallet and hire you? Contributions in any of the following areas would certainly appeal to most:

Typical Employer "Buying" Motivators

1. Generate more revenue

2. Reduce expenses

3. Increase productivity

4. Advance the use of technology

5. Resolve a long-standing problem

6. Enhance relationships or image

7. Deliver market intelligence

8. Envision new products or services

9. Bring new customers on board

10. Expand relationships/sales with existing customers

Impacts (benefits) are the most frequently overlooked element in resume writing (the sin of omission we referred to earlier). In developing resumes for the Net, we see a tendency for job seekers to focus so closely on including the right keywords that they forget to tie those keywords to specific benefits. To impress both machine and human, you need to do both. The next sections teach you how.

Keywords—The Key to a Successful eResume

"Help! What are the keywords for my industry?" We frequently are asked this question by job seekers. Given the multitude of industries and disciplines, it would be difficult to present a comprehensive list of keywords for every type of job. Further, you can be certain that any "definitive" list that we or anyone else might offer will change in the time it takes a book to go to press. With that in mind, we'll provide a template for the types of keywords you should look for, as well as where to look for them. Learning about keywords will benefit you in several ways as you

- *Familiarize yourself with the job market for your industry*

- *Pick up on new trends or vernacular in your profession*

- *Gather competitive salary information (an added bonus!)*

Keyword Categories

Table 2-1 shows how keywords can be divided into four groups—hard skills, soft skills, general information, and academic qualifications. This list is based on what recruiters tell us they typically use to search for candidates. The most common keyword is a *job title*, followed by a list of *hard skills*, then possibly a *degree or certification*, and a *location*.

You can use Table 2-1 as an outline to develop a master keyword list for your resume. A master keyword list is simply a collection of terms—usually nouns or noun phrases—that would be found in a

Table 2-1 Keyword Categories

Keyword Category	Your Keywords
Hard Skills • Areas of expertise • Computer programs • Languages • Qualifications • Skills • Terminology • Years of experience	
Soft Skills • Attitude • Communication skills • Interpersonal skills • Organizational skills • Personality traits • Planning skills • Work ethic/habits	
General Information • Affiliations • Area codes • Company names • Industries • Job titles • Locations • Products	
Academic Qualifications • Certifications • Colleges • Course titles • Credentials • Degrees • Training programs	

typical job description for your position. After you've searched job postings (described in Table 2-2), you can write the appropriate keywords to the right of each item in Table 2-1. Don't feel compelled to find terms for every item. For instance, under the Academic Qualifications heading, your field may not use certifications or training programs. The same holds true for Hard Skills—several items, such as Areas of Expertise and Skills, may have overlapping keywords. Simply use Table 2-1 as a guide to assemble keywords that employers might use to search for you.

Where to Look for Keywords

There are a number of resources for locating keywords, a few of which are listed below.

- *Career Web sites (job postings)*
- *Company Web sites (job postings, "about us" or "mission" page)*
- *Professional associations (newsletters, meetings, conferences, networking)*
- *Classified Ads (especially ads that include details)*
- *Dictionaries (online business, finance, or technical dictionaries)*
- *Formal job descriptions or job orders*
- *Informational interviews with industry contacts*
- *Publications (how-to job-search books,* Occupational Outlook Handbook, *[U.S. Department of Labor, compiler])*
- *Trade journals*
- *Online Yellow Pages*

By far, our favorite resource is online job postings. They're up to date, easy to access, and provide a good amount of detail.

How to Determine Keywords for Your Industry

Table 2-2 walks you through the steps of finding keywords at a career Web site.

Figure 2-1 illustrates the process of highlighting keywords in a job posting. The gray shaded words are hard skills, while the various underlining styles represent soft skills, academic qualifications, and general information. Figure 2-2 shows the resume that was developed to apply for the CFO opportunity in Figure 2-1. For purposes of illustration, the keywords in this resume are highlighted to show how they correspond to the job posting. *Do not* highlight, underline, or otherwise mark up keywords on your resume when submitting it to an employer.

How to Optimize Keywords

Although technology now plays a large role in finding and processing candidates, the procedure is not entirely automated. Human decision making takes place at several stages. For instance, when a resume is emailed, the recipient (hiring manager) typically completes a cursory review of the resume and decides whether to store it for future searches or immediately call the candidate if there appears to be a match for an open position. Several executive recruiters that we interviewed report they don't routinely keep every emailed resume—some are so off-base (e.g., the candidate is

Table 2-2   How to Find Keywords at a Career Web Site

Step	How To's	Tips for First-Timers
1. Assemble 3 to 5 job postings.	Log on to a career site and search job postings for target positions. Try FlipDog.com or GrassIsGreener.com for general sites, the latter of which conducts a split-second search of jobs at more than 100,000 sites. Alternatively, use a niche site that specializes in your industry. (See Chapter 10 for tips on finding general, specialized, or regional career sites.) At this point, it's not necessary that the jobs be in your geographic area. Copy and paste the text portions of 3 to 5 relevant, detailed postings into your word processing program (or print them out).	On the site's home page, locate a tab that says "Search Jobs" (or words to that effect), then follow the instructions. At a minimum, you'll be asked to input a job title or function; some sites will require that you complete a detailed profile before searching. Once search returns are displayed, click on the job title to view detailed information. Highlight the text and copy it to your word processing program. Avoid copying graphics or tables, as they'll bulk out the file size unnecessarily.
2. Cull keywords from each job posting.	Read the job posting once, then go back again and highlight keywords. Compare the job posting with the items listed in Table 2-1, Keyword Categories. The majority of your highlighted keywords will likely fall into the category of Hard Skills.	Use the highlight function in MS Word. (Click View, Toolbars, Reviewing to turn on the function. Highlight keywords with your mouse, then click the icon with the pen and yellow bar.) If you prefer a more traditional method, print the job postings and use a marker to highlight keywords.
3. Compile keywords into a master list.	After completing Step 2 for each of your postings, transfer the highlighted items to a new document (or fresh piece of paper). You should have a number of duplications (high-frequency keywords), assuming you chose 3 to 5 job postings similar in nature. Compare the list to the text in your resume. It should include most, if not all, of the keywords you've assembled. Those keywords that appear repeatedly should definitely be in your resume.	Just starting to write your resume? You can use the job postings as an outline for your description of responsibilities (but don't get too detailed and *don't* succumb to plagiarism). Caution! If your background does not include some of the keywords you've found, don't be tempted to "write them in" just to be found in a computer search. It's better to pursue training or experience in areas where you may be lacking.

underqualified or in the wrong industry) that the resume is summarily deleted.

After a resume has been found in a keyword search, the human factor again comes into play. Resumes are reviewed and first impressions are made. This is your chance to make a stunning impression . . . not just with a rhetorical regurgitation of a job posting, but with a well-crafted document, built on keywords that are backed up with tangible evidence of your ability to contribute.

Chief Financial Officer (CFO)

GreatCompany, Inc., Minneapolis, MN, US

Position Description:

The Chief Financial Officer will report to the CEO. The CFO will be involved in strategic planning, as well as oversee, direct, and manage all aspects of the manufacturer's financial operations. The CFO will lead a team that covers the areas of accounting, treasury, tax, investor relations, financial planning, and analysis.

In addition, the CFO will create and manage financial reporting, financial planning, forecasting and banking relations, develop short and long range strategic plans for effective financial management, oversee and help negotiate strategic alliances/partnering agreements, and perform financial reviews and recommendations for merger and acquisition dealings.

Position Duties/Responsibilities:

- o Oversee and direct treasury, financing, budgeting, audit, tax, accounting, purchasing, real estate, long range forecasting, and insurance activities for the company.
- o Direct the Controller in developing and implementing IT systems necessary to maintain proper records and to afford adequate accounting controls and services.
- o Analyze alliance and M&A activity from a strategic and financial perspective.
- o Coordinate tax-reporting programs.
- o Coordinate all investor relations activities.
- o Analyze operational issues impacting functional groups and aid in BPI initiatives.

Requirements:

- o Progressive experience of 10 years or more.
- o Broadly experienced, operationally-oriented financial executive who has experience in turnaround or reengineering environments.
- o Public accounting experience desired.
- o Outstanding analytical skills.
- o Outstanding management abilities.
- o Effective communications skills for banking relationships, investor relations, and internal coordination.
- o Consultant and advisor on startup issues for new divisions.
- o Functioning in a multinational environment.
- o Minimum of a BS or BA college degree – MBA or CPA is highly desirable.

Contact: jobs@greatco.com, (612) 554-5432, GreatCo., 543 E. 22ⁿᵈ, Minneapolis, MN 55435

Key:
Academic Qualifications ~ General Information ~ Hard skills ~ Soft skills

Figure 2-1   Internet job posting with keywords highlighted or underlined.

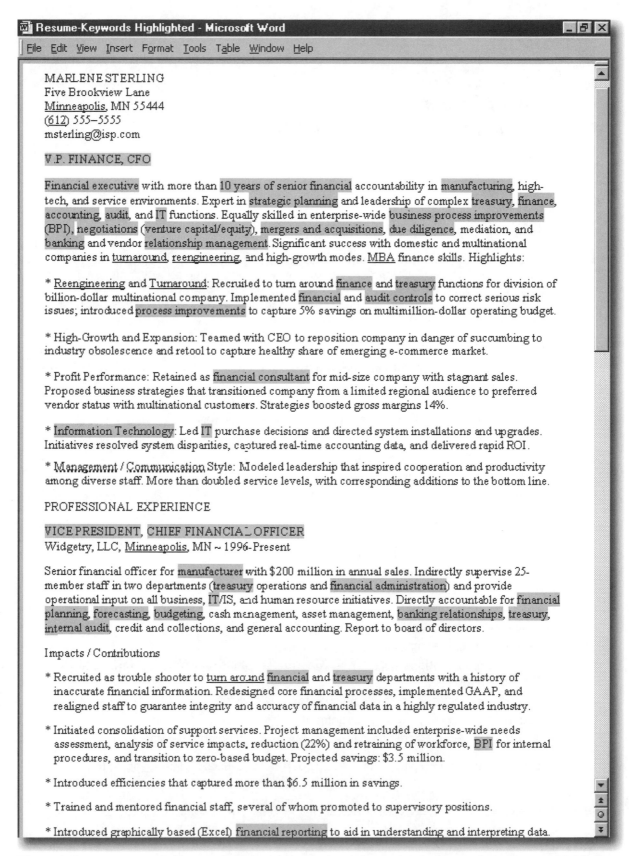

Figure 2-2 Resume with keywords that correspond to job posting in Figure 2-1. (Do not highlight keywords when sending to employers.)

The following tips will help you optimize keywords for greatest impact:

LEAD THE WAY

Although computer searches can find keywords anywhere in the resume, it's wise to position as many as possible at the beginning of the resume. This allows keywords to be seen on the first one or two computer screens when it comes time for the hiring manager to review your resume.

RESUME WRAP-UP

Although not a requirement, you can also include a category labeled Keyword Summary to conclude your resume. All too often, resumes start with a bang, then end on a dull note. A summary positioned at the end of the resume is a way to reinforce your profile as a qualified candidate. In addition, some resume-tracking software programs contain a field called Keywords or Skills. Providing a summary section allows hiring managers to copy and paste the information directly into that field and saves them from having to cull keywords manually from your resume.

KEYWORD QUALIFIERS

In keeping with the ROI theme, remember to flesh out your keywords with impact statements. We use the term *keyword qualifiers* for this process—in short, you qualify your keywords by describing positive impacts made on past employers. For instance, note how this retail manager responded to a job posting that required, among other things, a "self-starter with strengths in operations, budgeting, customer relations, and team building."

[resume excerpt]

- **Operations:** Implemented merchandise tracking systems that boosted productivity 35%. Trained and retained a competent staff whose average tenure was twice the industry norm.

- **Budget Management:** Controlled site costs to perform at 15–25% under budget . . . a record for the company.

- **Customer Relations:** Contributed to company's reputation as "best giftware retailer" for quality and personal service (voted by readers of *Sunnyview Times*).

- **Team Building:** Mentored inexperienced employees who went on to earn "outstanding" marks on performance appraisals.

- **Self-Starter:** Promoted from entry-level position to store manager within 16 months.

SHANE THACKERY WHEATON

555 East Cove Road   (555) 555-5555
San Francisco, CA 95555   http://www.yahoo.com/swheaton   stw78@yahoo.com

SYNOPSIS

Dual-degree graduate with D.C. internship experiences. Qualified for career opportunities where communications strengths, technology skills, and broadcast background will be of value.

EDUCATION

University of California, Santa Barbara
➢ Bachelor of Arts degree, Communications (Dean's List honors; GPA in major: 3.9)   June 2001
➢ Bachelor of Arts degree, Political Science   June 2001

INTERNSHIPS

Talk Radio News Service & TalkDaily.com, Washington, D.C.   June-August 2000

Assisted in production of daily radio and Internet broadcasts. Researched Internet and print news sources to assemble show content. Wrote daily news summaries for Web site. Highlights:

➢ **Broadcast:** Cohosted live daily radio broadcast (assignment normally given to full-time staffers).

➢ **Communications:** Covered White House press conferences; posed questions to senior officials. Interviewed guests for *Talk Magazine*, including hosts of top Boston and D.C. talk-radio programs.

➢ **Technology:** Updated Web site with daily highlights of talk personalities (Rush Limbaugh, Imus).

U.S. Representative Geraldine Smathers, 22nd District, Washington, D.C.   July-August 1999

Represented congresswoman at hearings. Provided written analysis of proposed legislation. Served as office contact for major supporters. Wrote constituent correspondence and franked communications.

➢ **Communications:** Selected (among five interns) as media spokesperson for several campaign events. Served as precinct captain on election day.

➢ **Technology:** Managed on-time installation of new telecom system at campaign headquarters.

ADDITIONAL SKILLS & INTERESTS

➢ **Computer Skills:** Dreamweaver Web site design, MS Office (advanced skills), MSIE and Netscape Navigator browsers, email applications (Outlook Express, Eudora), Internet research.

➢ **Language:** Basic business Spanish (completed four years of Spanish course work).

➢ **Favorite Subjects:** Political communications, lobbying, legal advocacy, oral debate, drama.

➢ **Activities:** Tennis, golf, canoeing.

KEYWORD SUMMARY

Communications, broadcast, reporting, on-air talent, research, programming, production, new media broadcasting, public speaking, presentations, Web site content development, BA Communications, BA Political Science, San Francisco, Bay Area.

Amplified Résumé and References Online:
http://www.yahoo.com/swheaton

Figure 2-3   Resume of college graduate with keywords optimized. Final "Keyword Summary" can be copied and pasted by employers into resume-tracking software programs.

LINDY SWERTFAGER

55 Trebuchet Court
Pasadena, CA 95555   www.e-folios.com/lindys.html   lindys@email.com
(555) 543-5544

QUALIFICATIONS

Sales Management / Project Management: More than 10 years' experience in direct sales, sales team management, and branch / regional training. Provided tactical direction for online and traditional media sales, including annual market planning, sales goal development, key account management, and dot-com sales launch. Highlights:

- **Top Performer (Internet & Print Sales):** As sales manager, ranked #1 in revenue among 3 area sales teams. Generated highest personal sales volume in Internet ad sales. As sales rep, frequently led branch in sales volume.

- **Turnaround Specialist:** Chosen from among 30 to lead important loss-control projects. Successfully reversed key accounts' decisions to reduce or cancel contracts. Additionally, upsold traditional print products and cross-sold Web-based advertising to recapture nearly $500,000 in annual revenue.

- **Creative Instructor:** Designed innovative sales aids, electronic tools, and procedural efficiencies that were adopted regionally (several now under consideration for national implementation).

- **Inspirational Leader:** Earned Outstanding Team Player Award (among 40 managers). Selected to train, coach, and manage new sales managers.

PROFESSIONAL EXPERIENCE

AdSmart.com / Advo Publishing, Los Angeles, California   1990-Present

Sales Manager / Special Projects (1996-Present)
Plan, manage, and monitor sales campaigns for key markets that generate combined revenue of $13 million. Manage sales team of 9-13; establish sales goals and provide individualized development, coaching, and feedback to drive sales. Forecast sales budget and manage resources. **Highlights:**

- **Internet Sales:** Led 50 reps and 8 managers in banner ad sales volume; first to sell direct premium impressions. Trained team in product knowledge (cobranding, banner ads/exchanges, reciprocal links) and cross-selling opportunities to interface with traditional advertising.

- **Special Assignments:** Called in to various markets to reinstate critical customers and recouped 94% of lost revenue, a company record. Chosen to jump start sales campaign that was behind schedule and far under quota—finished campaign with highest gain among three managers.

- **Sales Innovations:** Coached teams that ranked #1 in seven consecutive campaigns, achieving double-digit sales increases (13% to 18%) in annual revenue. Created a number of effective sales aids that documented product value and boosted team sales volume.

- **Sales Training:** Created training program, "Selling Against Competitive Media" and taught to 350 Western Region reps. Contributed sales training material for CD-ROM distributed statewide.

- **Personal Sales Performance:** Promoted from sales representative (1990-1996) based on consistent performance in top 10-20% of 100+ reps. Frequently ranked #1 among 10-member team.

EDUCATION

Bachelor of Arts Degree, Advertising—University of Southern California

* * * Web-resume and downloadable text version available at www.e-folios.com/lindys.html * * *

Figure 2-4   Resume of mid-career professional. "Qualifications" section doubles as a keyword summary, while accomplishments reinforce keyword competencies.

CHEL DORADO

(555) 545-4455   cheldorado@aol.com   Fax: (555) 565-6655

Project Leader / Program Manager
strengths in planning, promoting, and executing initiatives related to:
Business Development ~ Marketing ~ Corporate Communications ~ Technology

---

SKILLS, EXPERIENCES & CONTRIBUTIONS

Program/Project Management: More than 10 years' experience managing complex regional, national, and international projects. Recruited and guided teams (marcom, PR, financial/legal advisors, PhD researchers, engineers, think-tank experts); managed 7-figure budgets; aligned projects with organizational mission.

- **Budget Management**—Recruited as project manager to correct program with history of operational and budget mismanagement. Teamed with CPAs and attorneys to improve financial reporting, data integrity, and program accountability. Cut $500,000 from a $2 million budget without compromising outcomes.

- **Program Launch**—Directed launch of a first-of-its-kind consumer communications program that influenced the buying habits of millions of consumers in the U.S., Canada, and Europe. Directed 13 contract firms.

- **Quality Management**—Developed quality program that incorporated concepts from GE's renowned Six Sigma model (program earned national award). Coached executives on quality and management initiatives.

Marketing/Communications: Created and delivered persuasive marketing/communication messages. Directed production of videos, Web content, advertising, reports, publications, brochures, and collateral materials.

- **Media Management**—Obtained positive coverage in major media outlets, including *The Washington Post, New York Times, Wall Street Journal,* and *Discovery,* as well as NBC Nightly News, ABC, and the BBC.

- **Web Communication**—Worked with top international Web designers to improve W.H.O.'s Web site visibility and global reach. Implemented Intranet to instantly transmit vital data to managers nationwide.

- **Public Speaking**—International conference keynote speaker, panelist, and moderator. Appeared on network news in 10 major markets. Addressed technology, science, and energy innovations.

EXPERIENCE SUMMARY

Program Manager—U.S. Department of Health & Human Services, Washington, DC	1998-Present
Information Officer—World Health Organization, Copenhagen, Denmark	1996-1997
Program Manager—U.S. Department of the Interior, Washington, DC	1988-1995

EDUCATION & TRAINING

MS and BS degrees—University of Arkansas
Marketing—Wharton School of Business, University of Pennsylvania

---

OTHER ASSETS

Technology—MS Office; PageMaker; Eudora (including merge functions for rapid media communication).
Travel—Extensive U.S., Asian, and European travel (two years abroad). Global/multicultural orientation.
Community Involvement—Volunteered time/resources to Habitat for Humanity and Dallas Food Pantry.

---

55 E. Hampton Place ~ Denton, TX 76543 ~ Relocation Anticipated ~ Available for Full-Time or Contract Assignments

Figure 2-5 Resume of an individual in career transition. Functional format incorporates keywords, which are further "qualified" by contributions and career highlights.

JOHN BRADFORD

55 Route 9A
Springfield, MA 01234

jbradford@isp.com

Business: (555) 554-5454
Residence: (555) 445-4545

EXECUTIVE SUMMARY

C-level operations executive with 20 years' experience in general management, marketing, sales, finance, technology, and customer relations. Strong IT, system applications, and e-commerce skills. Significant industry leadership and community involvement. MBA (finance emphasis).

PROFESSIONAL EXPERIENCE

Chief Operating Officer—Manco Manufacturing Company, Springfield, MA   1986-Present

Hold P&L responsibility for flagship dealer that consistently ranks among top East Coast dealers in sales ($200 million annually). Direct a staff of 70 in four locations; recruit, develop, and supervise sales, store, service, and parts managers. Direct financial operations, including budgeting, cash management, accounting, inventory management, tax planning, and audit activities. Oversee IT and support functions.

Contributions

- **Organizational Management:** Directed organizational restructuring and adopted a participative management style that boosted morale and productivity. Identified "best practices" and communicated goals to all staff. Reduced employee turnover from 45% to less than 2%.

- **Marketing & Sales:** Collaborated on strategies that led company to retain #1 market share in fluctuating economy. Sustained a 14% average annual growth in sales. Supported sales increases that earned team numerous travel awards. Participated in critical meetings with key accounts.

- **Finance & Accounting:** Renegotiated vendor contracts that resulted in across-the-board savings of 15%. Converted manual accounting to fully automated system. Brought previously outsourced audit work inhouse at 6-figure savings to company (earned audits with no exceptions from CPA firm).

- **Technology:** Founded national users' group, now 350 members strong. Beta test and consult on proprietary software prior to release to 1,200 dealers. Launched Web site that features 3D equipment views, allows customers to check parts availability, and facilitates secure online ordering.

Accountant—Wren & Wren, CPAs, Springfield, MA   1980-1986

Conducted audits and prepared federal and state returns. Provided business advisory services. Client base consisted of primarily manufacturing, nonprofit, and financial institution accounts.

EDUCATION & LICENSURE

MBA—University of Massachusetts, Amherst   1989
BS, Accounting—Bowdoin College, Brunswick, ME   1980

COMMUNITY INVOLVEMENT

- Member—Western Massachusetts Business Leaders Program (one of 30 selected from 350 applicants)
- President—Northeastern Device Manufacturers' Association
- Board of Directors—Manufacturers' Alliance, Western Massachusetts Chapter
- Executive Board of Directors—Big Brothers, Big Sisters
- Board of Trustees—UMass-Amherst Alumni Foundation

Figure 2-6   Resume of executive. "Executive Summary" section functions as a keyword summary. "Contributions" document specific impacts in keyword areas.

In the resume excerpt on page 43, keywords lead off each paragraph and are enhanced by a tangible impact statement. To develop statements like these for your own resume, review the list of 10 buying motivators presented earlier in the chapter.

TIP

Are You Measurable?

Dr. Wendell Williams, Managing Director of ScientificSelection.com, develops hiring tools (sophisticated measurement tests, performance predictors, simulations) to help human resource managers select employees. Williams maintains that "Hiring managers need measurable data" to match the right candidate with the right job. You can hasten this process by providing measurable data in your resume. Use before and after numbers whenever possible, or compare your performance to annual goals, the employer's historical data, or an industry average.

Figures 2-3, 2-4, 2-5, and 2-6 display resumes (in MS Word format) for a recent college graduate, mid-career professional, career transitioner, and executive, respectively. Note how each uses the principles outlined in this chapter for organizing content and optimizing keywords. By doing the same, we guarantee your resume will find favor when viewed by both computers and people!

Now that you've mastered eResume content and keywords, it's time to learn about ASCII resumes—a must in any online job search.

Chapter 3

ASCII Resumes: Steps for a Glitch-Proof Conversion

Following a tour of duty in Vietnam, a young Marine Corps officer named Frederick Smith headed home to the United States with entrepreneurial aspirations. With the embryo of an idea, Mr. Smith filed paperwork and founded his company in 1971. Two years later, operations were launched officially, with the delivery of 186 packages to 25 U.S. cities. This start-up would not be particularly noteworthy in the annals of business history, except for the fact that the deliveries were completed overnight. In that 24-hour period, Smith—president of Federal Express Corporation—birthed the modern air-ground express industry. A Yale graduate, Smith encountered a number of naysayers when he first outlined his business plan. Few could predict the insatiable demand businesses would have for next-day deliveries. Today, FedEx is a $19 billion global enterprise.

Thanks to can-do leaders like Frederick Smith, business has been conditioned to operate at an accelerated pace. Sending documents across the country used to take five days—now it takes 24 hours or less. Without question, the Internet has pushed this tempo to warp speed.

Recruiter Preferences

Just as FedEx is the preferred vendor for expediting deliveries, the Internet is the preferred vehicle for sending resumes to hiring professionals. Statistics abound that support the increase in online recruiting. In a 2000 survey conducted by Manchester, Inc. of Jacksonville, Florida, more than 400 recruiters made clear their preferences for how applicants should send resumes:

- *82 percent of recruiters prefer to be contacted by email.*
- *8 percent prefer that resumes be sent by fax.*
- *7 percent prefer that resumes be sent by snail mail.*

In 1999, the Society for Human Resource Management (SHRM) also conducted a survey to determine its members' preferences for resume submission. Although SHRM's data is not as striking as that of the Manchester survey, email submission still won the majority of votes.

The trend for online interactions between employers and job seekers has climbed steadily since the mid-1990s. In 1998, roughly 50 percent of employers used the Internet for recruiting. In 2000, unofficial numbers varied between 70 to 75 percent. In 2001, the figure inched above 80 percent. Barring some unforeseen circumstance, this percentage will continue to increase.

> The mandate from hiring professionals is clear:
>
> Submit an electronic resume!

A Crash Course in ASCII Plaintext

Getting your resume into the hands of an employer (or the records of a database) is fairly straightforward. There are essentially three steps to the process:

1. Convert the resume from its original word processor format (MS Word, WordPerfect) to ASCII.

2. Clean up the formatting.

3. Paste the document into an eform or email.

To accomplish this, you'll need to know about ASCII, which stands for American Standard Code of Information Interchange. The acronym is pronounced "ask-ee" (as opposed to "ask-two" or "ask-eye"). Why do so many hiring professionals request ASCII, or text, resumes? Undoubtedly, it's an issue of compatibility. If systems aren't compatible, the recipient may not be able to open the file, or find that the contents have been translated into unintelligible garbage. Figure 3-1 illustrates an incompatibility issue—note that the only thing understandable in this mess is the candidate's name (Rodrigo Solario).

ASCII can solve these conversion problems because it creates a universally understandable language based on mathematics. In the basic ASCII character set, all letters, numbers, and symbols found on your computer keyboard are assigned a number from 0 to 127. For example, the ASCII decimal code for an uppercase A is 65, B is 66, C is 67, and so on. You don't have to learn these codes because your word processor will automatically convert text to ASCII equivalents.

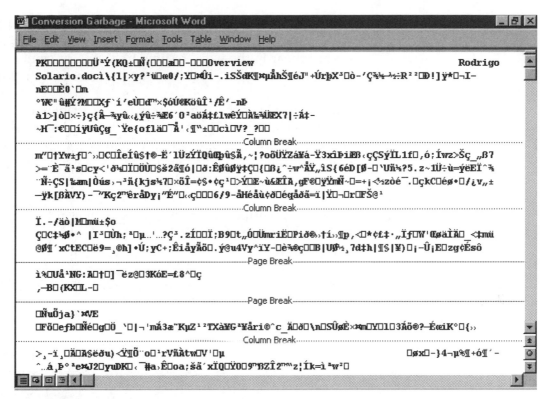

Figure 3-1 Conversion garbage—a "worst-case" scenario of incompatibility between computer systems.

What's important to know is that only the characters found on a keyboard are included in the basic 0 to 127 character set. All other characters are grouped into what's called "extended ASCII" (or non-keyboard characters) and are assigned a higher number that is not readable by all systems. These higher-numbered characters produce many specialty or typeset characters in word processing, such as one-character fractions (¾ versus 3/4) and ellipses (... versus . . .).

Tidbits for the Technically Inclined

TIP

ASCII is a subset of many other larger character sets, including the ANSI character set of MS Windows, the Roman-8 character set of HP systems, the IBM PC extended character set of DOS, and the ISO Latin-1 character set used by Web browsers. The good news is that all of these character sets apply the same numeric codes for their first 127 characters, which are English letters and numbers. Codes for European characters (such as letters with diacritical markings—accents, umlauts, etc.) start at 128. Systems that use the basic ASCII character set cannot read extended ASCII. Consequently, any unrecognizable character is assigned a random graphic . . . better known as a glitch!

Examples of extended keyboard characters that you might find in a cover letter or resume include em dashes (—), the accented e's that often appear in the word resume (résumé), or symbols that are sometimes used as bullets, such as a small square (▪) or arrow (►).

Because nonkeyboard characters have a tendency to cause conversion problems, it's important that you avoid using them in your resume. Figure 3-2 illustrates a worst-case scenario of what an employer might see when a resume is converted to ASCII without first eliminating non-ASCII characters.

Table 3-1 identifies the conversion glitches in Figure 3-2, the unsupported characters that were the culprits, and how the glitches can be corrected.

For a guaranteed clean conversion, limit characters in your resume to those found in Table 3-2.

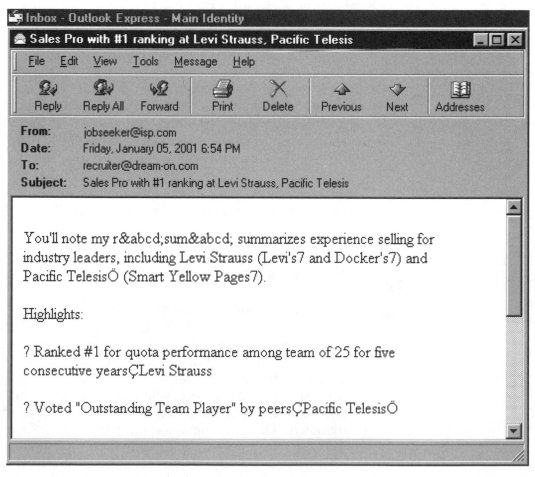

Figure 3-2 Conversion glitches. Sender failed to convert document properly before emailing.

Table 3-1 Conversion Glitches Based on Use of Unsupported ASCII Characters

Conversion Glitch (Viewed on a PC)	Location	Intended Character Not Supported by ASCII	How to Correct
&abcd;	Line 1 (the garbled word r&abcd;sum&abcd;)	é (accented e)	Use regular e without accent mark Result: resume
7	Line 2 (Levi's7, Docker's7)	® (registered trademark symbol)	Omit (or use -R) Result: Levi's or Levi's-R; Docker's or Docker's-R
Ö	Lines 3 and 7 (TelesisÖ)	™ (trademark symbol)	Omit (or use -TM) Result: Telesis or Telesis-TM
?	Beginning of lines 5 and 7	■ (square bullet)	Use an asterisk (*) or some other logical keyboard character, such as the plus sign (+), tilde (~), or a lowercase o (as in octopus). Do not use the greater than or less than signs (<, >). Result: * Rankcd #1
Ç	Lines 6 and 7 (years ÇLevi)	— (em dash)	Use a double hyphen (—) or a single hyphen preceded and followed by one space (-) Result: . . . years - Levi Strauss

Table 3-2 Standard Characters That Will Convert Properly

Basic ASCII Character Set					
!	1	A	Q	a	q
"	2	B	R	b	r
#	3	C	S	c	s
$	4	D	T	d	t
%	5	E	U	e	u
&	6	F	V	f	v
'	7	G	W	g	w
(	8	H	X	h	x
)	9	I	Y	i	y
*	:	J	Z	j	z
+	;	K	[	k	{
,	<	L	\	l	|
-	=	M	]	m	}
.	>	N	^	n	~
/	?	O	_	o	
0	@	P	'	p	

Recommended File Formats for ASCII Conversion

There are several types of ASCII, including plaintext, rich text, and hypertext. Plaintext is generally what you'll want for eforms and email. In MS Word and Corel WordPerfect, there are several file format options for converting to plaintext. Table 3-3 lists the recommended file formats for eforms and email.

You may be wondering why we recommend the ANSI-based Text Only formats in MS Word and WordPerfect (especially when you can find contradictory advice that recommends using the ASCII-based MS-DOS Text in Word and ASCII DOS format in WordPerfect). Actually, ANSI and ASCII are identical when it comes to coding values for characters found on your keyboard. Where they differ is in the "extended" character set that we described earlier. If your resume does contain some nonkeyboard characters (again, we don't encourage this), there is a much better chance of a clean conversion using the ANSI-based file formats listed in Table 3-3. In our conversion tests, the MS-DOS file formats caused more glitches.

Converting Your Resume to Paste into eForms

There is an easy five-step process for converting your word-processed resume to ASCII text to use in eforms (the steps for email are different and will be covered in Table 3-5).

Table 3-3   Recommended File Formats for ASCII Conversion

MS Word File Formats	Corel WordPerfect File Formats	When to Use
Text Only	ANSI (Windows) Generic Word Processor	• Eform posting to career or company Web sites—Use this format when pasting your resume into most (but not all) eforms at career and company web sites (see the file-format recommendations in Table 10-3 of Chapter 10). • Line breaks occur only at the end of a paragraph, not at the end of each line, giving the text freedom to adjust to the margin settings of the eform.
Text Only with Line Breaks	ANSI (Windows) Text	• Emailing to recruiters and networking contacts—Use this format when pasting your resume into the body of an email message. • Line breaks occur at the end of each line and help preserve the layout of the resume.

Before starting the conversion, it's wise to save a separate word-processed version of your resume (the paper type you'd take with you to interviews). To save this formatting, open the file, then click File, Save; use a descriptive filename (e.g., Doe-Jane-resume.doc in MS Word or Doe-Jane-resume.wpd in WordPerfect). Figures 3-3 and 3-4 show the resume in its formatted stage as an MS Word document. Once this is done, you can begin the conversion process, as outlined in Table 3-4. These instructions are specific to MS Word; parenthetical notes explain any differences for Corel WordPerfect.

If you were to open your newly saved document after completing the steps in Table 3-4, it would look jumbled and be difficult to read. Before we explain how to tidy up the formatting, let's review the steps to convert your resume for emailing.

Table 3-4   How to Convert a Resume to ASCII Text for Eforms

Steps	Microsoft Word Instructions	WordPerfect Differences	Tips
1. Use the Save As function.	With your word processing software open and the resume on screen, click File, Save As.		Figure 3-5 illustrates this step.
2. Choose Text Only.	Click the drop-down arrow in the Save As Type box; scroll down and select Text Only.	Scroll up in the File Type box and select ANSI (Windows) Generic Word Processor.	See Figure 3-6. If the name of your current, formatted resume file is "Doe-Jane-Resume," consider naming the new text version "Resume-for-Eforms." This filename may seem overtly obvious, but as time goes by, it will help you recall what the file is and how to use it.
3. Save the file.	Click Save.		See Figure 3-7. Make note of where the file is saved so you can find it easily later.
4. Accept the warning.	Click yes in response to the warning box.	Same, with one caveat: Users of older versions (6.1 or before) must manually type the ".txt" extension in the File Name box (e.g., reseform.txt).	See Figure 3-8. Don't be alarmed by the warning box—because you selected Text Only, the software is warning you that features (ruling lines, bolding, tabs, and other formatting) will be stripped from the document. A stripped-down version is exactly what you want. Your original formatted resume is still intact as a .doc file, whereas this new file will have a .txt extension.
5. Close the file.	Click File, Close to remove the file from the screen.		At this point, you'll note that your file looks suspiciously unchanged. You're right! It won't change in appearance until you close and reopen the file.

```
Morello - Microsoft Word                                    _ 🗗 ✕
```

BRIT MORELLO

555 West Palm	bmorello@yahoo.com	Voice Mail: (555) 555-5555
Clayton, NC 55555	http://www.morelloplace.com/resume.html	Fax: (555) 555-5556

SUMMARY OF QUALIFICATIONS

Senior Sales and Account Management Professional with impressive track record in consumer, commercial, and industrial product sales. Consistently promoted to key sales and account responsibilities throughout 11-year career with respected Fortune 500 leader. Career highlights:

- **Top National Ranking:** Performed in top 5% among sales representatives for XYZ National Corporation. Multiple recipient of company's highest sales achievement awards.

- **Revenue Generation:** Currently generating 111% of $24 million quota despite a flat, competitive market place.

- **National Account Development:** Improved market share for both consumer and commercial products, securing business with Fortune 1000 accounts (Georgia Pacific, Boise Cascade, Bergen Brunswig, Pfizer).

- **Strategy Development:** Authored sales strategies for divisions in Europe and Canada that increased sales 327% in one year.

- **Regional Trainer:** Selected over more experienced candidates as sales trainer for mid-Atlantic region. Developed new hires who went on to regularly meet or exceed quota.

- **Relationship Management:** Consistently provide a level of service that has built trust, advanced relationships, and increased sales in local, regional, and national accounts. Excellent communication skills (strong vocabulary, formal public-speaking training, experienced presenter, skilled in interpersonal relations).

PROFESSIONAL EXPERIENCE

XYZ NATIONAL CORPORATION, Lexington, Massachusetts   1989-Present
(The worldwide leader in widgetry with approx. $3 billion in annual sales, XYZ supplies digital imaging hardware, software and media to markets worldwide.)

National Account Manager (1/96-Present)

Manage key national accounts with complex sales and marketing structures. Construct annual business plans with customer-specific objectives, strategies, and plans to leverage brand image and sales. Develop and implement joint marketing programs. Built relationships with key individuals at all account levels. Preface all contacts with a commitment to supporting customers' sales and success.

- Increased sales $2.5 million (11%) in less than one year (performance is above national trends).

- Grew revenue in medical market more than $5 million, turning around past history of flat or declining sales.

- Launched new marketing programs that expanded Polaroid products into customers' catalogs, Web sites, and traditional sales channels.

- Increased account base in medical market 300% in first year.

(continued)

Figure 3-3   Page 1 of Resume in MS Word prior to conversion to ASCII.

Morello - Microsoft Word

BRIT MORELLO

| Voice Mail: (555) 555-5555 | Page 2 | bmorello@yahoo.com |

PROFESSIONAL EXPERIENCE (cont.)

XYZ NATIONAL CORPORATION, cont.

Senior Sales Representative (1989-1996)

Recruited to manage all aspects of a $10 million sales territory covering Washington, Oregon, Idaho, and California. Delivered sales presentations to Fortune 500 accounts in four core markets (professional photography, law enforcement, medical, scientific). Managed large retail accounts.

- Ranked in top 10% of sales force, consistently exceeding sales goals by as much as 120% of quota.
- Coordinated and presented more than 75 seminars.
- Selected as Regional Trainer, responsible for onboarding, sales development, and motivation of new sales representatives.

VALUE MATRIX CORPORATION, Detroit, Michigan   1984-1988
(Value Matrix is the nation's second largest producer of construction aggregates.)

Recruited to manage Midwest sales territory. Successfully sold aluminum sheet, plate, and ingot products to Fortune 500 accounts and large national metals distributors. Strengthened dealer relations.

- Sourced five new major accounts in first six months.
- Grew territory sales volume 98% during tenure.

ANOTHER MAJOR COMPANY, Detroit, Michigan   1981-1984
(division of General Motors)

Area Manager

Promoted from Sales Representative to Area Manager for Midwest sales territory. Managed wholesale distributors. Developed promotional programs.

- Set record for number of new accounts opened as rookie.

EDUCATION & PROFESSIONAL DEVELOPMENT

Bachelor's Degree—University of Washington, Pullman   1981
Public Speaking—Speaks School of Public Speaking
Channel Management—Carlson School of Management

KEYWORD SUMMARY

Account Management, Relationship Management, Client Relations, B2B, Business Development, Alliance Development, Dealer Relations, Distributor Management, Fortune 500, Industrial Products, Consumer Products, Medical Products, Prospecting, Cold Calling, Negotiating, Communication Skills, Presentation Skills, High Energy, Self-Managing, Willing to Travel, Virtual Office

---

Figure 3-4   Page 2 of Resume in MS Word prior to conversion to ASCII.

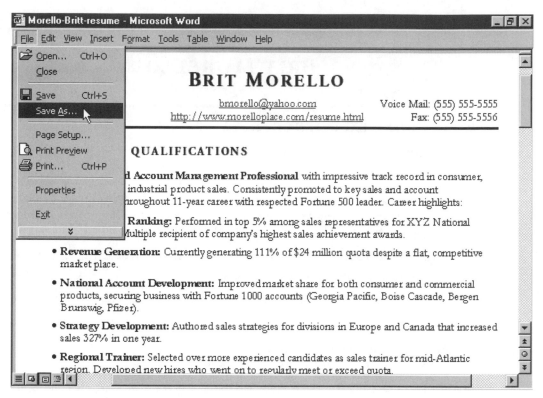

Figure 3-5 Step 1 in the ASCII conversion process.

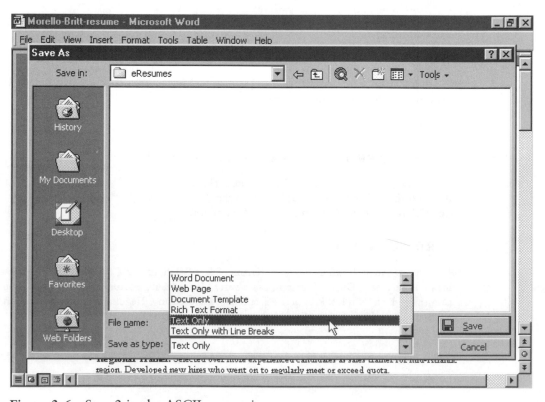

Figure 3-6 Step 2 in the ASCII conversion process.

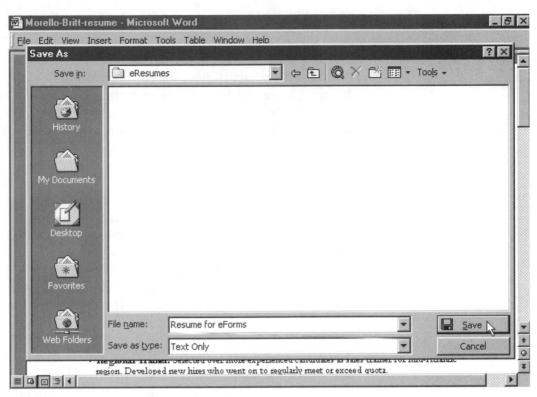

Figure 3-7   Step 3 in the ASCII conversion process.

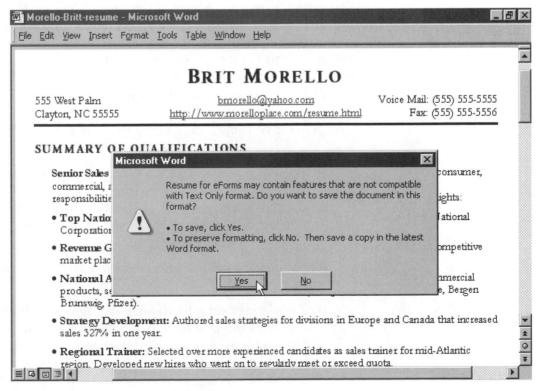

Figure 3-8   Step 4 in the ASCII conversion process.

Converting Your Resume to Paste into Email Messages

To convert your resume for email requires a few extra steps than for eforms. As we mentioned, we recommend the Text Only with Line Breaks file format for pasting into emails. Why line breaks? Because experts in the online recruitment industry recommend this format. Neil Fox, CIO for BrilliantPeople.com (the Web site for Management Recruiters International's network of 5,000 search professionals), advises job seekers to "include hard line breaks when emailing your resume." Bill Vick, CEO of Recruiters Online Network (the world's largest association of recruiters, executive search firms, and employment agencies) concurs: "Straight ASCII text with line breaks" is the format most compatible with all systems. (Both of these visionaries testify to the increasing prevalence of software products that accommodate HTML files and advise job seekers to also think in terms of providing an HTML or XML version—refer to Chapter 6. In the meantime, we'll confine our discussion in this chapter to ASCII-plaintext format.)

The term *line breaks* refers to the placement of hard returns at the end of each line, forcing the start of a new line, or break, at that point. Your goal is to restrict the number of characters that appear on each line to approximately 60 to 65 (including spaces). The end result will be a single column of text measuring approximately 5.5 inches from left to right (just one inch less than paper resumes). In many cases, this width matches the default screen size used by popular email programs. Many of the job seekers we've worked with are surprised at this shortened line length, and concerned that the resume will be much longer than necessary if printed out. Our response to this is that an emailed resume isn't meant to be printed out; and, if it is printed, most recruiters realize that formats for emailed resumes won't be the same as paper resumes.

The benefits of using Text Only with Line Breaks are threefold:

- *For those recipients who read your resume with a text editor, you can prevent the annoying "tennis-match" scroll (moving the scroll bar from left to right to read every new line) or the appearance that text has dropped off on the right margin.*

- *To some degree, you can control the look of the text on the recipient's end and avoid odd line breaks, such as those seen in Figure 3-9.*

- *Line breaks set a predefined line length, which will normally retain its original formatting when forwarded one time, say, from a recruiter to a client company. (Line-break formatting will eventually disintegrate in documents that are forwarded over and over again; the only way to prevent this is to have each person who forwards your email delete the ">" marks*

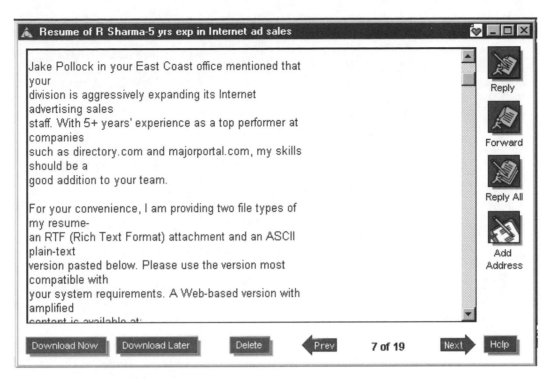

Figure 3-9   Example of bad line breaks, the result of placing too many characters on a line when using line breaks.

that precede each line of a forwarded email . . . something you have no control over.)

The steps to convert your word-processed resume to ASCII (Text Only with Line Breaks) for emailing are outlined in Table 3-5. Note that steps 4 to 8 correspond to steps 1 to 5 discussed previously for eforms, with one exception: you'll choose Text Only with Line Breaks when it comes time to select a file type.

After completing the steps in Table 3-5 and opening the new text document, the format will look pretty rough. Read on to learn how to give your ASCII resume a much-needed face-lift.

10 Steps to Clean Up Formatting

Whether preparing your resume for eforms or email, a few post-conversion tweaks can have a huge impact on the readability and visual appeal of your new text resume. *Use a text editor program for this task instead of MS Word.* Unsupported ASCII characters may display properly in Word yet appear as glitches in Notepad or other text editors. A text editor will give you an accurate picture of the ASCII text.

To open Notepad, the text editor bundled into Windows' operating system, click Start, Programs, Accessories, Notepad. (Mac users,

Table 3-5   Steps to Convert a Resume for Email

Steps	Microsoft Word Instructions	WordPerfect Differences	Tips
1. Highlight the document.	With your word processing software open and resume on screen, click Edit, Select All.		Press Ctrl A as a shortcut for Edit, Select All.
2. Change right margin to 2.0 inches.	Click File, Page Margins. Setup, Enter 1.0 (for 1 inch) in the boxes labeled Top, Bottom, and Left. Enter 2.0 in the box labeled Right. Click OK.	Corel WordPerfect users: click Format, Margins, Page Margins, then enter 1.0 in the boxes labeled Left, Top, and Bottom; enter 2.0 in the box labeled Right. Click OK.	See illustration in Figure 3-10.
3. Set a fixed-width font, such as Courier.	With the document still highlighted (step #1 above), change the font by clicking Format, Font. Scroll through the font selections found in the drop-down box labeled Font or Font Face. Click on Courier or Courier New. In the drop-down box for Font Size, choose 10 pt. Click OK.		Figure 3-11 displays the font dialogue box in MS Word. When finished with this step, click anywhere on the document to turn off the highlighting. Why Courier 10 pt? Because Courier is a fixed-width font. This means each character will take up the same amount of horizontal space (e.g., the letter "i" will take up the same width as an "m"), giving you some control over where the line will break. The 10-pt size will position approximately 65 characters (letters, spaces, or punctuation) on each line. This line width is easily readable and fits in most email screens without the unsightly line-wrap effect.
4. Use the Save As function.	Click File, Save As.		Shown earlier in Figure 3-5.
5. Choose Text Only with Line Breaks.	In the Save As dialogue box, click the drop-down arrow to the right of Save As Type. Scroll down and select Text Only with Line Breaks.	Scroll up in the File Type box and select ANSI (Windows) Text.	See Figure 3-12. As discussed in converting files for eforms, you can give the file a new name. In this case, the name "Resume-Emailable" or "Paste to Email" will help you remember the purpose of the file.
6. Save the file.	Click Save.		Make note of where you save the file.
7. Accept the warning.	Click Yes in response to the warning box.	Same, with one caveat: Users of older WP versions (6.1 or before) must type the .txt extension in the File Name Box (e.g., resemail.txt).	Illustrated earlier in Figure 3-8. The warning is simply cautioning you that formatting will be eliminated from the document. This is your goal.
8. Close the file.	Click File, Close to remove the file from the screen.	Same.	Your file will look unchanged. To review the changes, you'll need to open the new text document in a text editor (explained later).

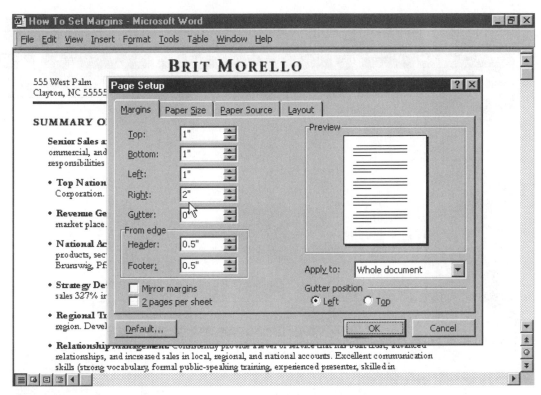

Figure 3-10   Step 2 in conversion of resume to ASCII for emailing. Margins should be 1 inch on the left and 2 inches on the right.

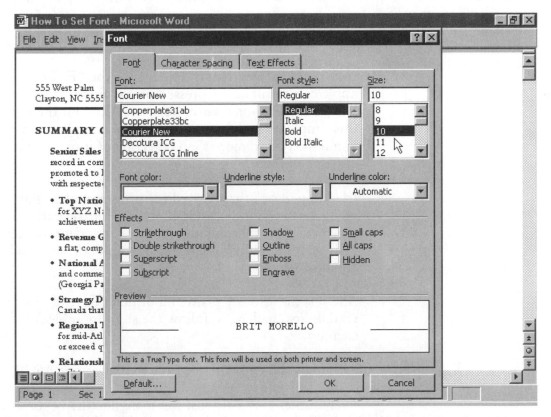

Figure 3-11   Step 3 in conversion of resume to ASCII for emailing. Font should be set to 10-point Courier.

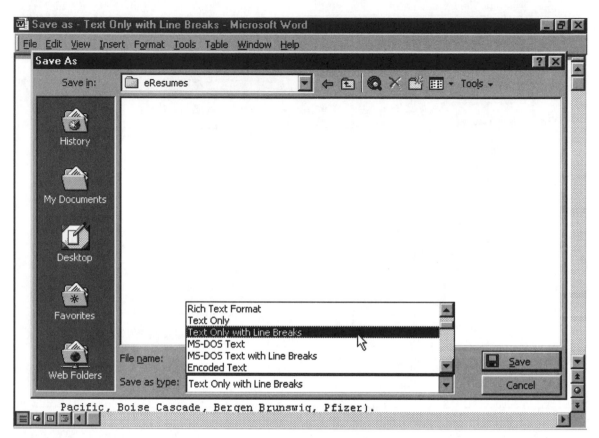

Figure 3-12 Step 5 in conversion of resume to ASCII. Choose "Text Only with Line Breaks" for an emailable resume.

click on Your Desktop and then click the "F" key with your apple/command key depressed. In the finder window, type SimpleText—one word, no space—and hit the Find button. Since this simple text editor comes with most application installations, you'll likely find more than one copy of it on your computer. Open any one of them.)

In Notepad or other text editor program, click File, Open and navigate to the folder that contains your recently saved text file. You'll see that the .doc to .txt conversion process automatically stripped ruling lines, bolding, underlining, and other enhancements.

ASCII is notoriously plain and difficult to read. To counter these readability challenges, follow the steps in Table 3-6 for format cleanup.

Although you can take the time to make your ASCII resume pretty, formatting efforts beyond the 10 tips listed in Table 3-6 will be relatively futile. There are just too many factors beyond your control, including the type of email program and the user's default settings for line breaks, type size, display dimensions, and more.

Table 3-6 10 Tips to Improve Readability of ASCII Text

Step	Description	Example
1. Format contact information.	Place all of your "dashboard" information on the left margin, using a separate line for name; street address; city, state, and zip; telephone; alternative telephone; email address; and URL.	```Brit Morello``` ```555 West Palm``` ```Clayton, NC 55555``` ```Voice Mail: (555) 555-5555``` ```Fax: (555) 555-5556``` ```Email: bmorello@yahoo.com``` ```www.morelloplace.com/resume.html```
2. Review bullets.	Make sure that bullets converted properly to asterisks (*). Word automatically converts round bullets to asterisks. Other types can turn into question marks (?). Bulleted items can be accentuated by adding space in front of the asterisk (touch the spacebar five times to emulate a tab set); this extra spacing may hold when pasted into an email but will disappear if pasted into Web site eforms.	Before: ```? Top National Ranking:``` ```Performed in top 5% ...``` After: ```* Top National Ranking:``` ```Performed in top 5% ...``` See Figure 3-13 for an example of "bad" bullets.
3. Replace unsupported ASCII characters.	Scroll through the document to check for glitches. In addition to fixing bullets, you'll want to replace other characters that may have converted improperly. (See Table 3-2 for basic ASCII characters.)	Note the examples of ASCII characters that converted incorrectly in Figure 3-2 and the appropriate ASCII replacement characters in Table 3-1.
4. Add white space.	To improve readability, separate each paragraph with two line spaces. Always place two line spaces before category sections to set them off clearly. You may also want to use two line spaces between bulleted items. To add a line space, place your cursor at the end of a paragraph and touch the enter key.	Before: ```PROFESSIONAL EXPERIENCE``` ```XYZ National Corp ...``` ```(The worldwide leader ...``` After: ```PROFESSIONAL EXPERIENCE``` ```XYZ National Corp ...``` ```(The worldwide leader ...```
5. Left-justify all text.	Delete any large spaces or gaps that resulted from center codes, tabs, or columns in your original Word document. For instance, dates that were right-justified in MS Word will need to be moved to a new line on the left margin.	Note the improvement between the "Before" and "After" resumes in Figures 3-13 and 3-14.
6. Tighten spacing.	If you haven't already done so, use just one space instead of two between sentences and after colons. When readers view the document in a Courier default font, two spaces between sentences leaves gaping holes, reminiscent of a child's smile with two front teeth missing.	Before: ```Develop and implement joint``` ```marketing programs. Built``` ```relationships with key``` ```individuals. Preface all``` ```contacts with . . .``` After: ```Develop and implement joint``` ```marketing programs. Built``` ```relationships with key``` ```individuals. Preface all``` ```contacts with . . .```

(continued)

Table 3-6   10 Tips to Improve Readability of ASCII Text (*Continued*)

Step	Description	Example

7. Clean up columns or tables.	If columns were used in the print version, place text in a single column. Likewise, tables should be reformatted for a textual presentation. Do not try to realign text that previously appeared in columns or tables—chances are slim that it will stay put once transmitted to a hiring manager, and failed attempts look horrid!	Before:
		`Distribution  Warehousing`
		`Shipping   Inventory`
		`Receiving   Logistics`
		
		After:
		`Distribution`
		`Shipping`
		`Receiving`
		`Warehousing`
		`Inventory`
		`Logistics`

8. Delete unnecessary information.	If the original version of your resume included more than one page, delete any references to "continued," as well as header information on the top of subsequent pages.	Before:
		`...first year.`
		`(continued)`
		
		`BRIT MORELLO`
		`Voice Mail: (555) 555-5555 Page`
		`2    bmorello@yahoo.com`
		`PROFESSIONAL EXPERIENCE (cont.)`
		`XYZ National Corp. (cont.)`
		`Senior Sales Representative...`
		
		After:
		`...first year.`
		
		`Senior Sales Representative...`

9. Set off category headings.	Format resume category headings (Qualifications, Education, Experience, etc.) in all CAPS. Consider accenting category headings by adding a few equal signs separated by spaces (= = =) or tildes (~ ~ ~) or some other combination of keyboard characters. Use the same treatment for each resume category.	`QUALIFICATIONS`
		`~ ~ ~ ~ ~ ~ ~ ~ ~ ~`
		`QUALIFICATIONS`
		`-^-^-^-^-^-^-^-^-`
		`QUALIFICATIONS = = = =`
		`QUALIFICATIONS`
		`------------------`
		`QUALIFICATIONS`
		`~~~~~~~~~~~~~~~~~~`

10. Save the file.	Click File, Save to retain all of the format enhancements you've made in steps 1 to 9.	When making changes to the formatted (Word) document, remember to make the same changes to your ASCII file in Notepad.

Figures 3-13 and 3-14 give you a "before" and "after" picture of format cleanup. Your emailable resume—with line breaks—should resemble the "after" illustration. Alternatively, your resume for eforms—with no line breaks—will look similar with the exception that each paragraph will appear as one long line. (Don't worry about this; scrolling right will display everything. Once the text is copied into eforms, it will reformat to the preset margins of the forms.)

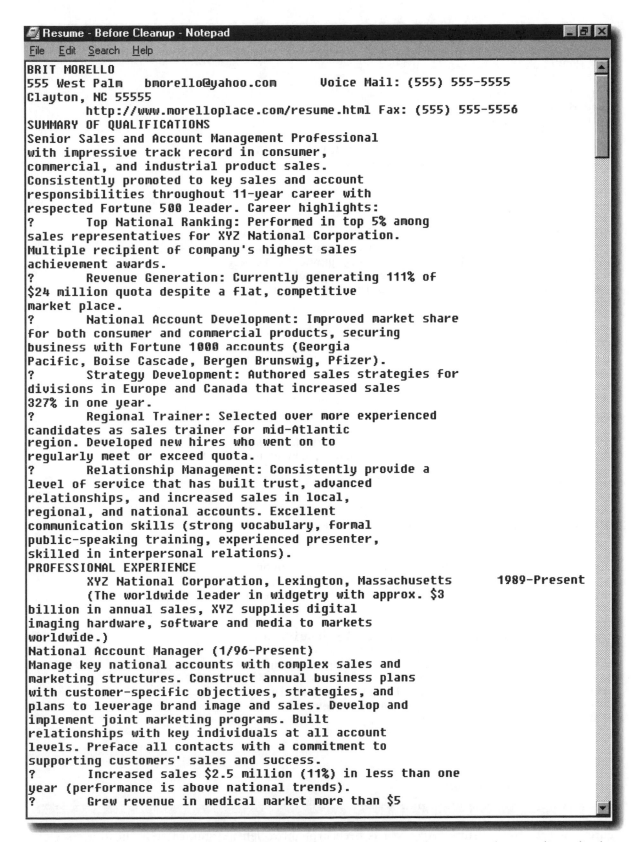

Figure 3-13   "Before" resume. Prior to cleanup, raw ASCII in the Notepad text editor displays unsupported characters as ? and is difficult to read.

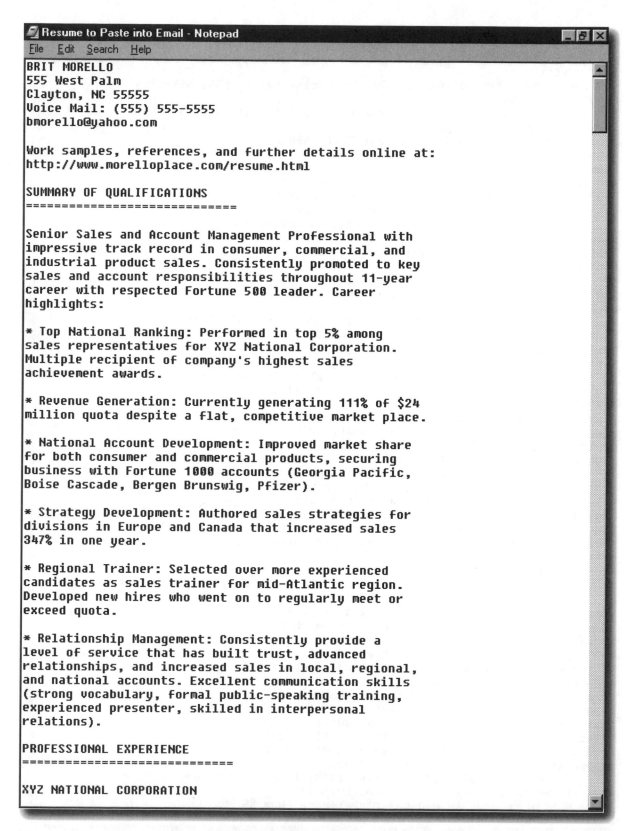

Figure 3-14   "After" resume. All text has been brought to left margin, category headings set off, unsupported characters changed, and extra spacing added to improve readability.

Now that your resume is ready for a ride over Internet lines, let's talk about the process of getting it into the hands of an employer (or the records of a database). The pasting process for eforms and email is covered in Chapter 4, along with some insider tips, tricks, and traps to avoid.

Chapter 4

Pasteable Resumes: Using Eforms and Email in Your Job Search

In Chapter 10, "Getting the Word Out," we cover a number of options for where to post your resume (including helpful comparisons of career, recruiter, and resume distribution Web sites, as well as confidentiality options and tips for finding industry- and region-specific sites.) In this chapter, you'll find pointers on how to get your ASCII resume from your computer to Web site eforms or in an email in minutes, if not seconds. It's done through a simple copy-and-paste function.

Resume Builders

Eforms come in different sizes for different functions. They are used primarily to collect and send information to an application (e.g., a resume-tracking database program), which can then store, sort, search, preview, or print the information. Getting your resume into the "hands" of a database can extend your networking reach and add to the shelf life of the resume.

At career sites like Monster.com (and some company sites, as well), you'll encounter a "resume builder." This tool takes you through a series of steps (some short and simple, some long and drawn-out) to produce an electronic resume and profile. You may be required to click through "radio" buttons and drop-down boxes, as well as input or copy text into several eforms. Behind the scenes, the resume builder is separating information into database fields that describe items such as your title, skill set, number of years' experience, keywords, education, salary requirement, relocation limitations, and contact information. There are dozens of e-recruiting application service providers (the companies that design resume builders), and each has products with varying levels of sophistication. One of the more recognized is Webhire.com (the Internet-based descendant of Restrac, once a leading applicant-tracking software program), which now powers the likes of Yahoo! Resumes and the recruiting efforts of more than a thousand customers, including American Express, Boeing, and Northrop Grumman. Other providers include Recruitsoft.com and Resumix, a subsidiary of HotJobs.com.

Pasting Your Resume into Web Site Eforms

Have you been exploring the World Wide Web and found a career site that requires you to use its resume builder? When you're at the site, the first thing to do is open your text editor (in future references, we'll be using Notepad). Click File, Open to bring up your Text Only resume (if you took our advice in Chapter 3, you may have labeled the file "Resume-for-eforms.txt"). Your screen should look something like Figure 4-1 (with the appropriate company Web site in the background).

The resume builder in this illustration breaks the posting process down into separate sections for Objective, Experience, and Education. With your text resume open in Notepad, you can copy and paste the appropriate information into the corresponding text box. To copy from Notepad, highlight the text, right-click, and select Copy. Move your mouse to the Web site window and click anywhere—this will automatically minimize the Notepad program and make the Web site active. Position your cursor inside the eform, left-click so that your cursor is blinking inside the form, then right-click and paste. Repeat the process until you've filled in every section.

One thing to be aware of is that some resume builders automatically generate a category title (e.g., Objective or Experience). For

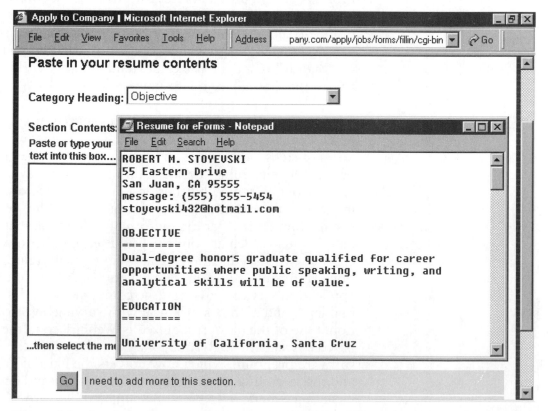

Figure 4-1 Posting a text resume at a career Web site. The text resume is displayed in Notepad, while the Web site is displayed in the background.

Tips for First-Timers

TIP

After text is pasted into an eform, the cursor automatically positions itself at the end of the text. Since the window size on eforms is sometimes small, you may need to use the vertical scroll bar to move up to view the beginning of the text. To reactivate Notepad to grab and copy more text, click on the Notepad icon on your task bar. The program will return to the same size as when it was last open. You can resize the Notepad window by moving your mouse on top of a border—once the left-right or top-bottom double arrows appear, left-click and drag to the desired dimension. To move the entire window, click on the title bar and drag it. Resizing windows can allow you to see both Notepad and the Web site at the same time.

those that do, select from your ASCII resume only the appropriate text (exclude the heading) or you'll end up with duplicate category headings. Figure 4-2 illustrates how to copy information from Notepad, while Figure 4-3 shows the result of pasting the text in the eform.

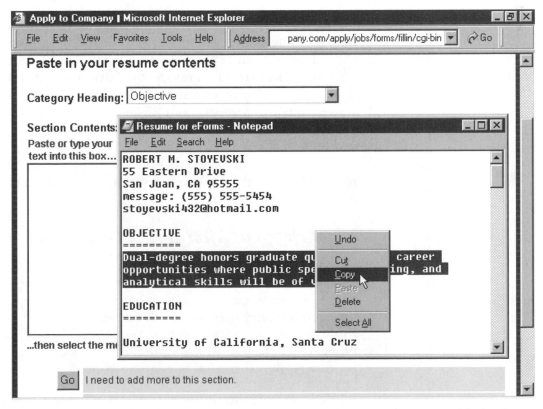

Figure 4-2   How to copy information from Notepad to a Web site. Highlighted text ("Objective" section) will be pasted into an eform.

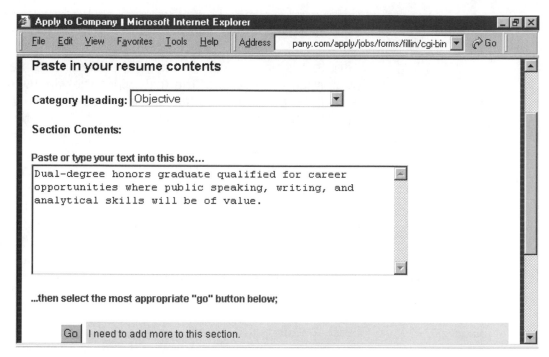

Figure 4-3 Text pasted into an eform (resume builder). The Notepad program has been minimized while the cursor is active in the Web site.

COMMON FAUX PAS IN USING RESUME BUILDERS

Filling in dozens of eforms can get tedious. Don't be hasty or careless. Rushing the process is one of the land mines that job seekers should avoid with resume builders. To make sure your online resume doesn't backfire, review the "Top Five Faux Pas in Using Resume Builders," courtesy of Kim Isaacs, director of Resume-Power.com and Monster.com Resume Expert. (Monster.com—behemoth of all career sites—is the most popular site for posting resumes on the Web. See Table 10-3 for posting tips to different career sites.) Although Isaacs's advice is specific to Monster.com's resume builder, these insider secrets are relevant to resume builders at most career sites.

What Happens After You Click Submit

Ever wonder what happens to your information once you've clicked Submit? It depends entirely on the programming behind the scenes. Figure 4-4 shows a job seeker submitting a resume to the TopEchelon.com recruiter network. In this case, the resume landed in a sophisticated proprietary program developed by Canton, Ohio–based Top Echelon Network, Inc., a network of nearly 1000 independently owned recruiting companies across the United States.

Mark Demaree, Vice President of Top Echelon Network, explains that the software searches according to profile data given by the job seeker at the Web site. This information is then compared to exist-

TIP

Top Five Faux Pas in Using Resume Builders
(shared by Kim Isaacs, Monster.com Resume Expert and Director of Resume-Power.com)

1. **Lack of industry keywords:** One of the top mistakes people make with the resume builder is lack of keywords. Keywords are vital if job seekers are to be found in an online database. Monster.com's resume builder gives ample opportunity to add industry keywords—you can use the "Skills" and "Additional Information" sections to sneak in keywords that don't appear elsewhere in the document.

2. **Really bad "Title":** When hiring managers sift through resumes that match their search criteria, they are primarily reviewing the title of each resume. This makes the title one of the most important sections of the resume builder, yet job seekers often gloss over it, sometimes including a vague label or something that doesn't reflect their career goals. Ideally, the title should contain the keywords for the desired job or career objective.

3. **Self-centered focus on the "Describe Your Ideal Job" and "Describe Your Ideal Company" fields:** When job seekers are asked to fill out these sections, many go into detail about their own needs, including benefits, ideal working conditions, or even desired dress codes. Instead, users should turn this question around and focus on the employers' needs or their key qualifications (for example: "Seeking a sales position that will benefit from my 7-year record of meeting business development, productivity, and profit goals . . .").

4. **One-size-fits-all resumes:** Monster.com allows users to store up to five resume versions, yet many job seekers try to make one resume fit all circumstances. Because of the large number of job seekers online, hiring managers are more likely to be seeking an "exact match"—they don't have time to decipher where a job seeker might fit. Those job seekers with more than one goal will be better served by setting up targeted resumes for each of their objectives.

5. **Rushing through the forms:** Monster.com's resume builder usually takes about 20 minutes to complete. Some folks try to rush the process, and the end result is a poorly developed resume, complete with typos and other signs of poor writing. Job seekers should take the time to think about their responses and double-check to be sure the final document is error free. Monster.com offers a feature that saves the resume as it's being built, allowing users to come back and fine-tune the document, then "activate" the resume only when it's perfect.

Lastly, here's a little-known resume builder "tip" specific to Monster.com: If your resume has been in the system for several months, you can "renew" it and bring it to the top of the stack. To do this, sign in, go to My Monster, Resumes, find your resume in the list, and select "renew."

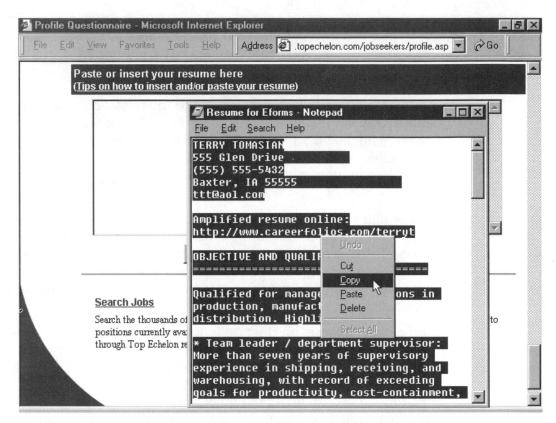

Figure 4-4   Entire text resume is highlighted, ready to be pasted into an eform, which will later process it into special recruiting software.

ing job openings—the job seeker from Figure 4-4 came up with 13 potential job matches. Figure 4-5 shows a control page in the TopEchelon software (viewable only by the member recruiter who posted the job) that displays "dashboard" information on the candidate—everything from position title, profile, and skill set to geographic and salary requirements. The recruiter can click on the View Resume tab and see a full screen shot of the candidate's ASCII text resume (Figure 4-6), as well as access a number of other search and candidate management features. This illustration gives you an interesting peek at the high-tech tools available to recruiters and how those tools can affect your job search.

Emailing Your Resume

Differences in Email Programs

There are a number of email programs in use—MS Outlook Express, Eudora, Lotus Notes, AOL, and more—and each release has its own idiosyncrasies that will affect the look of your resume. This challenge is compounded by the fact that every user can change his or her default settings, making it impossible to know how your text resume will display on other computers.

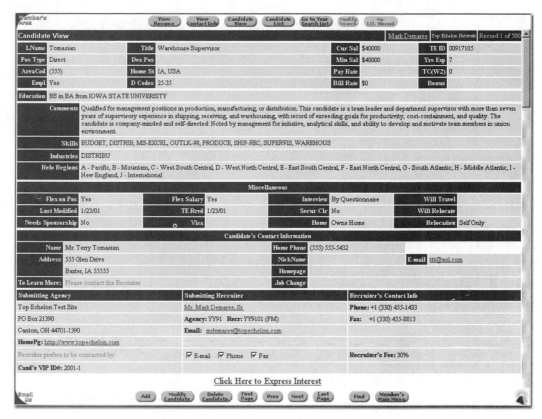

Figure 4-5   Special recruiting software—control page displays candidate profile information, as well as link buttons to other recruiting options.

Karen Osofsky, cofounder of Chicago-based Tiburon Group, an e-recruiting consulting firm that also powers RecruiterResources.com, understands the problems that occur with different email systems. She observes, "Often, the emailed resumes we receive are dramatically altered from the originals." When a qualified candidate surfaces, she teaches third-party recruiters to do some cleanup before passing the resume on to the client company's hiring manager. "It's better for recruiters to spend 5 minutes today reformatting a resume than 10 hours tomorrow looking for another candidate." Osofsky reports that "Some hiring managers really rely on a well-formatted resume. In many cases, they can't get past the distractions of a poorly formatted resume and will reject a candidate who is otherwise qualified." These comments drive home our message that first impressions are critical. You should do all you can to ensure that your ASCII resume has a clean, appealing format that will survive the vagaries of any and all email systems.

The growing sophistication of email programs has afforded many new format options, primarily the ability to mark up, or "style," text with different fonts, colors, and sizes. In essence, the styles automate the application of HTML codes and dress up the appearance of plain text. In addition, pictures can be added to text, and stationery templates can be applied to messages. MS Outlook

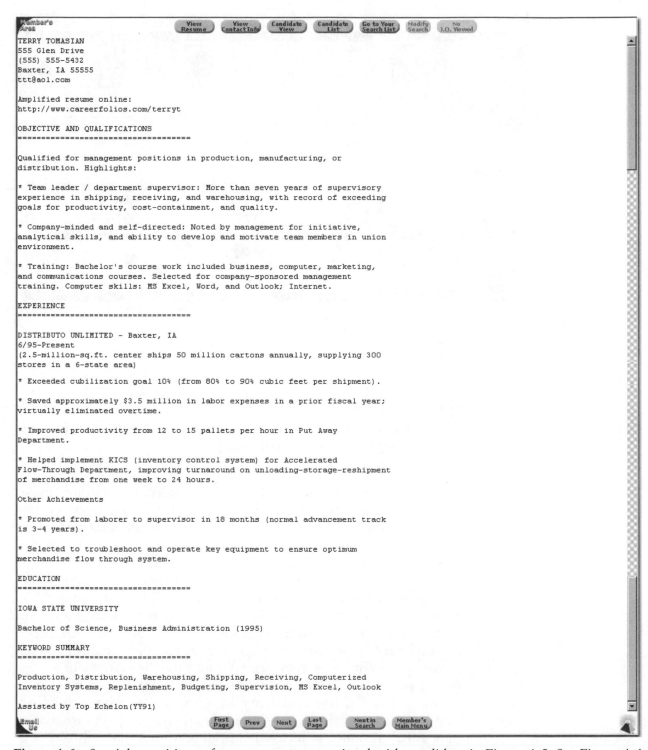

Figure 4-6 Special recruiting software—resume associated with candidate in Figure 4-5. See Figure 4-4 for original submission.

Express offers 25 stationery styles, from subtle backgrounds to bright, fiesta-like themes. Despite the fun of using these bells and whistles, we strongly discourage you from "ringing and blowing" when writing to employers! Your recipient may very well use a different email system that doesn't support HTML formatting.

Figure 4-7 shows a sample email prepared in MS Outlook Express using the Chess template stationery. Styled text (bold, italic, font changes) was also used. Figure 4-8 displays the jumbled mess seen by the recipient, an America Online subscriber. This is what would happen to your resume.

Messages created in MS Outlook Express with a stationery template can split into separate bits of text and graphics, with the graphics files turning into an attachment when opened in AOL and other HTML-enabled email programs. In Figure 4-8, you'll note that the attachment is the "Chess.gif" file we mentioned earlier. The phrase "DL Time (TCP/IP): < 1 minute" on the email means that downloading this particular file will take less than 1 minute on a high-speed cable connection (slower-speed modems will require a longer download time).

Depending on the original message, the text file might also be bundled into a .zip file. In this case, the recipient sees no message on opening the email—only a blank email screen with an attachment that must be downloaded, unzipped with special software, and extracted to open and view . . . a time-consuming and unappealing prospect when the recipient has no clue as to who sent the email or why.

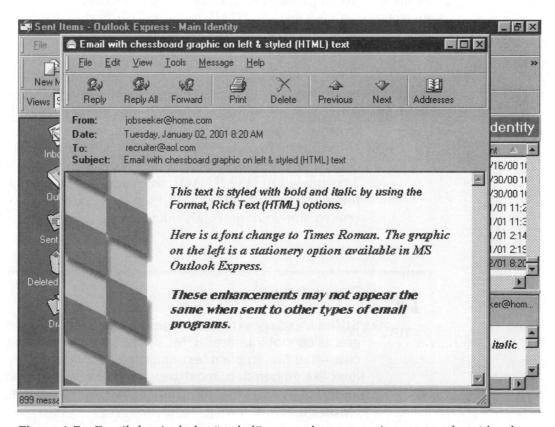

Figure 4-7   Email that includes "styled" text and uses a stationery template (the chessboard on left side). Stationery templates can cause compatibility problems.

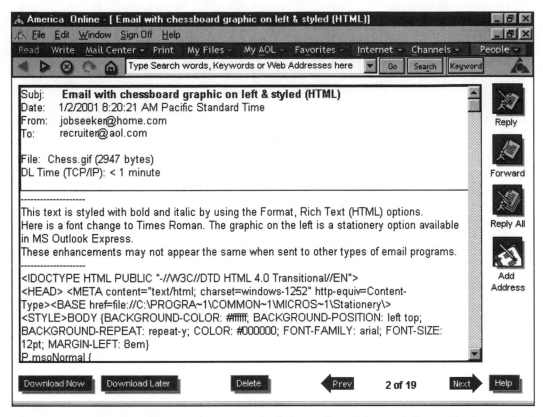

Figure 4-8 Incompatible email systems. Styled text from Figure 4-7 morphs into a dual presentation of plain text and HTML codes, and places the stationery template into an attachment labeled Chess.gif.

In addition to glitches with stationery templates, the original enhancements to the text (bold, italic, font changes) have been stripped. Note that the entire message is repeated with all of the HTML code that was required to "style" the text. To avoid this, change the MS Outlook default for Mail Sending Format to Plain Text instead of HTML. AOL users can also style email text but only for the benefit of fellow AOL users; when the same styled text is sent to non-AOL users, all enhancements are stripped.

Double Trouble!

TIP

Styled messages (resumes) sent to recipients whose email programs cannot interpret HTML will display the message in duplicate—the first in plain text and the second as HTML codes that look like gibberish to most people. This effectively doubles the length of the resume, requiring the recipient to delete the second message before saving it to disk.

Format Email for the Lowest Common Denominator

Because of the differences in email programs and the unforeseeable happenstances of Internet transmission, we recommend that you set your email default settings for Plain Text delivery. While this recommendation may be disheartening to those of you who are "visually oriented," there are a number of advantages to formatting for the lowest common denominator:

- *Control. You're virtually assured that the WYSIWYG (what you see is what you get) principle will hold true. In this case, it's WYSIWES (what you see is what everyone sees).*

- *Consistency. In most cases, you won't be familiar with the email preferences of your recipient. Plain Text guarantees that your message will be easily readable by all email software. This is especially important when using an online distribution service, where your resume may be sent to hundreds or thousands of contacts.*

- *Clean. Plain Text delivery ensures that messages created with stationery templates won't be turned into attachments, which can raise concerns about viruses (see Chapter 5).*

- *Conversion. When inserting text files that do not contain line breaks, the Plain Text option automatically inserts line breaks, placing a predetermined number of characters on each line.*

To change the Mail Sending Format in MS Outlook Express from HTML to Plain Text for your job search email, start at the main screen (close any new message that may be started) and follow these steps:

1. At the main window, click Tools, Options.

2. Click the Send tab.

3. Under Mail Sending Format, select the Plain Text option.

4. Click the Plain Text Settings button that appears to the right of the Mail Sending Format.

5. Change the "Automatically wrap text" option to 65 characters, as Figure 4-9 illustrates.

The process for changing Eudora's word wrap settings is similar.

1. Click Tools, Options.

2. Scroll to and click on Composing Mail.

3. Uncheck the Word Wrap option.

4. Click OK.

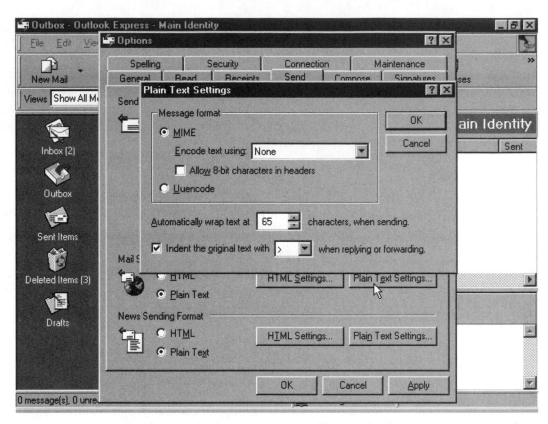

Figure 4-9   How to change Plain Text Settings in MS Outlook Express. Increase characters per line to 65.

We'll admit that using the HTML option—which allows you to apply stationery, use color, and format text—makes an emailed resume much more attractive. Nonetheless, it's virtually impossible to guarantee those enhancements will hold (or won't morph into something worse) when viewed with different email programs. If you really want to gussy up your text, a Web resume is the best way to do it (see Chapter 6).

Steps for Emailing a Glitch-Proof Resume

Your resume and email default settings should now allow your resume to travel glitch-free on the Internet. Follow the steps in Table 4-1 to transport your text resume from your computer to a hiring manager's computer. Instructions are provided for users of MS Outlook Express, Eudora, and America Online.

Table 4-1   How to Send a Glitch-Proof Email

Step	MS-Outlook Express Users	Eudora Users	AOL Users	Tips
1. Start a new email message.	Launch MS Outlook Express and click the New Message icon. You can also use the standard toolbar and click File, New, Mail Message.	Launch Eudora. Click Message New or Ctrl N.	Click the Write icon near the top left of the main screen (this is faster than using the Mail Center icon, which can load slowly due to all the Mail Center graphics).	Complete the message before filling in the Send To information. Some email programs will send messages with a combination of shortcut keys (Control Enter in Outlook Express and AOL); once those keys are struck, intentionally or not, your message is sent. One of the authors (whose initials start with S) can admit to doing this on several occasions—it can leave you with a sinking feeling if you hadn't yet finished or proofed your message.
2. Insert the cover letter and resume.	In MS Outlook Express, click Insert, Text from File (the cursor must first be active in the message window to access this option). Navigate to the folder that contains your text resume. Highlight the file and click Open. The resume will be inserted into the email message.	Launch Notepad. Click File, Open, then navigate to the folder with your text resume. Open the file. Right-click your mouse and Select All. Right-click again and Copy. Close Notepad and click on Eudora. With your cursor blinking in the email message area, right-click and Paste (or Ctrl-V).	Use Notepad or the AOL text editor to access text files. With either program running, click File, Open, then navigate to the folder with the text resume. Open the file. Right-click your mouse and Select All. Right-click again and Copy. Close the text editor window and make AOL the active window. With your cursor blinking in the email message area, right-click and Paste (or Ctrl-V).	Compose, proof, and fine-tune both your resume and cover letter in a word processing program, where you have the benefit of a thesaurus, spell check, and so on. Composing in an email program makes it tempting to dash off letters in a too-casual tone. The cover letter should precede the resume. Use a short row of dashes (———) to visually separate the letter from the resume. Note that the cursor moves to the end of the document after the resume is inserted. Scroll back through the entire document to make sure the resume looks intact.

Table 4-1   How to Send a Glitch-Proof Email *(Continued)*

Step	MS-Outlook Express Users	Eudora Users	AOL Users	Tips
3. Write a subject line.	Outlook Express allows up to 90 characters in its subject line.	Eudora allows you to write a short novel, but we recommend restraint—most email programs display a limited number of characters.	AOL allows 80 characters in its subject line.	The Subject line is very important—choose your words (or abbreviations) wisely. We recommend a 3-point subject line: Title-# yrs exp—other features See "Tips for Writing Tantalizing Titles."
4. Fill in the recipient's email address and click Send.	Consider using the address book to organize your job-search emails.	Consider using the address book to organize your job-search emails.	Consider using the address book to organize your job-search emails.	Use lowercase letters to type your recipient's email address. **Warning!** Never address the email to more than one employer at a time. Instead, send a separate email to each employer with a targeted cover letter. Before you email your first resume to an employer, send a test copy to your own email address, as well as to a friend with a different email program. This will give you and your ally a chance to view and correct any glitches before you submit to boss@dreamcompany.com!

Tips for Writing Tantalizing Titles

The subject line, or title, of your email is the employer's first impression of you. Avoid gimmicky phrasing: It may be interpreted as spam and be deleted posthaste. A conservative approach will often be better received.

FOLLOW A FORMULA

This three-part formula will guide you in determining a subject title for your email.

- *Resume/name/title. If making a first-time "cold" contact, use the term* resume *followed by your name. If you're responding to a job posting, it's not necessary to include the word* resume—*recruiters expect to receive resumes. Using your name in the title line can soften the anonymity factor associated with cold email, as well as facilitate the saving and naming of your file. Your position title should reflect the new job target. If your present title is inconsistent with your new job target, leave out the title.*

- *Years of experience. List the number of years of experience you have if it coincides with the job posting or complements your skills. When your number of years of experience undermines your abilities (e.g., "too old" or "too inexperienced"), substitute one of these phrases: "adv skills . . ." or "expert in . . ." or "strong bckgrd in . . ."*

- *Other features. Features should be keywords for your industry or selling points, such as an advanced degree, in-demand computer skills, certification, an employer with name recognition, or a major honor. It's fine to use abbreviations.*

Here are a few email subject lines that follow the preceding formula:

> Subj: Ref 21929-Juan Ortiz-Operations Mgr-12 yrs' exp w FedEx, MBA-Logistics
>
> Subj: Job ID55XYZ-Jon Orlando-Pharm Sales Rep-7 yrs' exp, top 5% nat'l ranking
>
> Subj: Resume-J.Green-Internet-Legacy Sys Architect-Java, CF, C++, RDBMS, XML
>
> Subj: Tod Simerton-Prod Mgr-10 yrs exp-APICS Cert-MBA

Recruiters tend to dislike self-appointed adjectives or "me-focused" wording in title lines. Accordingly, avoid titles such as these:

> Subj: Dedicated, fast learner, willing to train
>
> Subj: Seeking new challenge with industry leader
>
> Subj: Self-motivated, people person

Finally, never leave the subject line blank. We've spoken with recruiters who say they routinely delete untitled emails.

Avoid Slashes in the Subject Line

Slashes may cause extra work for your recipient in the file transfer process. Some employers will copy the email subject line and paste it as the filename when saving to disk. If the subject line contains a slash, a warning screen will pop up because the Windows operating system won't accept slashes as part of a filename. The employer then has to delete the slashes or substitute characters. Instead of a slash (/), consider using a dash (-), parenthesis, comma, or period.

WATCH YOUR CASE

Never use ALL CAPS in a subject line (or in the body of an email message). Statistics shows that upper- and lowercase letters are much easier to read and comprehend than all capitals. What's more, WRITING IN CAPS IS THE ONLINE EQUIVALENT OF SCREAMING!

TIP

Advanced Email Tips

- Here's My vCard! Consider using a vCard, the digital equivalent of a business card, when networking online. To create your own MS Outlook Express vCard, first use the Tools, Address Book keys to create a contact for yourself. Then click Tools, Options, Compose. In the Business Cards section, choose Mail; select your business card from the drop-down list. Your vCard will be added to your outgoing mail.

- Save Time with Message Templates. Advanced users of Outlook 2000 can set up a message template for their resume (earlier versions of Outlook do not support this). Complete the subject and message fields in a new message and choose File, Save As. In the Save dialog box, choose Outlook Template (*.OFT), type a filename (resume), and click Save. To use the resume template again, click File, New, Choose Form. From the Look drop-down menu, choose User Templates in File System, select your resume template, and click Open.

- Keep Track of Deliveries. To keep track of whether your job-search mail has been received, set your email program to request a return receipt. If recruiters have their email programs set for automatic response of return-receipt requests, they won't be aware you've requested a receipt. If they don't, there's a chance they may find the query for a receipt irritating. It's a trade-off. Here are the steps, should you decide to request receipts.

  · In Eudora, click to activate the Return Receipt button (RR) in the message toolbar.

  · In AOL, check the status of mail sent to other AOL users by clicking Read, Sent Mail, and Status. You cannot check the status of mail sent to non-AOL users.

Use the Universal Language

When it comes to submitting your resume to potential employers, think "multicultural." In other words, the "language" your system or email program speaks may not be the same as that of your reader, and the formatting "customs" you hold dear may not be embraced by those of your recipient. This is especially true for email. Messages sent with an HTML default may turn into an annoying attachment or appear as HTML code. In some companies, Word attachments may be welcomed; in others, attachments may be viewed with disdain.

The universal language—plaintext—is spoken everywhere. It may not be pretty, but it is understandable. If you want employers to view a nicer-looking version of your resume, opt for a Web-based format that you can refer to in your text resume (see Chapter 6). Alternatively, consider emailing an MS Word attachment, but do so only after reading the next chapter, which will help you avoid some common pitfalls and cmployer pet peeves associated with attachments.

Chapter 5

Resume Attachments: By Invitation Only

For nearly two decades, federal law enforcement officials were stymied by the identity of someone sending deadly package bombs. The culprit's first few bombing targets were *UN*iversity professors and an *A*irline executive, thus earning him the code name "UNA-bomber" by the FBI. After an intense investigation, it was learned that a former mathematics professor turned antitechnology hermit was behind the anonymous parcels. With revenge as his motive, Theodore Kaczynski hunted those who had helped advance the industrial-technological systems that he so vehemently opposed. Kaczynski's innocent-looking parcels injured, maimed, and killed. In a letter to one of his victims, he wrote:

> People with advanced degrees aren't as smart as they think they are. If you'd had any brains . . . you wouldn't have been dumb enough to open an unexpected package from an unknown source.

What does the Unabomber have to do with resume attachments? We're certainly not accusing those who send email attachments of having malicious intentions. Kaczynski knowingly acted with vengeance in sending his phony parcels. Unfortunately, job seekers can unknowingly create mayhem by causing hiring managers frustration, wasting their time, and, at worst, creating a major computer disaster, just by sending email attachments.

The Problem with Attachments

There are three troublesome issues associated with these innocuous "unexpected packages" known as attachments:

- *Safety*
- *Compatibility*
- *Time*

Let's look at each of these concerns in more detail.

Safety

Computer viruses are abundant, and many are virulent. To an email recipient, an attachment can be as dangerous as a deadly airborne disease. McAfee.com, the Internet's leading security application service provider, notes the existence of more than 53,000 viruses, with some 200 new ones discovered each month. Names like Melissa, LoveLetter, and Mother's Day sound harmless, but these viruses have spelled catastrophe for thousands of computer users.

Based on advice from reputable news sources such as *U.S. News & World Report,* some employers have policies against downloading attachments. The magazine's May 29, 2000 issue, in the wake of the Love Bug virus, advised users to "refuse to open e-mail attachments in the form of Microsoft Word documents that have a '.doc' extension." Love Bug ran rampant around the globe in a matter of hours, bringing hundreds of corporate systems, as well as four classified Pentagon networks, to a grinding halt. Damage from the virus was estimated to be between $300 million to $2.5 billion. No doubt, if "pain and suffering" damages were added in, the total cost would rival that of the national debt.

In an effort to curb destructive and costly viruses, many Internet service providers provide pop-up warning boxes when a user is about to download an attachment. The warning asks email recipients if they know the sender of the attachment, and then informs them that they are about to download a document that may contain a virus. Should you unknowingly submit a virus-infected file and it is detected by the employer, it will be deleted without being read. You can count yourself fortunate if the recipient takes the time to notify you of the mishap.

Think your computer is impervious to a virus? Once upon a time, co-author Susan Whitcomb thought so. She admits to formerly downloading resume files emailed from clients without using any virus protection program. One day, her computer started acting "funny." Finally, a pop-up box appeared on the computer screen that said "Susan Whitcomb is a stupid. . . ." (We won't bore you with the details.) The virus was relatively harmless but inserted the computer user's name to display a warning box with a less-than-pleasant message (and yes, at that point, Susan felt very stupid!) She quickly logged on to McAfee.com, gladly paid her $30 for a year's worth of virus protection, exorcised the little bug, and now devotedly downloads virus protection updates on a weekly, if not daily, basis. Moral of the story: If you don't have some sort of virus protection (and update it regularly), you're living dangerously.

Compatibility

An attachment carries with it the assumption that the receiver has the same software you have. Never assume! Although it may seem so, the entire planet does not use Microsoft Word for word processing. Apple Macintosh aficionados will confirm that not everyone is devoted to PCs. Even different software releases (for instance, Microsoft Word 2000 versus Microsoft Word 6.0) can cause glitches in files. And many people are unaware that a document prepared in MS Works (Microsoft's scaled-down word processing program) and opened in MS Word can either wreak havoc with formatting or not open at all.

When you send an attachment that is incompatible with your email recipient's system, your communication will likely be aborted. Most recruiters we interviewed while researching this book said they simply delete an attachment that is incompatible with their system. Rarely do recruiters have the time to write back and inform job seekers about incompatible file formats. Typically, these recruiters just press on, diligently shoveling out their email bins to make room for the next batch of resumes.

Time

We live in an age when Internet users don't have the patience to wait 15 seconds for a Web page to load. This "impatience quotient" also holds true for email. With the advent of dot-com resume distribution services (see Chapter 10), hiring managers are inundated with emailed resumes. If your resume can't be accessed quickly, it will likely be ignored. Granted, it takes only seconds to download a

---

Recruiter Preferences

Recruiters responding to a survey by Manchester International regarding preferences on emailed resumes had this to say about attachments:

- "We have ALL kinds of computers here, and there are ALL kinds of resumes that never get seen because the candidate has sent the important stuff in an attachment that we CANNOT OPEN."

- "[hiring managers] do not wish to take the time to open formatted attachments suitable for printing out."

- "We routinely scan all incoming e-mail for viruses; when we detect a virus, we delete the file."

- ". . . there is one basic rule. No Attachments. No Addenda. No additions. No extra files to try to open."

file and, when things go smoothly, less than a minute to open and view the file. This time may amount to mere minutes, but minutes multiplied by dozens of daily occurrences can add up. A resume pasted into the body of an email message can be seen immediately. If there is interest on the part of the recruiter, the text resume will be saved into the recruiter's system. Once the recruiter has contacted you, you can then send a more visually attractive, formatted resume. Alternatively, your text resume can include a URL to your in-depth and engaging Web resume (for how-to's, see Chapter 9). Here, the recruiter can obtain more information and even download your traditional resume without risking communicable diseases!

When to Use an Attachment

With all the liabilities associated with attachments, when should you send one?

> By invitation only!

Make a point of learning how your target company or recruiter wants to receive resumes. Many employers will have more than one accepted method. For instance, Figure 5-1 captures Microsoft Corporation's preferences for receiving resumes.

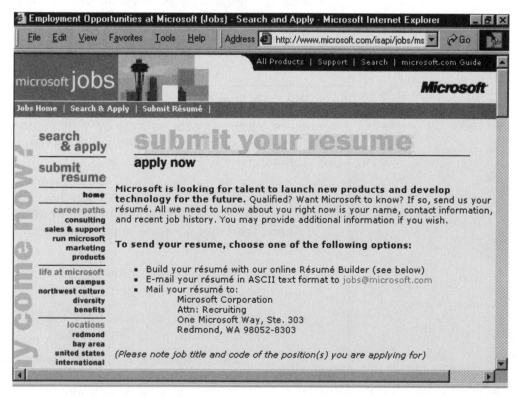

Figure 5-1   Microsoft's Employment Opportunities page, with recommendations for how to submit resumes.

Interestingly, even the granddaddy of the technology giants and maker of the ubiquitous MS Word prefers ASCII text delivered in an email message instead of a Word attachment. The company notes that email attachments can be received, yet it doesn't offer this method as one of its top three options.

If resume submission instructions are not posted at the employer's site, we recommend pasting an ASCII plain-text version into an email message (see Chapter 4). Or you can ask the employer or recruiting firm about its preference for receiving resumes.

Tips for Sending an Attachment

For those employers that request a formatted document (i.e., an attachment), the following tips will ensure that your resume can be downloaded, opened, and read.

Use the Recipient's Preferred File Format

Note what file format the recruiter prefers for attachments and use the Save As function to format your resume accordingly. In our review of corporate jobs pages and recruiting Web sites, we noted that MS Word (.doc) files and Rich Text Format (.rtf) files were specified most often—IF and WHEN an attachment was acceptable.

If you're not familiar with the RTF format, there are two important benefits you should be aware of:

- *Rich Text Format (RTF) typically cannot be infected with a macro virus, making it a safe format for sending documents via email. (See the tip "Viruses in RTFs?" for exceptions.)*

- *RTF files are universally compatible—all Web browsers, email programs, and word processing applications can read an RTF file.*

TIP

Viruses in RTFs?

Discouraging to note, even Rich Text Format documents can contain viruses, making attachments all the more mistrusted. Some macro viruses can intercept the RTF Save As process and instead save the resume as a DOC file with an RTF extension. You can catch this trick by first reading the file in a text editor, such as Notepad. DOC files will be nearly unreadable; RTF files will be readable.

If a job posting instructs you to send your resume in MS Word format, it's likely that the recipient has virus scanning software. In this case, do not send an .rtf file, lest you confuse the recipient with a different file extension or be accused of not following directions.

Name Documents Intuitively

Use your last name as part of the resume filename. One of the following methods for labeling your resume will be helpful to your email recipients (the extension will be either .doc or .rtf, depending on the recipient's preference):

- *Smith resume*
- *Smith (Jane) resume*
- *Smith-Jane resume*

A common error that job seekers make is sending a resume labeled simply "resume." Chances are good that the hiring manager has already received multiple file attachments that day with the same filename. The label "resume" causes extra work if your employer-to-be wants to save the file to his or her computer. When the file is labeled using one of the three preceding formulas, all the recipient need do is click File, Save Attachments, and Save (in MS Outlook Express). If the file is labeled with a generic "resume," the recipient must open and view the file to determine what your name is, so that the file can be accurately labeled. A recruiter responding to the Manchester survey confirms the benefit of using a descriptive name on resume attachments: "If the [applicant] writes their name as the name of the document, I always give them ten points for awareness of who's on the other side of the communication line!"

Limit Formatting

To allow for variations in printers, software releases, or system default settings, we recommend the following formatting settings:

- *Set margins to 1.0 on the top, bottom, left, and right.*
- *Limit use of tables, tabs, or columnar formatting.*
- *Use traditional fonts, such as Times Roman or Arial.*

Differences in hardware, software, or peripherals can cause your resume to appear different on the receiver's end. For instance, when we test printed a resume on three Hewlett-Packard printer models, we saw three different results. The best-of-breed Color LaserJet squeezed roughly 10 percent more information onto each line. The older LaserJet 4 expanded each character a bit, causing a two-page resume to become a four-page resume. Part of the problem was that the document contained a forced page break at the bottom of page one, yet page one had already spilled over to a second page. Once the printer "read" to the end of the new spillover page, it found a start-a-new-page code and promptly made a new third page. The same scenario occurred on the original page two. There were similar results with the color InkJet printer.

Another rationale for keeping things simple is that the more bells and whistles in formatting, the greater the file size. Some email services limit the size of attachments that can be received. And, of course, once the file is downloaded to the receiver's system, a larger file will eat up more hard disk space.

Some resume management software used by executive recruiters will automatically convert MS Word attachments to Rich Text Format. During the conversion process, style enhancements can be lost or distorted. In our conversion tests, we found that multiple tabs, columns, and tables had a tendency to fall out of alignment. Especially troublesome were nontraditional bullets—anything beyond the most conventional small circle morphed into question marks or hollow squares. The Employment Summary section in Figure 5-2 illustrates how tab stops can misalign, while the Professional Experience section shows how bullets created as arrows converted to empty rectangles. Figure 5-3 offers formatting solutions that address these problems.

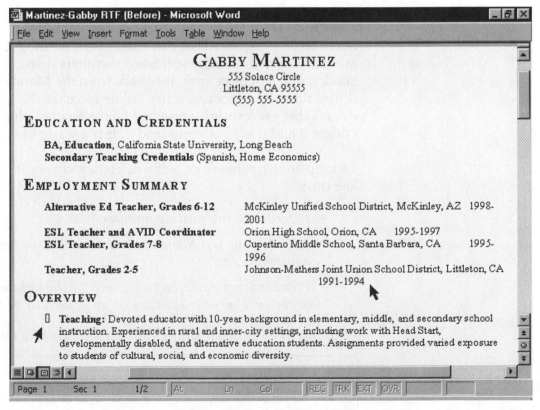

Figure 5-2   Problematic formatting in Word or RTF documents. Arrows point to tables that misaligned and nonstandard bullets that distorted on the receiver's end.

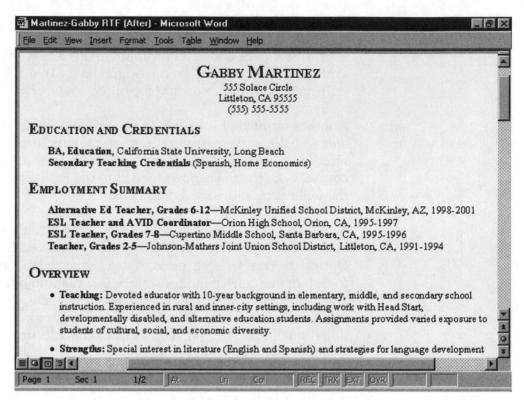

Figure 5-3 Recommended formatting that corrects problems seen in Figure 5-2.

Complete the Subject Line

Recruiters repeatedly tell us that emails with no subject line are automatically deleted. Yes, deleted. Some recruiters delete emails with nondescriptive subject lines. Feedback from the Manchester survey included this advice from an active online recruiter: ". . . often, I receive e-mails that say 'executive resume.' I have no idea what that means so I delete it and don't bother to read it. It is a waste of my time."

To keep your resume from being deleted, incorporate these subject-line tips:

- *Reference a job posting number, if any.*

- *Include your last name in the subject line to help reduce the anonymity factor.*

- *Provide tangible descriptors, such as the number of years' experience in your industry or an advanced degree.*

With this in mind, your subject line might look like this:

> Subj: Job Code FXG34 Res of J. Doe-7 yrs pharm
> sales exp, MBA

Refer to Chapter 4 for more specific information on writing a subject line.

Write a Cover Letter

Recruiters prefer that a cover letter be included in the body of the email message. Applicants who omit a cover letter are considered a bit clueless, much like those who mail a hard copy of their resume to a company without a cover letter. In general, follow these tips for your e-letter:

- *Make it short and to the point.*
- *Identify the position you're interested in or reference a job code or posting number.*
- *Summarize your most relevant qualifications.*

Most importantly, don't send a canned, generic letter.

Paste the ASCII Resume into the Email Message!

It may sound like a duplication of work when also sending an attachment, but there are several advantages to including the ASCII version within the email message:

- *First, the recruiter can quickly scan your qualifications to determine if there's a potential match for open positions.*
- *Second, should your attachment be incompatible for any reason, you've covered your bases by providing the text-only version.*

Use one of these sample paragraphs to explain why you've sent both an attachment and a plain-text version:

- *A plain-text version of my resume is pasted below for your convenience. Should you prefer a formatted resume, I have also attached an MS Word version (both the plain-text and formatted versions contain the same wording).*

or

- *I have attached an MS Word version of my resume, as well as pasted a plain-text version below. (If the plain-text version is sufficient for your database, it is not necessary to download the formatted attachment.)*

or

- *For your convenience, I am providing two file types of my resume—an RTF (Rich Text Format) attachment and an ASCII plain-text version pasted into this email. Please use the version most compatible with your system requirements.*

Attach Only One File

There is no need to send more than one file attachment to a hiring manager on your first contact. Some job seekers naively attach two separate files—one containing a cover letter and another with the resume—not realizing this is more time-consuming for the hiring manager (more clicks = more time). Those who use MS Outlook Express and Eudora can handle multiple email attachments easily, but for AOL users, viewing multiple file attachments can be as frustrating as untying the proverbial Gordian knot. The recipient of zipped file attachments must have or download a decoding program (such as WinZip or MimDecode), then log off to decompress the files (no matter how small each file might be). Only then can the files be opened and viewed.

To make life as easy as possible for hiring professionals, put the text of the cover letter in the email message and attach only one file— the resume.

After following the advice in this section, your resume should arrive in the employer's email program looking something like the examples shown at the end of this chapter (see Figures 5-5 through 5-7).

Insider's Tip

TIP

All MS Word documents have a "properties" template that provides a summary of information contained in the file. Completing this section may boost your chances of being found in document searches and reinforce your key skills when reviewed by a hiring manager. These steps explain how to change the Properties information on your document:

1. With the resume file open, click File, Properties.

2. Click the Summary tab.

3. Enter appropriate information in the Title, Subject, Author, Category, Keywords, or Comments boxes.

4. Click OK.

Figure 5-4 illustrates the Properties dialog box. Use the comment box for geographic preferences, relocation, or other relevant information. Although you might openly communicate your salary requirements when emailing a third-party recruiter, do not include this information in the properties box as it's possible the file will be forwarded on to the recruiter's client companies. If your resume was prepared by a resume professional or some other person, change Author to your name so as not to confuse recipients.

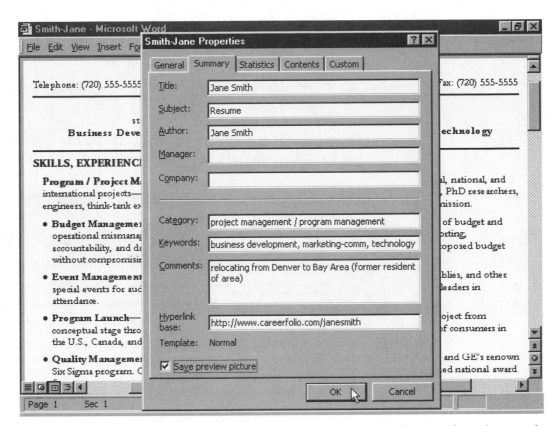

Figure 5-4 Properties dialog box in MS Word that can be used to reinforce keywords or communicate geographic preferences.

Courtesy Counts

We repeat: Courtesy counts. Just as you would include a letter explaining the contents of an unexpected package, you should clearly describe your intentions and qualifications before asking an employer to download or open your file attachment. Remember that in many job-search scenarios, you're an "unknown sender" of an "unknown parcel." To avoid potential problems, follow these seven tips before you send an attachment.

1. Use the file format indicated by the employer. When the employer asks for a formatted resume but does not specify file format, send the RTF file format.

2. Include your last name as part of the filename. Do not label the document "resume."

3. Avoid extensive formatting or style enhancements within the formatted resume, as styles may appear different on the recipient's system.

4. Fill in the subject line with descriptive, tangible information.

5. Write a brief cover letter. Avoid "canned" boilerplate letters.

6. Include an ASCII plain-text resume below the cover letter. This allows the recipient to review your qualifications without first opening the attachment.

7. Attach only one file on your first contact with the employer or recruiter.

These guidelines will earn you etiquette points from recruiters and add to your credibility as someone who is savvy about online job-

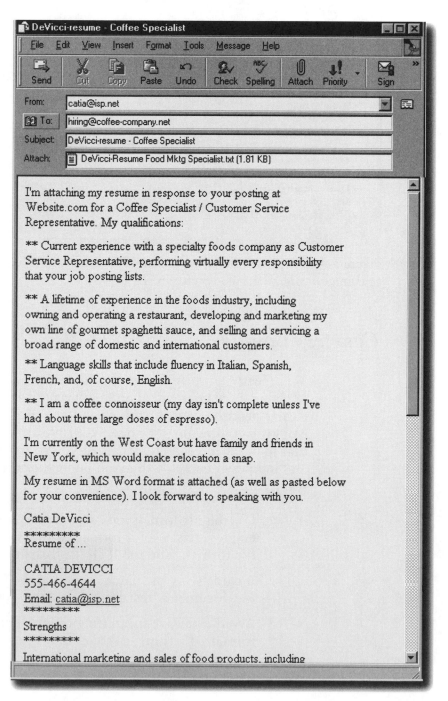

Figure 5-5   Example of email with an attachment prior to sending.

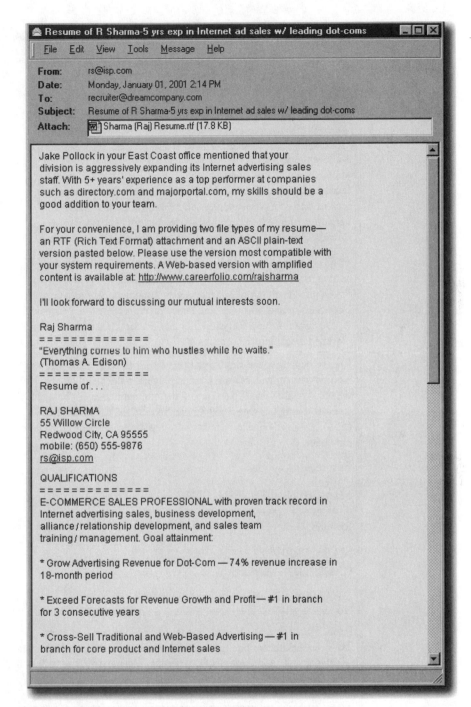

Figure 5-6 Example of email received with an attachment. Cover letter precedes text-only resume, which is included in body of email message as a courtesy to employers.

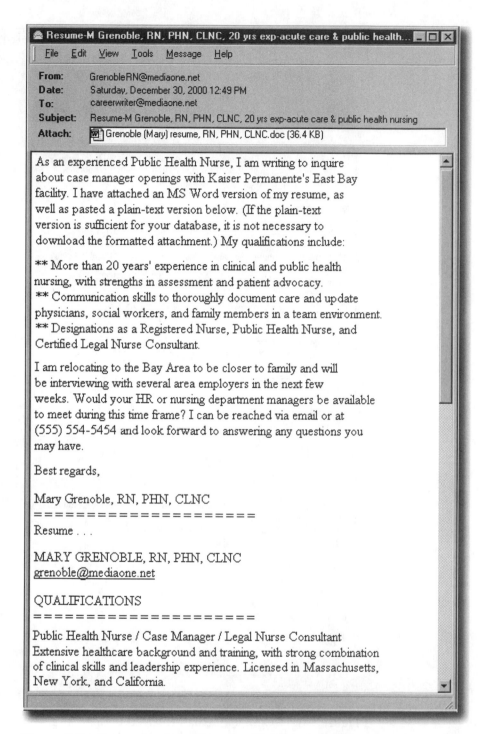

Figure 5-7   Example of email received with an attachment.

search and email protocol. By making a good first impression, you improve the likelihood that the recruiter will take the time to click through and view your Web resume. What's that, you say? You don't have a Web resume? Turn to Chapter 6 to learn how to take your resume to the next dimension . . . one that will make your old paper resume seem as outdated as carving on stone tablets.

Part 2

eResumes as Web Pages

Chapter 6

Web-Based Resumes and Portfolios: The New Gold Standard

Change is inevitable . . . and unavoidable. Author and advertising executive Bruce Barton once said, "When you're through changing, you're through." To illustrate his point, here are a few accounts from the chronicles of international business:

- *Royal and Underwood typewriters don't exist today because they refused to acknowledge that electricity would have an impact on their product lines.*

- *Admiral and Philco—at one time, household names in radios—aren't around anymore; Motorola—their chief competitor—is a market leader because it adapted to change.*

- *In 1950, 80 percent of the world's motorcycles were manufactured in Britain. Today, Britain's market share has shrunk to 1 percent because it insisted on using old-fashioned production methods. The Japanese now rule the motorcycle market because they researched new products, updated their marketing methods, and modernized production.*

Change also affects how we produce and distribute resumes. For example, the documents we once hammered out on our old typewriters underwent a metamorphosis when personal computers and word processors hit the scene—then underwent another transformation with the advent of desktop publishing. Ten years ago, job seekers thought faxing was the "be-all and end-all" for speedy delivery of resumes. Next came email, and zipping a resume off to hundreds of employers could take place in a matter of seconds.

The World Wide Web's technology innovations have raised the bar even higher. Web-based documents not only challenge us with new levels of visual and multimedia possibility but also give us the unprecedented ability to link—and virtually leap—to other Web-based documents. The samples and documentation that (in the "old" days) may have required a cumbersome, multipage portfolio can now be accessed online—and employers don't have to wade through pages they don't need. In this chapter, we will look at how Web resumes outperform traditional paper resumes and give job seekers a competitive edge. Here's what we'll cover:

105

- *Advantages of Web resumes and portfolios*
- *How job seekers use Web-based marketing tools*
- *Web portfolios 101*

The Advantages of Web Resumes and Portfolios

Before we look at the benefits of using Web-based personal marketing tools, we want to take a moment to distinguish between Web resumes and Web portfolios. The lines are blurred between these two types of documents, so for the purposes of clarification, we'll offer these definitions:

> **Web resume:** a Web-hosted resume with content similar to a traditional one- or two-page resume, with the added benefits of design enhancements, universal format compatibility, ultimate accessibility, and email connectivity. Information in a Web resume is typically confined to one page (however long it may be), with hyperlinks reserved for email, links within the same page or, occasionally, to a separate Web page.

> **Web portfolio:** a Web-hosted, in-depth career-marketing tool (typically with the resume as its focal point) with links to work samples, charts, significant accomplishments, reference letters, a mission or philosophy statement, and other supporting data. Information is presented using a multipage format, with a structured navigation system and a design theme that ties the pages together. All content resides within the same upper-level domain name (e.g., *www.yourname.com*).

A *resume* is (by definition) a synopsis of your career, while a *portfolio* is a collection of career documents. Not just the tip of the iceberg, but—at the viewer's discretion—as much of the iceberg as he or she wants to see.

Since Web resumes and Web portfolios are created with HTML, the language used to create Web pages, they have several unique features that aren't available in other formats.

Control/Privacy

Web resumes can be set up in private nonsearchable databases—accessible (with exceptions) only by those who have the URL Web address. In comparison, most ASCII resumes are hosted in public databases where anyone can find them by conducting a simple keyword search. While public posting provides job seekers with a higher level of exposure, this exposure can backfire should their current boss find them on the Net. If your employer is one of the 80 percent who uses the Net for recruiting, this is a real concern.

Universal Compatibility

Web resumes—like other Web pages—are accessible to people all over the world, no matter what kind of software or computer system is used. Web resumes transcend the whole issue of system compatibility, so there's no need to worry about file conversion problems, formatting glitches, or viruses. While some employers and recruiters request (or accept) an MS Word attachment, the use of attachments is fraught with compatibility and virus hazards—as described in Chapter 5.

Enhanced Appearance

Web resumes can be embellished with color and design to enhance appearance and project an image that reinforces your candidacy. As HTML evolves (and we learn to use it properly), Web pages become more sophisticated and "tasteful," allowing people in conservative professions to join the creative types and techies who have long enjoyed the edge that an online presence provides.

Three-Dimensional

Replete with images, audio, video, or high-tech animation, a Web portfolio is the perfect medium for showcasing tangible work samples, letters of recommendation, graphs, charts, photos, and so on. You can provide hiring managers with a wealth of content in a compact "package," to be reviewed at their convenience. Additionally, producing traditional portfolios is expensive, making them impractical for most job seekers. Conversely, there are no printing costs when you showcase your skills in a Web portfolio.

24/7 Accessibility

Because Web resumes "reside" on the World Wide Web, they are accessible 24 hours a day, seven days a week. Unlike traditional resumes, Web resumes don't have to be mailed, attached, faxed, or emailed. This not only cuts printing, copying, faxing, and mailing

---

The Perfect Portfolio

Marilyn Seguin (*The Perfect Portfolio*, Career Press, 1991) describes the portfolio as "an interview tool" . . . "an attractive package of written documents, photographs, slides, tapes, sketches, and projects that reflect your best efforts." Marilyn further defines the portfolio as "a sales kit for the most important product you will ever have to sell—yourself."

costs but also ensures that your resume is continually available to potential employers, recruiters, and networking contacts—even when you're not able to access your computer or, heaven forbid, your computer crashes.

Image Building

By their very nature, Web resumes reinforce your image as an intelligent, cutting-edge candidate. Whether you create it yourself or hire a designer or writer to help you, a Web resume will position you as someone who has embraced the wired world and is capable of using technology on the job.

In short, Web resumes are accessible, compatible, interactive, and attractive. These attributes make them an ideal career marketing tool—the pièce de résistance in an electronic job market full of ugly ASCII resumes.

How Job Seekers Use Web Resumes

Does everyone need a Web resume? No. Can a large percentage of folks benefit from a Web-based presentation? Yes! Since job seekers are individuals with unique backgrounds and needs, each will use this new medium in his or her own way.

Professionals

Professionals who need to project the "right" image can link to success indicators—charts, graphs, recommendation letters, photographs of representative work, and so on. The screenshot in Figure 6-1 shows how hyperlinks can be included in the text of a resume to verify performance-based skills.

Freelancers and Contract Workers

Freelance workers—hired on a "temporary" basis to complete short- or long-term projects—are constantly on the lookout (actively or passively) for new opportunities and assignments. Because they are in a continual mode of "self-marketing" (and because confidentiality is not a concern), many contract workers and free agents find that Web resumes are great tools for self-marketing and career management.

Teachers

Teachers can use a Web resume as an online portfolio with links to completed projects; photographs of classroom activities; videos of

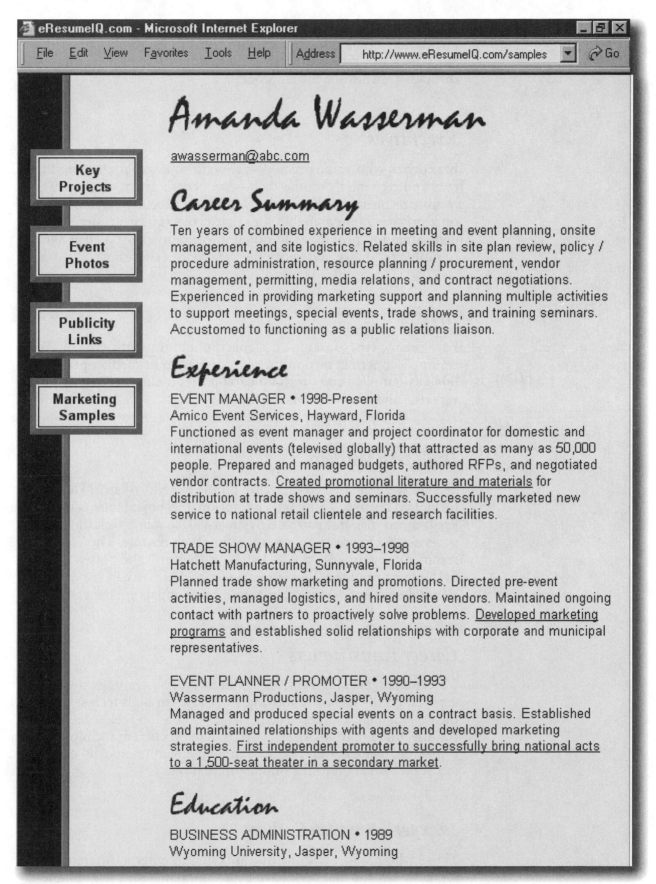

Amanda Wasserman

awasserman@abc.com

Key Projects

Event Photos

Publicity Links

Marketing Samples

Career Summary

Ten years of combined experience in meeting and event planning, onsite management, and site logistics. Related skills in site plan review, policy / procedure administration, resource planning / procurement, vendor management, permitting, media relations, and contract negotiations. Experienced in providing marketing support and planning multiple activities to support meetings, special events, trade shows, and training seminars. Accustomed to functioning as a public relations liaison.

Experience

EVENT MANAGER • 1998-Present
Amico Event Services, Hayward, Florida
Functioned as event manager and project coordinator for domestic and international events (televised globally) that attracted as many as 50,000 people. Prepared and managed budgets, authored RFPs, and negotiated vendor contracts. Created promotional literature and materials for distribution at trade shows and seminars. Successfully marketed new service to national retail clientele and research facilities.

TRADE SHOW MANAGER • 1993–1998
Hatchett Manufacturing, Sunnyvale, Florida
Planned trade show marketing and promotions. Directed pre-event activities, managed logistics, and hired onsite vendors. Maintained ongoing contact with partners to proactively solve problems. Developed marketing programs and established solid relationships with corporate and municipal representatives.

EVENT PLANNER / PROMOTER • 1990–1993
Wassermann Productions, Jasper, Wyoming
Managed and produced special events on a contract basis. Established and maintained relationships with agents and developed marketing strategies. First independent promoter to successfully bring national acts to a 1,500-seat theater in a secondary market.

Education

BUSINESS ADMINISTRATION • 1989
Wyoming University, Jasper, Wyoming

Figure 6-1   Web resume. Hyperlinks are included in the text to verify performance-based skills.

instructional or classroom management skills; and copies of recommendation letters, awards, training certificates, published works, etc. Check out the Web portfolio shown in Chapter 1 (Figures 1-7 through 1-10) to see this approach.

Executives

Executives who value privacy—yet want to leverage their best talents and credentials on the Web—can benefit greatly from a Web resume or portfolio. Figure 6-2 depicts an executive resume (hosted on a private, nonsearchable site) that projects a professional demeanor and provides additional information (just a click away) to build credibility and verify the candidate's success.

Artists

For creative types (graphic designers, photographers, etc.), a Web resume is a perfect medium. Color, design, multimedia options, links to samples, and portfolio capabilities make the Web resume a versatile and attractive marketing tool.

High-tech Workers

Techies were the first to capitalize on the benefits of an HTML-formatted resume. Those with exceptional technical talents tend to be left-brained (i.e., not particularly creative), so many lack the design skills needed to create an eye-appealing Web resume. The Web resumes in Figures 6-3 and 6-4 show a "before" and "after" version of the same resume for a high-tech worker. As you can see, professional design intervention can have a huge impact on appearance.

Career Transitioners

Career changers and transitioners need every advantage they can get—especially if they're moving from low- to high-tech segments of the employment market. The very fact that a job seeker has a Web resume infers that he or she is up to date on current technologies. In this sense, using a Web resume can help a technologically challenged job seeker break in to the online job market.

Inexperienced Job Seekers

Those who are just starting out or trying to enter a different field typically lament that they have little "content" for their resumes. While it may be true that they lack paid experience, inexperienced

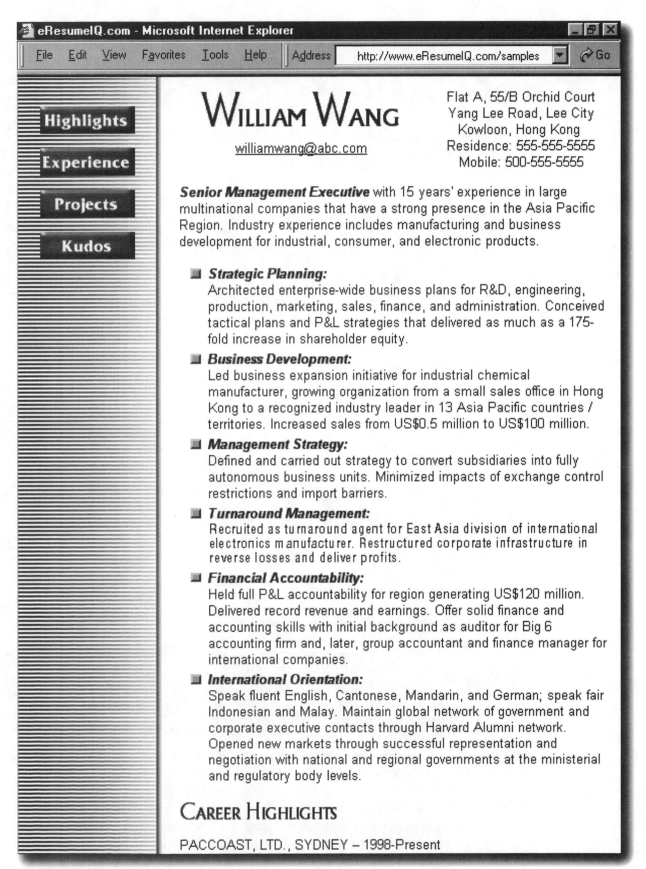

Figure 6-2   Executive's Web resume (hosted on a private, nonsearchable site). Site provides additional information (just a click away) to build credibility and verify the candidate's success.

James Galina

1234 Any Way
Anytown, Anystate 55555

jgalina@abc.com

Education:	Washington State University, Seattle, WA Bachelor of Science in Computer Science, 1989 Minor: Electrical Engineering

TECHNICAL SUMMARY:		
	Hardware:	IBM PC/x86, and Compatibles, MC68xxx ,DSP 320C240,68HC812 HP730,Sun, Sparc, DEC6xxx, 8xxx, 11/750, 11/785, GPIB-488, MIL-
	Operating System:	Windows 95, 3.x , OS2/WARP, MS/DOS 6.2, UNIX, VMS, VRTX
	Languages:	C++, C, Windows 3.1 SDK, Visual Basic, ZAPP, MFC, OWL, YA PASCAL, FORTRAN, MC68xxx Asm, Natural, LISP, ADA
	Design Tools:	Evergreen Case Tools, CADRE Case Tools
	Debugging Tools:	HP 7400 series ICE, Tektronics Logic Analyzer (Prism 3000, DAS circuit emulator, HP4951a Protocol Analyzer, IO-Tech 488 Analy

PROFESSIONAL EMPLOYMENT

1997 to Present	**Advo Technology Systems**, Washougal, WA Senior Software Engineer/Project Lead

Responsible for design, development, and testing of real-time, embedded code for the
in full motion concert and stage variable lighting. Products use 68360,68302,68332, and
processors running code generated by MicroTec C and C++ compilers hosted on HP7
Booch Design model. Used Microsoft C++ for Windows 95 for user interfaces. Experie
design for custom boards, utilizing TI Dsp 320C240 and Motorola HC12 using GODSP
HiCross compiler.

1995 to 1997	**New Age Design**, Vancouver, WA Software Engineer - Contractor

Team member developing a large commercial fourth generation compiler (QIK2) to pro
friendly interfaces for complex host environments in call centers. Development under \
multi-platforms (DOS, Windows 3.X, OS2/16 and OS2/PM) using ZAPP class framewo
DOS and OS/16 capability, and YACC as the lexical engine.

Software Engineer/Project Manager - Contractor

Designed and maintained an Automated Travel Authorization Certificate (AutoTAC) ;
develop in Microsoft Visual Basic (VB) using Q&E database extensions. Work closely
and operators to increase TAC processing efficiency, increase user-friendliness, and ;
operator training time. Increased program ability to process 2100 TAC's/month to 21,0(
through a series of hardware and software design improvements. Other duties include
administrator and configuration administrator

Figure 6-3   "Before" version of a high-tech worker. The screen setting is too wide and chops off text, requiring viewers to scroll repeatedly from left to right.

job seekers can round out their presentation by providing links to course work, academic projects, or "personal assignments"—self-initiated projects undertaken for the sole purpose of demonstrating acquired skills. Want to be a graphic designer? Create some dynamic design samples and link to them from your Web resume.

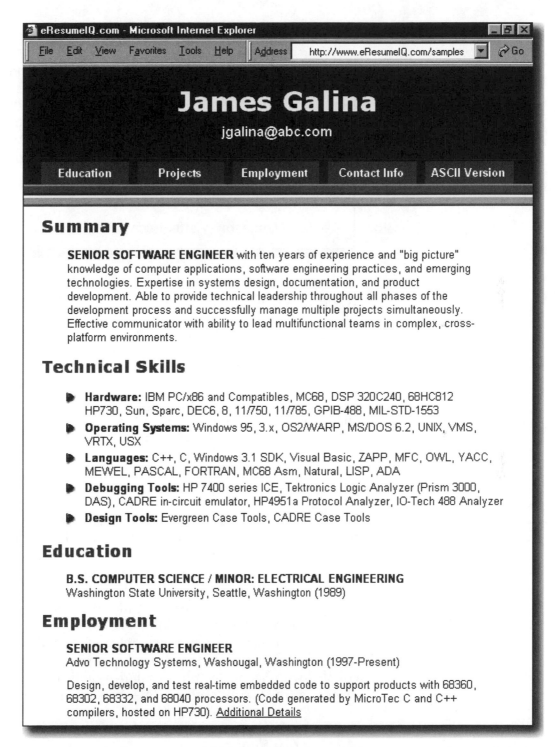

Figure 6-4 "After" version of high-tech worker's Web resume. Professional design intervention significantly improves appearance.

Self-assignment projects can benefit Web designers, photographers, writers, composers, animators, and others who create visual and audio "products." Those in other fields might capture highlights of volunteer or internship experiences using links to printed summaries, photographs with brief captions, or video files.

> **When in Rome . . .**
>
> "When in Rome, do like the Romans; when applying for jobs at Web companies, create your own website. Just as those applying for jobs as chefs audition by making a meal, those interested in working in the online world can impress by showing that they're well versed in the medium's idiom. A personal website that features your resume and other targeted information about yourself can go a long way to impress dot com recruiters."
>
> —Jake Jamieson (Wetfeet.com)

Recent Graduates

The global job market can make it tough for recent college grads to stand out—especially when recent statistics show that a large majority (80 percent) of graduates use the Net for job searching. With more competition than ever, college graduates should be encouraged to optimize their career marketing efforts, move beyond the experience-based resume model, and steer clear of the nondescript Web resumes that are catalogued on their alma mater's Web site.

Passive Job Seekers

Web resumes can be hosted privately and confidentially, making them a valuable asset to passive job seekers. Passive job seekers aren't out there pounding the pavement (so to speak), but they are proactive in making sure their resume is updated and ready to go. In addition to keeping tabs on industry trends, passive job seekers monitor the employment market and are continually improving or expanding their marketable skills. The resume depicted in Figure 6-5 shows a "confidential" approach, where the candidate's name and other identifiers have been removed to protect her privacy. When coupled with hosting in a high-volume public database, this job seeker has the best of both worlds—privacy and exposure.

Active Job Seekers

While some job seekers use their Web resume as a primary job search tool, others use them as deal-clinchers. Either way, online resumes can reinforce job seekers' perceived value by enhancing their image and building on information provided in a paper-based resume. The screenshot in Figure 6-6 shows how different document formats (ASCII, PDF, and Word) are offered in a Web resume as downloadable files, providing employers and recruiters with immediate access to whatever format is needed.

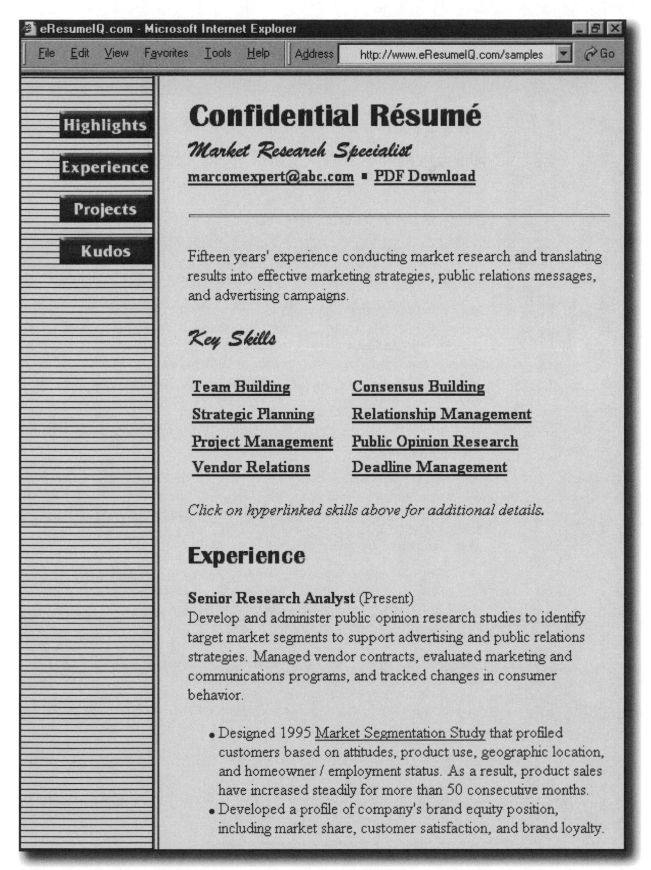

Figure 6-5   A "confidential" Web resume, where candidate's name and other identifiers have been removed to protect her privacy.

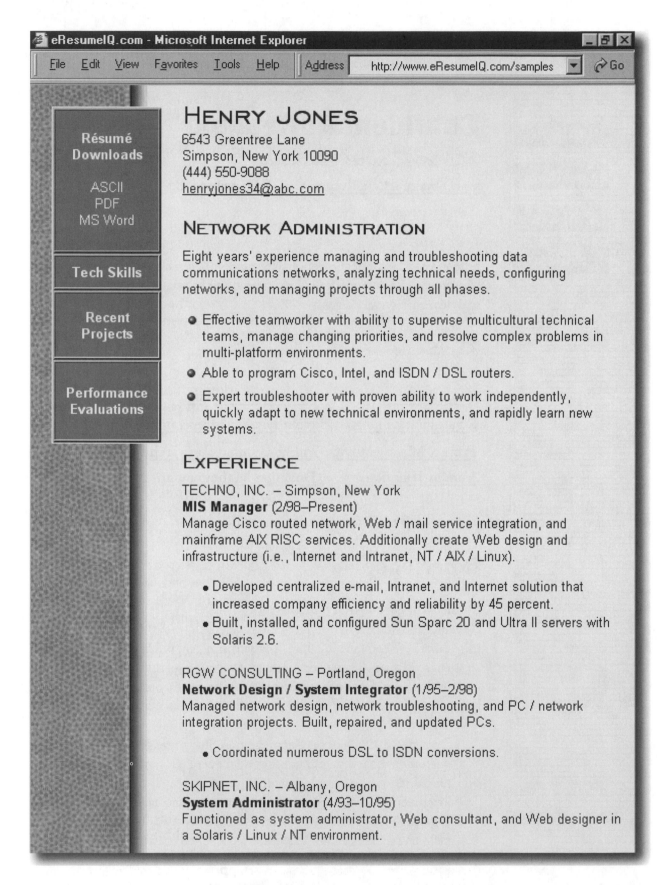

Figure 6-6 Web resume that offers different document formats (ASCII, PDF, Word) as downloadable files. This technique provides employers with immediate access to a format that can be stored in a database.

Consultants

Obviously, consultants are not job seekers per se, but we are including them here since many consultants use modified resumes to promote their consulting practice. The Web resume—or even better, an expanded Web portfolio—is a great tool for consultants as its "expandable" nature provides unequaled opportunities for image marketing and the telling of success stories. Not surprisingly, The Dot Com News reports that business management consultants were among the top five business markets registering Web addresses in 2000.

Web Portfolios 101

Traditional (paper-based) portfolios have been used for years by visual artists, journalists, writers, teachers, graphic designers, and creative professionals of all kinds. Now, the popularity of the Net has created a portfolio renaissance, where all types of job seekers—from graduates to executives—are using Web portfolios.

Portfolios are the ultimate career marketing tool, as they can speed up a job search, facilitate a successful performance review, or play a major role in landing a new project contract. Filled with tangible evidence of an individual's skill set, work philosophy, and inherent talents, portfolios present a three-dimensional picture of a candidate's qualifications. Because they are expandable, contractible, customizable, and persuasive, portfolios can repackage a job seeker and transform him or her from an average candidate to a top pick.

Portfolios include tangible documentation of credentials, projects, and capabilities, enabling them to go far beyond what a simple resume can offer. When Web portfolios are properly architected, they not only provide potential employers with a "flat" resume but also supply immediate access to supplemental information via Web hyperlinks. And like traditional portfolios, Web portfolios can be modified and reconfigured to meet your self-marketing needs as your career progresses. In short, Web portfolios are valuable because they document the full scope of your experience, training, talent, or skills.

What's Included in a Web Portfolio?

Most job seekers are familiar with typical resume categories and headings; yet for some, Web portfolio categories have an aura of mystery. If you're wondering what kinds of things can be included in a Web portfolio, take a look at the "idea list" that follows. Obviously, not all components are appropriate for every job seeker. The question you must ask yourself is this: Which items will bolster my candidacy?

Idea List: Web Portfolio Categories

- *Abstract of your career*
- *Academic projects*
- *Accomplishments*
- *Articles you've written*
- *Awards*
- *Biographical sketch*
- *Bulleted lists of strengths*
- *Business plans*
- *Career coups*
- *Career summary and goals*
- *Certificates*
- *Challenge + action = results charts*
- *Commendation letters*
- *Committee projects*
- *Computer skills*
- *Course work details*
- *Credentials*
- *Downloadable formats*
- *Global literacy*
- *Goals*
- *Grant samples*
- *Honors*
- *Interests and activities*
- *Job-related activities*
- *Languages*
- *Letters of recommendation*
- *Licenses*
- *Management philosophy*
- *Marketing plans*
- *Military records and*
- *Multicultural experiences*
- *Newspaper or magazine articles*
- *Organizational charts*
- *Performance reviews*
- *Personal mission statement*
- *Philosophy statement*
- *Photo gallery*
- *Press clippings*
- *Press releases*
- *Processes and programs*
- *Professional affiliations*
- *Project highlights and outcomes*
- *PowerPoint presentations*
- *Proposals*
- *Publications*
- *Publicity (traditional or online)*
- *Reading lists*
- *References*
- *Reports you've written*
- *Research*
- *Sales reports, charts, and statistics*
- *Sample lesson plans*
- *Streaming video of presentations*
- *Success stories*
- *Summary of your career*
- *Summary of your work experience*
- *Table of contents*
- *Technical skills*
- *Testimonials*
- *Training courses, conferences, and workshops*
- *Transcripts*
- *Video clips*
- *Work samples (links to projects, awards etc.)*
- *World travel*
- *Writing samples (reports, etc.)*

Without question, there is no "standard" set of portfolio categories. Portfolios are as unique as the job seekers they represent and their content varies according to each job seeker's competencies and talents.

The Portfolio's Technical Side

Unlike paper-based documents, Web pages have infrastructure and require an HTML technical foundation that supports the various elements. If you look beyond outward appearance, you'll find HTML-coded text, programming, and other technological components. Here are some of the most common technologies used:

- *ASCII and HTML (txt and HTML)*
- *Graphic file (GIF or JPEG)*
- *Photographs (JPEG)*
- *Audio file (streaming audio)*
- *Video file (streaming video)*
- *PDF files (for downloading)*
- *Scanned documents (saved as graphics or saved in PDF format)*

While most portfolio pages can be developed with HTML coding, others will need to be created as graphic images, PDF downloads, or streaming audio or video files. Check out the additional resources at the end of Chapter 9 for more information.

Portfolio Infrastructure

Creating any kind of portfolio—Web-based or not—requires a personal investment of time and effort, or the assistance of a professional. Whether you do it yourself or hire a Webmaster, careful thought should be given to site organization and structure. Since the "home" page is where most visitors enter a site, this entry page creates the first impression and sets the "tone" for the viewer's experience. Consequently, the entry page is the starting point in the site design process. Your home page can include any number of different elements, including those listed here:

- *Executive summary or qualifications profile*
- *Cover letter or introduction*
- *List of qualifications or special skills (linked or not)*
- *Philosophy statement/mission statement*

- *Graphic or sample of your work. For example, a photographer might use a photo collage as a splash (entry) page for a Web resume or portfolio.*

When building a Web portfolio, be sure to configure it so that critical information can be found immediately. For example, if you'd like to include a "Professional Awards" section in your portfolio, it should be accessible (i.e., linked) from the home page—not buried behind other pages where it's less likely to be found. To determine what your focal point should be, consider what your "best" qualification is and build the Web resume around it. For instance:

- *Artist/Graphic Designer: Small collage of representative drawings, sketches, or design projects*

- *Teacher: Quote on teaching or teaching philosophy*

- *Writer: Introductory cover letter with links to writing samples*

- *Business executive: Management philosophy*

- *Sales representative: List of accomplishments or links to (nonproprietary) performance charts*

Once you determine which categories and elements will serve your purposes, you can create a simple line drawing (see Figure 6-7) to diagram a hierarchy and "linking" strategy. For the average job

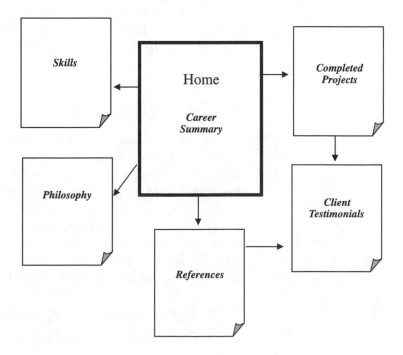

Figure 6-7   Sample of Web portfolio structure.

seeker, the best focal point for a home page is a carefully written summary statement. But consider the possibilities! Don't be afraid to think outside the box, at least a little bit.

At this point, you should have a good understanding of how a Web resume or portfolio can expand and maximize your personal marketing efforts. In Chapter 7, we'll discuss the various options for creating, designing, and hosting Web resumes.

Chapter 7

Web Resume Options: Fee or Free?

As we've discussed in earlier chapters, Web resumes and Web portfolios can be highly effective career marketing tools. Before we start describing the various options for creating a Web resume, we'd like to share with you a common but helpful analogy to get you in the right frame of mind.

> Web resumes are like product brochures, but instead of describing a product or service, they market your ability to contribute to an employer's operation.

Let's take this analogy a step further and look at how quality affects marketing results. Marketing experts know that, regardless of a product's quality or performance record, the sales team will have great difficulty selling the product if the marketing materials aren't up to par. A poorly produced resume will make it more difficult to market yourself.

Whether it's fair or not, we must resign ourselves to the fact that the quality of a marketing message can have more impact on "sale-ability" than the product itself. How does this affect you? Recognizing that product appearance and quality can give you a competitive edge, you need to be sure that the marketing vehicles you employ are top-notch in all regards—that is, copywriting, design, production, and printing.

Large corporations have marketing departments or ad agencies to handle these functions, but small business owners tend to produce their own promotional materials (just as job seekers often do) to save money. Keeping costs down is a practical goal, but saving money doesn't always come cheap, as "free" products typically include hidden costs. Unfortunately, many business start-ups are oblivious to the fact that their homespun marketing efforts are anemic (or even embarrassing), causing them to end up among the 70 percent of small businesses that fail within five years of start-up.

So, if you've decided to create a Web resume—your own personal marketing piece—we encourage you to do it well. In other words, dedicate a realistic amount of time to learn the art and science of

Web design, find a "low baggage" resume builder site, or track down a professional to do the job for you.

Web Resume Options

The first thing you need to decide is whether you want to produce the Web resume yourself or hire someone to do part (or all) of the work. You have several options:

- *Hire a professional Web page designer.*
- *Learn HTML and do the coding yourself.*
- *Use Web page development software (HTML editors or Web resume programs).*
- *Use MS Word's "Save As Web Page" option.*
- *Use a "no charge" cut-and-paste Web-resume creator.*
- *Use a fee-based cut-and-paste Web-resume creator.*

On the pages that follow, we've outlined the pros and cons of each approach so that you can become familiar with your alternatives.

Hiring a Professional

Web page designers (and wannabees) are relatively easy to find—but finding a *good* Web designer is another story. Fees for Web page design typically range from $25 to $150 an hour, with most Web resumes running $50 to $150, and Web portfolios (potentially as complex as a small business site) costing several hundred dollars or more. In addition to the resources listed at the end of this chapter, we've provided links to Web page designers and related resources on the eResumeIQ book site (www.eResumeIQ.com).

Here are some factors to consider when hiring a Web page designer:

- ***Comparison shop:*** *Take the time to shop a couple of different services and compare prices, services, and response time. (Red flag: If you ask for a quote and it takes someone a week to get back to you, go elsewhere.)*
- ***Review samples:*** *Carefully review the designer's site as well as "sample" sites, noting attention to detail, consistency, and download time. (Red flag: If samples aren't available, consider using another designer.)*
- ***Ask for References:*** *Request one or two names of recent clients, then call to see how the process worked for them. Was the project completed on time? Were they charged more*

than the project quote? (Red Flag: If the designer is not willing to provide references, consider going elsewhere.)

- *Determine level of expertise: New designers are certainly capable of producing quality work—but, in most cases, you will be better off hiring someone who's been at it a while. An experienced pro is more likely to know the ropes and be able to resolve technical glitches in short order.*

- *Assess available services: Ask about maintenance/updating fees and other services like search engine submission. If you don't have free Web site hosting (through your Internet service provider or other means), you'll want to determine whether your Web page designer can provide this service.*

Hiring a professional is not a one-shot project, but should be viewed as a potentially long-term business relationship. For example, you'll need to update your Web resume whenever you change jobs, acquire new skills, or sign up for a new email account. While a simple Web resume may meet your needs now, you may decide later to go "whole hog" and invest in a full-scale portfolio. Either way, you want to hire someone who's reliable, honest, and technically astute. For a list of professional resume writers who can create Web resumes, go to the National Résumé Writers' Association Web site (www.nrwa.com), click on Members, and use the term "Web Resume" as your search criteria.

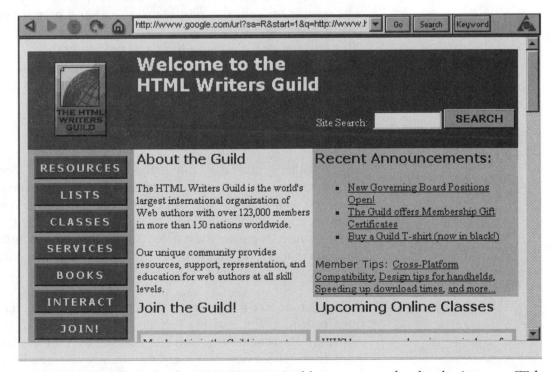

Figure 7-1 Home page of HTML Writers' Guild—a resource for developing your Web resume.

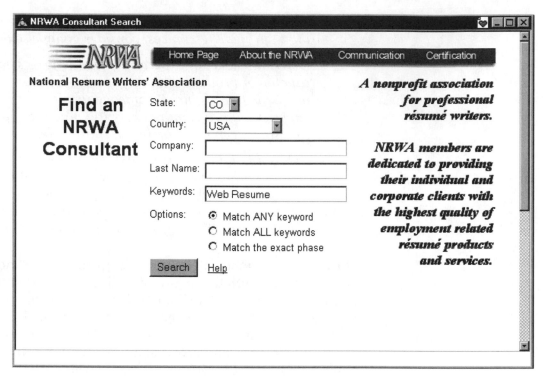

Figure 7-2   National Resume Writers' Association—search function can be used to find professional, credentialed writers who provide Web resume services.

However, most Web page designers are not writers or English teachers, so don't expect them to find your errors and fix your grammar. The onus is on you to carefully proofread and prepare your text before handing it over to your Web page designer for production. This will not only save you time and money in the long run but will also ensure that you maintain a positive relationship with your Web designer because there won't be unrealistic expectations on your part.

Do It Yourself

On the other end of the scale is the "do-it-yourself" option. If you're technically oriented, artistically inclined, or have the time to learn the technical ins and outs of HTML, you may want to consider creating the Web resume yourself. Be cautious if you decide to go this route, because your success may hinge on whether you do the job right. Don't tackle this option unless you're confident you have the time and talent to pull it off.

If you decide to do it yourself (more on this in Chapter 9), you'll need to find a Web hosting service and secure a URL (i.e., Web address). In some cases, Web site hosting may be available through your Internet Service Provider and already covered by your monthly fee. Another option is to buy a URL (e.g., www.YourName.com) and pay for monthly hosting. Typically, a URL (also known as a domain name) costs between $20 and $35 a year and average monthly hosting ranges from $10 to $20. Free hosting services are available, but we recommend that you look carefully before you leap. Why is it free? In some cases free Web services are used to attract job seekers to the host site in an effort to build a long-term "captive" audience. After all, the typical online job seeker is a "demographically ideal" target customer.

In other cases, free Web creation services include the obligatory pop-up banner ads that greet potential employers when they download your page. The question you must ask yourself is this: Is it worth it to annoy potential employers with banner advertising?

Teach Yourself HTML/Web Tutorials

HTML tutorials can be found all over the Web, and, in most cases, they are free of charge. If you're up to the challenge, there are vast storehouses of HTML resources, including training, advice, and graphics. Finding these sites is easy: Go to any search engine and conduct a simple keyword search for *HTML*.

In addition, books on HTML and Web site building can be found in any library or bookstore. Although these books do not focus on resumes specifically, most of the information on Web site development also pertains to Web resumes. If you're motivated to follow this course, check out some of the titles listed at the end of this chapter.

Using Web Page Development Software (HTML Editors)

Instead of learning HTML coding, there are dozens of programs that automate the process of creating and designing Web pages. In most cases, these tools dramatically reduce learning time and the attendant frustration. The resources section at the end of this chapter lists some commonly used HTML editors.

You can also purchase software programs designed specifically to create Web resumes. We reviewed several of these programs, but found that most were lacking in the areas of quality, flexibility, and ease of use. Based on our sampling, we encourage job seekers to look at other options.

Using Microsoft Word's Web Authoring Option

Those who have a recent version of Microsoft Word already have an HTML editing tool. Unfortunately, HTML documents created in

Word have an underlying code structure that (while it isn't apparent to the reader) can adversely affect download time. Proceed with caution!

Online Web Resume Creators

Not everyone can afford to hire a professional—or has the time or patience to learn HTML. Luckily, there are online resume builders (such as MyOnlineResume.com, CmyResume.com, or CareerFolios .com) that automate the Web resume creation process via a simple cut-and-paste interface. (Authors' disclosure: CareerFolios is a Web site that we developed.) Online resume creators automate the design and layout process and, in most cases, include hosting, a URL, and amenities not found in free services. The price tags for fee-based Web resumes typically range from $19.95 to $129.

There are also many free resume creation services on the Web. However, most free sites are like free television: You pay (ultimately) by having to endure the attendant advertising. In the case of Web resumes, these ads typically take the form of banner advertising. Some banner ads blink obnoxiously across the entire top of the screen, while others occupy a corner at the top, or are tucked away at the bottom. Regardless of its placement, banner advertising on a resume is unprofessional and counterproductive to making a good impression.

When considering Web-resume services, here are some features you'll want to look for:

- *Short, intuitive URLs: If the URL is long and full of numbers and other code, you won't be able to include it on other documents (like a personal business card or ASCII resume)— nor recite it to a recruiter or networking contact during a*

Ugly URLs

Take a look at the Web resume URLs listed below. Which ones would you feel more comfortable using?

- www.webresumesrus.com/resumes/john_henderson768.html

- www.careerfolios.com/johnhenderson

- www.aol.com/members/johnhenderson988.html

- www.johnhenderson.com

telephone conversation. And, unless you have a photographic memory, you'll have a hard time remembering the darn thing!

- *Flexibility: Look for a service with flexible design layouts and category headings. Don't limit yourself to a set-in-stone format that doesn't provide the options you need. It is critical that you are able to list categories and information in a way that benefits your candidacy.*

- *Full functionality: To ensure that your Web resume is useful to hiring managers and recruiters, it should include at least one download option. The most useful formats are ASCII (for database input) and PDF or MS Word for downloading and printing.*

- *Confidentiality/privacy options: If you have concerns about confidentiality, you'll need to find out whether your resume will be hosted in a public or private database. Public databases are accessible and keyword-searchable by virtually anyone—which is good if you don't have confidentiality or privacy concerns. On the other hand, if your resume is hosted privately, its contents are not (usually) searchable. The ideal situation for most job seekers is to use a service that provides both public and private posting—allowing you to use whichever option meets your needs.*

- *No advertising: It's better to pay a fee than to force your potential employers to endure banner advertising! Some services (free and fee-based) also promote the Web resume's "brand" name. Here, too, you'll need to decide whether someone else's brand name is the image you want to project.*

While it may be tempting to get a Web resume for free, experience teaches us that we usually get what we pay for. If category or formatting options are limited (or unsightly)—or if banner ads are blasted across the top of the page—this "free" site is no bargain and won't project the kind of professional image you need.

Using an automated Web resume generator not only saves time but can also reduce the hassle of doing it yourself, and can eliminate the costs associated with hiring a professional Web page designer. Regardless of time or cost savings, though, your objective is to create a quality product. So before you buy (or subscribe or sign up), take a good close look at the finished resume samples. To make the review process easier, we've created a chart (Table 7.1) that compares online Web-resume builders (with features, costs, pros and cons). When reviewing these options, pay special attention to the following:

- *How long is the hosting period?*
  Most services host Web resumes for six months or more, some indefinitely. The ideal hosting period will vary for each

job seeker, depending on whether the resume is used short term (during an active job search) or long term (as a career management tool).

- **How flexible are the design options?**
  Can you choose from several formats? Can you control how your Web resume will look? Are you limited to using a restrictive format or preset options that don't meet your needs?

- **What kind of Web address will you get?**
  Do you have any say over the URL? Is it fairly short and intuitive, or is it so long that it will be difficult to share with others?

- **What does the finished product look like?**
  This is critical. A well-designed Web resume should be easy on the eyes (not too gaudy or colorful)—but with an attractive appearance that personifies your candidacy.

- **Exactly what is included in the fee?**
  Do you have to pay more for downloadable files? Do you have to pay not to have an advertising banner on your site? Are there confidentiality options?

Your Web resume is a dynamic document, one that should be updated and expanded as you acquire new experience and skills. Look at the complete costs before you commit yourself to a particular service. Is there a monthly fee? Does it cost extra to make revisions? Carefully compare (and factor in all costs) before you make your decision.

Cut-and-Paste Web-Resume Creators

The Web-resume creators listed in Table 7-1 have the following characteristics in common:

- **Cut-and-paste interface.** *All of the services require the job seeker to cut and paste text into online forms to build the resume.*

- **Enhanced HTML.** *All services offer background designs and color or graphics, except as noted. When multiple options were available (for example, simple HTML layout with no color or an enhanced option with color and design), we used the enhanced option.*

- **No charge updating.** *All services allow job seekers to use a click-and-build interface at no charge for updating and revisions.*

Table 7-1 Web-Resume Creators

Service	User URL	Pros	Cons	Cost
America Online	http://hometown.aol.com/ yourname/myhomepage/ resume.html	Easy and quick America Online ad included under heading "My Favorite Product" at bottom of resume Can include photos and links to other pages AOL advertising is optional	Design options (heading graphics and dividers) are basic and not "integrated" in central design theme Enhanced ASCII, not full HTML No confidentiality features	Free
Yahoo	http://resumes.yahoo.com/ username/yourname	Flexible category choices / order changes No advertising	No confidentiality features	Free
MyOnlineResume	www.myonlineresume.com/ ViewSite/your_name_2613	4 template designs in different colors Full portfolio capabilities Fee includes 12 months of hosting Built-in job seeker tips and spelling checker "Panic Button" for help Includes virtual interview	MyOnlineResume Brand logo is placed at the top Photos and pictures not always relevant (no tie-in) Long URL	$99 (Introductory price)
ProWebResumes	www.prowebres.com/ yourname	4 design themes Submission to search engines included. Download options Includes six months of hosting	Design themes rely on photo to provide visual impact ProWebResumes logo appears (with contact info) at bottom of each page.	$39.95

Table 7-1   Web-Resume Creators   *(Continued)*

Service	User URL	Pros	Cons	Cost
10minuteresume.com	www.10minuteresume.com/ resume/yourname	Built-in tips and help	Limited resume categories (6 only) Only 4 styles on white backgrounds	Free
CareerFolios	www.careerfolios.com/ yourname	9 design themes 90 category headings Help file / instructions Can include links Confidentiality option ASCII download	Fee includes 6 months of hosting Additional 6 months $19.95 Links must be hand-coded in HTML	$39.95 114

For the purposes of comparing the URLs, we used the term *your name* to indicate the job seeker's name in the URL.

Look at the complete costs before you commit yourself to a particular service. Is there a monthly fee? Does it cost extra to make revisions? Some services charge to add download options, but others include downloads at no charge. Compare (and factor in all costs) before you make your decision.

Additional Resources

- *Create your First Web Page in a Weekend* (Steve Callihan Prima Publishing, 1999)

- *Creative HTML Design* (Lynda and William Weinman, New Riders Publishing, 2001)

- *Creating Web Pages for Dummies* (Bud Smith and Arthur Beback)

- *HTML for Dummies* (Ed Tittel and Steve James, IDG Books)

- *HTML 4 for the World Wide Web* (a "Visual Quickstart" book)

- *Looking Good on the Web* (Daniel Gray, Coriolis Group, 1999)

- *Web Pages That Suck* (Vincent Flanders and Michael Willis, Sybex, 2001)

HTML Editors

- *Macromedia Dreamweaver (about $300)*

- *FrontPage (about $100)*

- *Netscape Composer (built into Netscape Navigator and free on the Netscape site)*

- *NoteTab—Pro version ($19.95)*

- *Arachnophilia Web site Workshop (free at www.arachnoid.com/arachnophilia/index.html)*

Chapter 8

New Medium, New Rules: Designing Resumes for the Web

Most job seekers would never consider wearing a pair of old sweats or a clown costume to an interview, but surprisingly, many have resumes that project the same sloppy or gaudy image. Job seekers know how important it is to put their best foot forward, but sometimes knowing and doing are two different things.

The uninviting appearance of ASCII resumes was addressed in Chapter 3. Frankly, some of the ugliest resumes on the Net aren't ASCII files, but poorly designed Web resumes. And worse, they are ugly in color!

Job seekers fail to realize that employers view resumes as "representatives" of the candidates they portray. When a resume does not reflect good craftsmanship, the impression employers get is that you either have bad taste or poor judgment—or are flat-out lazy. Even worse, if you use an ineffective resume, you lose your opportunity to make a good first impression. Conversely, a well-planned, appropriately designed Web resume immediately sets you apart from the crowd. In fact, attractive Web resumes are such a rarity that having one gives you a distinct advantage in the online job market.

In this chapter, we'll look at how to improve the effectiveness of your Web resume by making it easy to read and visually compelling. We'll cover the following topics:

- *Common characteristics of poorly designed Web resumes, along with "before" and "after" makeovers to demonstrate key concepts*

- *Basic rules for Web resume design that dramatically improve appearance*

- *How to check your resume against our Web resume checklist*

135

Design Faux Pas

The following list describes common characteristics of poorly produced Web resumes and provides samples of how to fix them:

- *Amateurish: Poorly executed HTML and sloppy, inconsistent formatting.* The "before" example in Figure 8-1 shows a typical Web resume found on the Internet. If your resume looks like this, there is one piece of good news: You are not alone! Figure 8-2 shows how a design makeover can save the day.

- *Austere: Too plain and no visual enhancements.* The "before" example in Figure 8-3 shows a common mistake: Plain Jane Syndrome. Some job seekers have plain Web resumes because they require minimum effort and can be created quickly. Other job seekers have plain resumes because they believe that they have only two options (i.e., "all" or "nothing")—and they do not *want their resume to look like the gaudy sample in Figure 8-4. Our "after" example (Figure 8-5) shows that it is possible to build a conservative—but attractive—Web resume.*

- *Gaudy: Too much color and garish or inappropriate graphics.* Luckily, the limitations of black and white do not allow us to capture the havoc that can be wreaked by overzealous HTML aficionados (Figure 8-4). Just take our word for it— it's worse in color! The design makeover in Figure 8-6 projects an image that works for the candidate—not against him.

- *Too flashy: Nonrelevant, overly "slick" technology.* Unless you're an animator, it's unlikely that you'll benefit by including animated GIFs and other artistic forms of technology on your Web resume. When considering whether to include a flashy feature, ask yourself: Does it support my candidacy? Or will it distract from the message I'm trying to deliver? Although the resume in Figure 8-7 will undoubtedly elicit some "oohs and ahs" at first glance, its high-tech bells and whistles are overkill for this particular job seeker. The "after" design in Figure 8-8 is attractive, appropriate, and doesn't get in the way of the message.

- *Clumsy navigation: Inaccessible or poorly placed links.* One of the defining features of HTML is its ability to hyperlink to other pages. Since a typical computer screen shows only the top portion of a Web page, your viewers will need a navigation system to help them get around and find what they want. Figure 8-9 shows a Web resume with a poorly designed navigation system. The "after" example in Figure 8-10 shows how properly placed hyperlinks add style and functionality.

- *Poor strategy: No strategy.* With few exceptions, your most important credentials should be immediately visible when the Web resume is brought up. The resume in Figure 8-9 does not meet this criteria, as its hyperlinks are too large and eclipse the summary statement. The resume shown in Figure 8-10 has readily accessible links, positioned so that the summary is visible.

- *Poor quality: Typos, poor grammar, and inconsistent formatting.* Despite the valiant efforts of software developers to develop fail-safe spelling and grammar checkers, resumes with errors and inconsistencies run rampant on the Web. Figure 8-11 shows a resume that is sloppy and bland. The resume in Figure 8-12 shows the results of some judicious editing—along with a badly needed design makeover.

- *Long downloads: Too many (or the wrong kind of) graphics.* There are many factors that affect download time, but, in most cases, the problem is caused by nonoptimized graphics or too many bells and whistles. There are some highly motivated readers (your Mother perhaps?) who will patiently wait for your page to display, but don't count on it. If the graphics on your Web resume negatively affect download time, it's time to downsize your graphics (more on this in Chapter 9). The "before" resume in Figure 8-13 shows a Web resume with a graphic that is too large. In the "after" example (Figure 8-14), we've incorporated a smaller graphic image. This not only looks better but also dramatically speeds up download time.

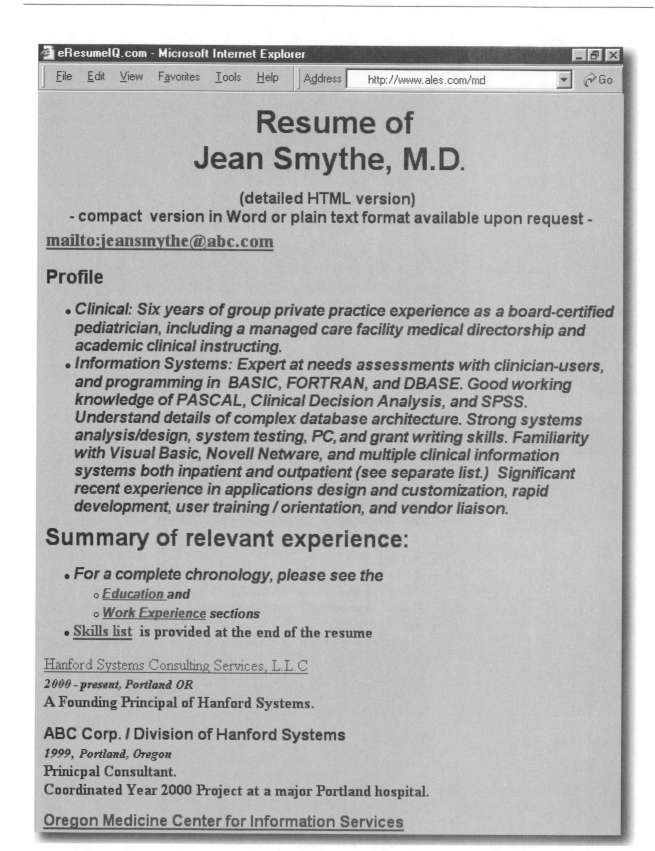

Figure 8-1 "Before" example of amateurish Web resume.

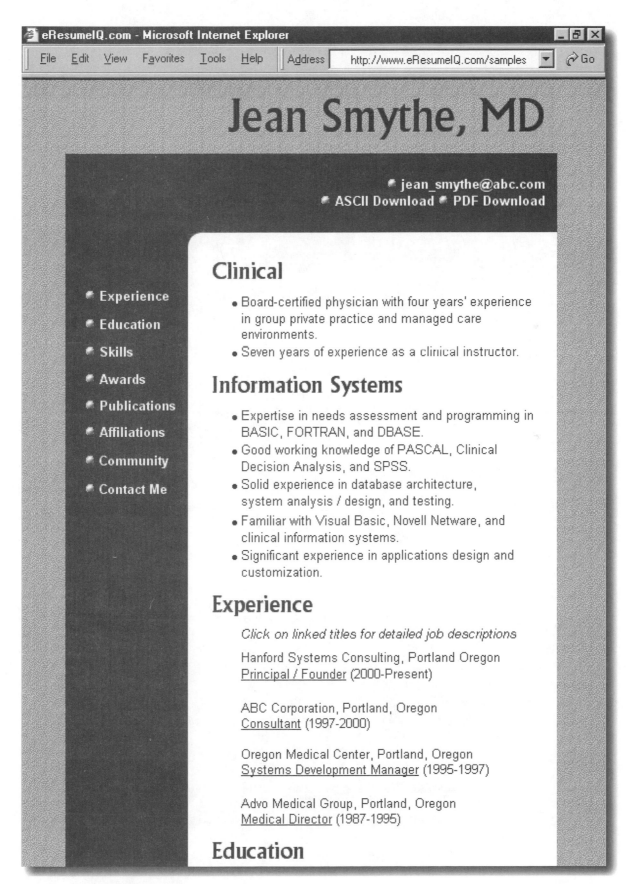

Figure 8-2   "After" example of Figure 8-1.

Sheena Martin-Jones

sheenamj@mail.com

OBJECTIVE *Position as a controller*

EXPERIENCE

Lawson Container Corporation

Divisional Controller (Current)

Click for more information

Interactive Solutions, Inc. Finance Manager- (1995-1998)
Click for more information

ITEMS OF INTEREST

Active member of the American Institute of Certified Public Accountants

EDUCATION

University of California

Masters in Business Administration (2000)

Oklahoma University-

B.S. Degree in Accounting (May, 1995)
Overall GPA: 3.4/4.0

REFERENCES

Click on References

CONTACT INFORMATION

EMAIL: sheenamj@mail.com
URL: http://web-resume.com/sheena-martin-jones

Web-Resume
Examples | Order | Benefits | FAQ | Value-Added Services

Figure 8-3 "Before" example of Plain-Jane Syndrome.

Figure 8-4 "Before" example of too-gaudy presentation.

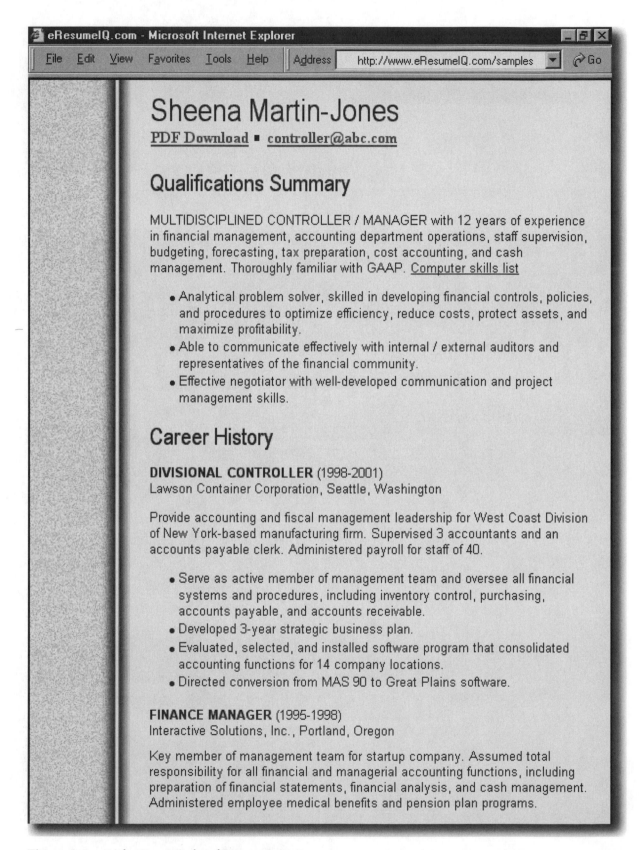

Figure 8-5   "After" example of Figure 8-3.

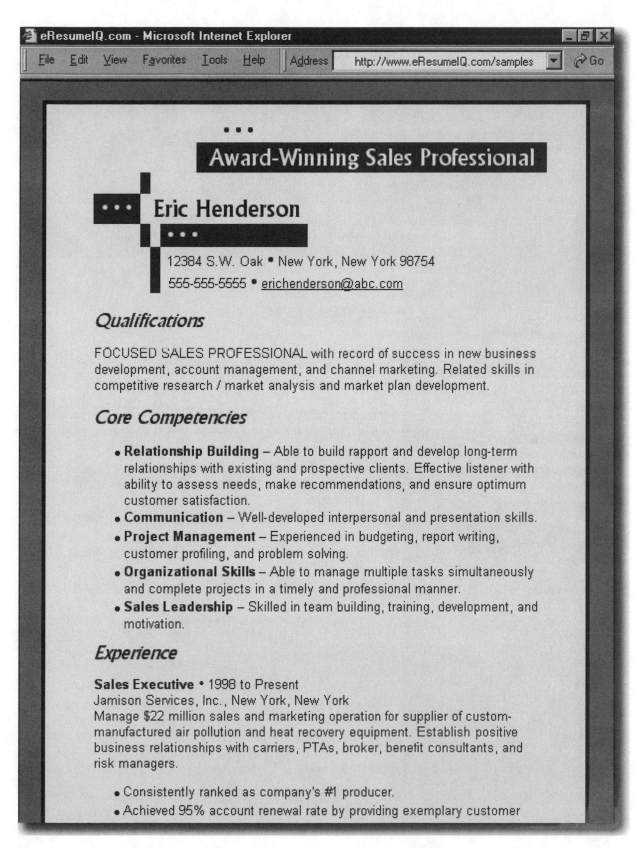

Figure 8-6   "After" example of Figure 8-4.

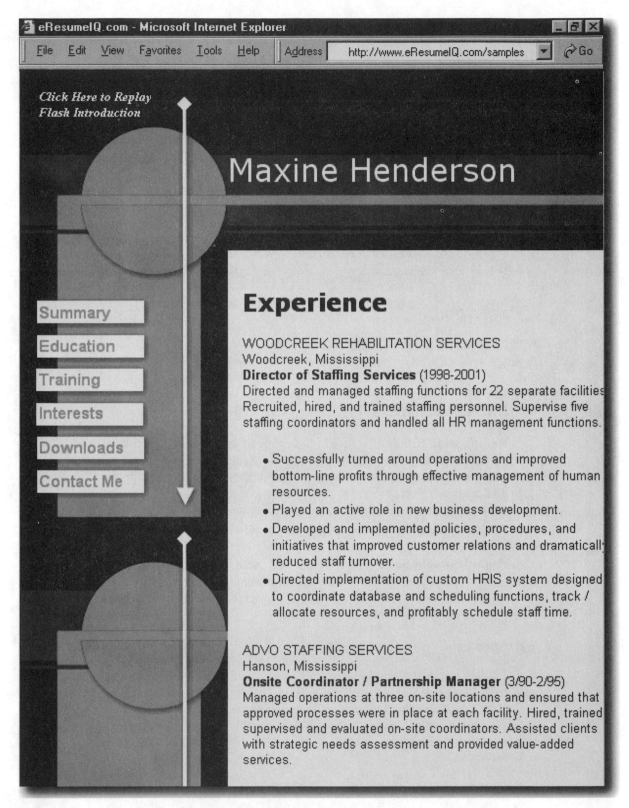

Figure 8-7 "Before" example of high-tech "oohs and ahhs" with Flash technology.

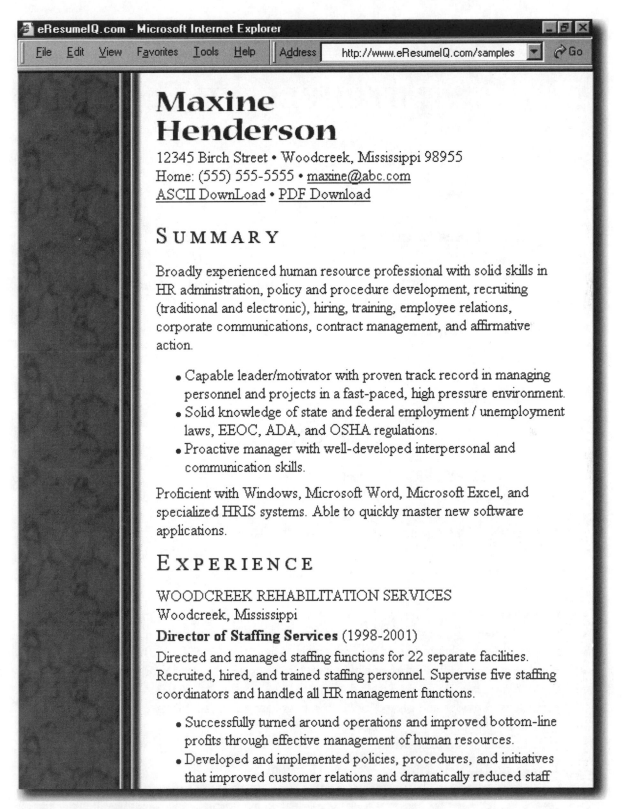

Figure 8-8 "After" example of Figure 8-7.

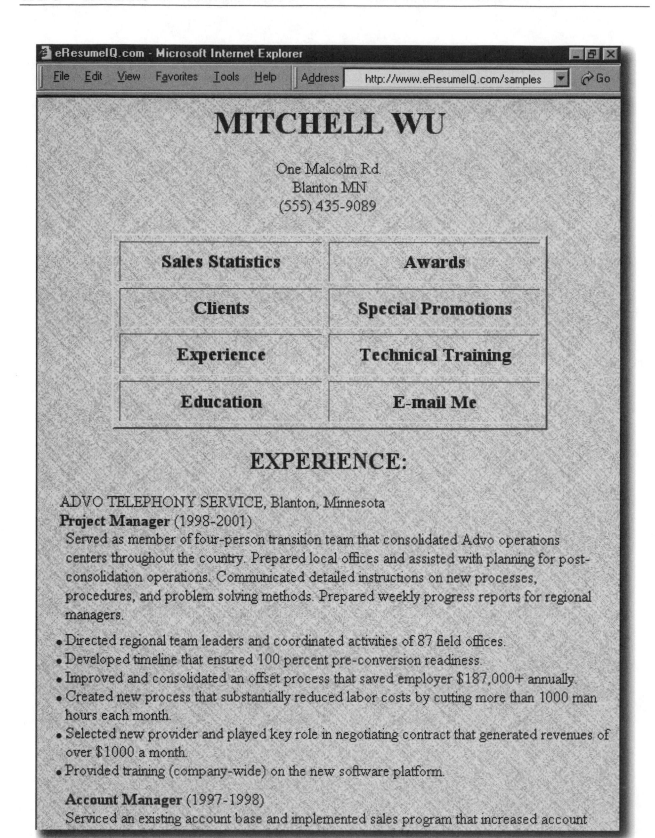

Figure 8-9 "Before" example of bad navigation.

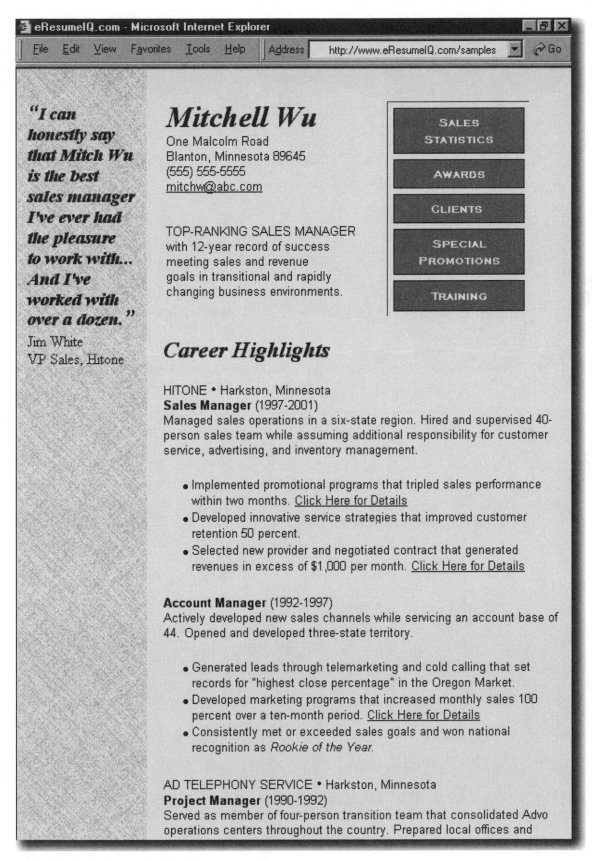

 (as a browser window)

> *"I can honestly say that Mitch Wu is the best sales manager I've ever had the pleasure to work with... And I've worked with over a dozen."*
>
> Jim White
> VP Sales, Hitone

Mitchell Wu

One Malcolm Road
Blanton, Minnesota 89645
(555) 555-5555
mitchw@abc.com

TOP-RANKING SALES MANAGER with 12-year record of success meeting sales and revenue goals in transitional and rapidly changing business environments.

- SALES STATISTICS
- AWARDS
- CLIENTS
- SPECIAL PROMOTIONS
- TRAINING

Career Highlights

HITONE • Harkston, Minnesota
Sales Manager (1997-2001)
Managed sales operations in a six-state region. Hired and supervised 40-person sales team while assuming additional responsibility for customer service, advertising, and inventory management.

- Implemented promotional programs that tripled sales performance within two months. Click Here for Details
- Developed innovative service strategies that improved customer retention 50 percent.
- Selected new provider and negotiated contract that generated revenues in excess of $1,000 per month. Click Here for Details

Account Manager (1992-1997)
Actively developed new sales channels while servicing an account base of 44. Opened and developed three-state territory.

- Generated leads through telemarketing and cold calling that set records for "highest close percentage" in the Oregon Market.
- Developed marketing programs that increased monthly sales 100 percent over a ten-month period. Click Here for Details
- Consistently met or exceeded sales goals and won national recognition as *Rookie of the Year.*

AD TELEPHONY SERVICE • Harkston, Minnesota
Project Manager (1990-1992)
Served as member of four-person transition team that consolidated Advo operations centers throughout the country. Prepared local offices and

Figure 8-10 "After" example of Figure 8-9.

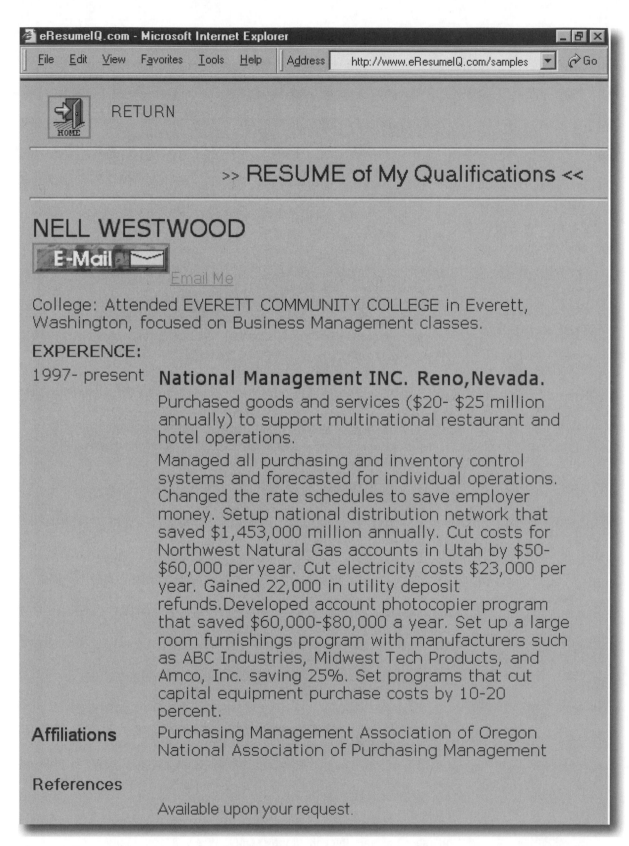

Figure 8-11   "Before" example of sloppy Web resume.

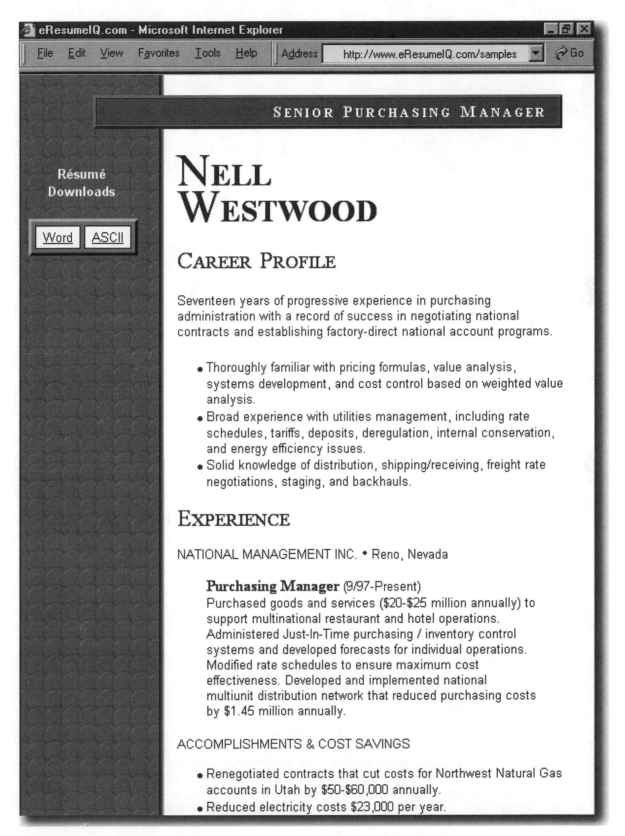

Figure 8-12 "After" example of Figure 8-11.

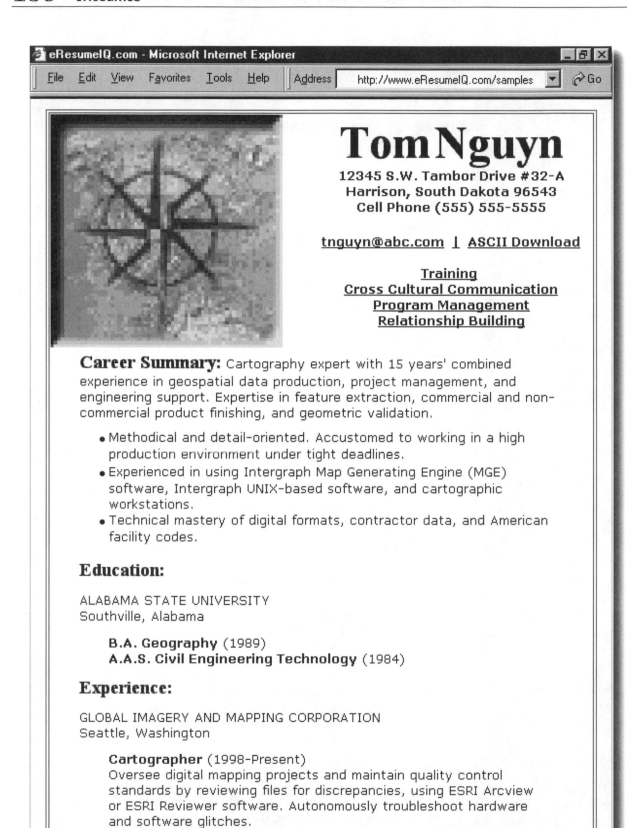

File   Edit   View   Favorites   Tools   Help   Address   http://www.eResumeIQ.com/samples   ⟳ Go

Tom Nguyn

12345 S.W. Tambor Drive #32-A
Harrison, South Dakota 96543
Cell Phone (555) 555-5555

tnguyn@abc.com | ASCII Download

Training
Cross Cultural Communication
Program Management
Relationship Building

Career Summary: Cartography expert with 15 years' combined experience in geospatial data production, project management, and engineering support. Expertise in feature extraction, commercial and non-commercial product finishing, and geometric validation.

- Methodical and detail-oriented. Accustomed to working in a high production environment under tight deadlines.
- Experienced in using Intergraph Map Generating Engine (MGE) software, Intergraph UNIX-based software, and cartographic workstations.
- Technical mastery of digital formats, contractor data, and American facility codes.

Education:

ALABAMA STATE UNIVERSITY
Southville, Alabama

B.A. Geography (1989)
A.A.S. Civil Engineering Technology (1984)

Experience:

GLOBAL IMAGERY AND MAPPING CORPORATION
Seattle, Washington

Cartographer (1998-Present)
Oversee digital mapping projects and maintain quality control standards by reviewing files for discrepancies, using ESRI Arcview or ESRI Reviewer software. Autonomously troubleshoot hardware and software glitches.

Figure 8-13 "Before" example of too-large graphic

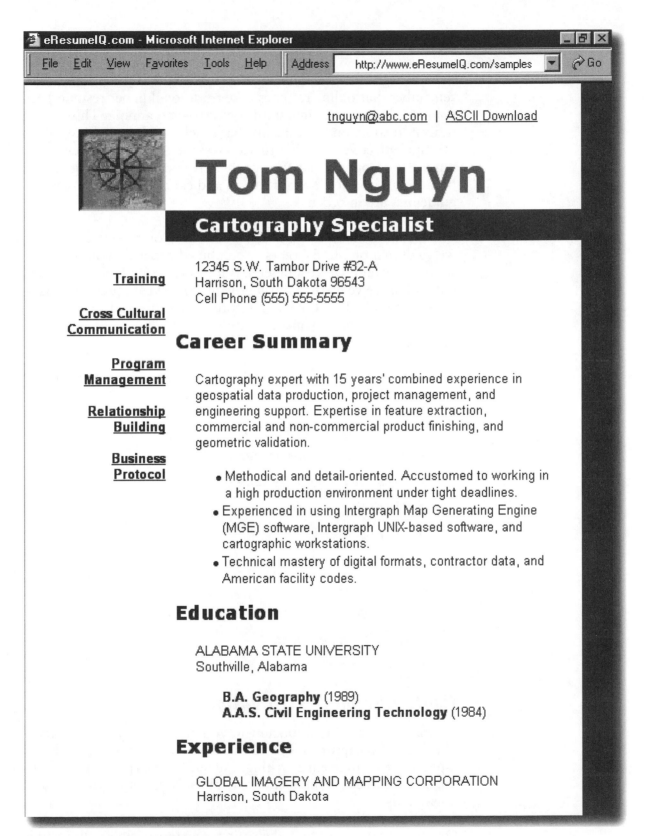

tnguyn@abc.com | ASCII Download

Tom Nguyn

Cartography Specialist

Training

Cross Cultural Communication

Program Management

Relationship Building

Business Protocol

12345 S.W. Tambor Drive #32-A
Harrison, South Dakota 96543
Cell Phone (555) 555-5555

Career Summary

Cartography expert with 15 years' combined experience in geospatial data production, project management, and engineering support. Expertise in feature extraction, commercial and non-commercial product finishing, and geometric validation.

- Methodical and detail-oriented. Accustomed to working in a high production environment under tight deadlines.
- Experienced in using Intergraph Map Generating Engine (MGE) software, Intergraph UNIX-based software, and cartographic workstations.
- Technical mastery of digital formats, contractor data, and American facility codes.

Education

ALABAMA STATE UNIVERSITY
Southville, Alabama

B.A. Geography (1989)
A.A.S. Civil Engineering Technology (1984)

Experience

GLOBAL IMAGERY AND MAPPING CORPORATION
Harrison, South Dakota

Figure 8-14   "After" example of Figure 8-13.

Web Resume Rules

Even though the Web is an electronic medium, it's important to remember that online resumes (like traditional paper resumes) are made for human viewing, not for electronic scanning. This is a significant distinction, as it means that much of what we know about "resume effectives" applies to Web resumes as well. However, we must also recognize that Web-enabled resumes are a new genre, and because of their additional features and capabilities, some new guidelines are in order.

The recommendations that follow are based on three criteria. First, we've drawn on our 37 years of combined experience in resume writing. Second, we've tempered traditional resume-writing wisdom with what we've learned during the past five years preparing electronic resumes. Third, we've reinforced the list—and validated our recommendations—by incorporating data on how people read Web documents.

To create a "maximum potential" Web resume, incorporate these concepts into its development:

- *Capture employers' attention*
- *Make your resume easy to read*
- *Keep the typography simple*
- *Maximize contrast*
- *Avoid clutter*
- *Project the right image*
- *Use spot color*
- *Select your graphics carefully*
- *Limit visual elements*
- *Don't be a Plain Jane*

Capture Employers' Attention

No matter what kind of document you're writing, your primary objective is to capture and hold the reader's attention—and this is especially true in resume writing. In fact, most experts agree that the best resumes communicate critical "selling points" in the first 15 seconds.

One of the best ways to make your credentials visible is to include a strategically written summary statement at the top of the resume. Summaries also provide another benefit: They allow you to present your credentials in a way that enhances a less-than-perfect career path. Since summary statements don't include dates and job titles, they level the playing field (at least for a moment) and allow you to present your qualifications in a strategic manner.

The best way to accomplish this (whether the resume is read electronically or by a person) is to build the summary around carefully selected keywords. Using carefully selected keywords in your introductory summary quickly establishes you as a contender and gets you past the traditional and electronic gatekeepers.

Make Your Resume Easy to Read

In traditional resume writing, we've been taught to avoid dense paragraphs and to break up long copy with bullets and subheadings. Although readability seems like an "obvious" criterion, it is one of the most abused and neglected guidelines of all.

Fortunately, the application of good page design principles will quickly improve the readability and eye appeal of a Web resume. Check out the guidelines in Table 8-1 for more specific advice on how to make your resume more readable, more attractive, and more appealing to employers.

Project the Right Image

When it comes to paper resumes, most job seekers understand the need for restraint, but the Web's colorful multimedia environment—combined with literally thousands of backgrounds, borders, and color combinations—is very tempting to many. Instead, follow the guidelines below to keep your resume off the "worst dressed" list.

Table 8-1   Improving Readability

Keep the typography simple: You can improve Web resume readability by keeping the design recipe simple. A good formula is to use one or two complementary type designs in 10- to 12-point type for body text (size 2 or 3 in HTML) and 18- to 24-point type for major headings (4, 5, or 6 points in HTML). You can use boldface type on job titles and subheadings, but avoid bolding (or colorizing) keywords, as it has a tendency to confuse and overwhelm the reader. Italics should be used sparingly (especially in small sizes), as they are hard to read. Underlined text is a big "no-no" since readers will mistake it for a hyperlink.
Maximize contrast: You can maximize contrast by using a light-colored background and very dark or black text. White text on a dark background (i.e., reverse type) is dramatic, but difficult to read. Accordingly, save reverse type, fancy type, and other special effects for your name and category headings. Also, check your Web resume to see how it looks when it's printed out. Some color combinations are readable online, but impossible to read when printed.
Avoid clutter: Lines, tables, boxes, and graphics are effective in small doses, but are frequently overused. One of the most common problems with Web resumes is design overkill. If in doubt, remember the old axiom: Less is more. Overdesigning your resume won't make it stand out—it just makes it harder to read.

Use Color in Small Doses

Colored text for major headings or bullets adds pizzazz, but if you use too many colors, your resume will look like a gaudy carnival flyer. Spot color is usually a better choice.

Carefully Consider Photography

While the use of photographs is pretty common on Web resumes, that doesn't mean they are beneficial. Job seekers should consider carefully whether including a photograph is in their best interests.

From a graphics standpoint, photographs tend to serve as a Web resume's focal point—and using your own image as a focal point can backfire. Most of the photos we've seen on Web resumes are amateur efforts with less-than-perfect lighting and less-than-flattering results. If a photo is appropriate in your case, make sure it's a professional photograph with appropriate lighting, background, and attire.

Select Your Graphics Carefully

Businesslike graphics can enhance your resume, but steer away from anything that might be distracting to the reader. Remember—your objective is to impress employers with your qualifications, not your animated GIF collection! In addition, large graphics slow down resume loading time—leaving you with a frustrated (and unimpressed) audience.

Limit Visual Elements

Unless you're a trained graphic artist, play it safe and stick with one or two primary design elements. For example, if your Web resume has a colorful side bar and category headings, forget the fancy ruling lines. If you're including graphic images or icons, avoid busy (textured) backgrounds. If you're using colored text, optimize page contrast by using a simple white (or very light colored) background. In most cases, less is more.

In addition—if you remember nothing else, remember this: Your Web resume should not include banner ads, horoscopes, family reunion photos, weather reports, baby pictures, or links to a Tom Cruise Web site.

Don't Be a Plain Jane

On the other hand, many resumes that aren't overdesigned tend to be too plain. And as you might guess, a bland-looking resume doesn't do much for your image either!

Whether it's fair or not, there will be times when your suitability for a job will be determined on the basis of your resume's appearance. What does your resume say about you? Does it say that you're careless about details? That you were in a hurry to get the job done? That you are uninspired? Or does it say that you're a professional?

Your Web resume should leave no doubt in the employer's mind that you are a capable and professional candidate—the kind of person who takes the time to do things right. Bottom line: If your resume is sloppy, overdressed, or underdesigned, it won't do a good job of conveying your potential value. And conveying your potential value is exactly what a resume is supposed to do.

Regardless of your profession, your resume should demonstrate a careful balance of design, common sense, and good taste. If you're an artist, this is your chance to be creative! Develop a visually dynamic Web portfolio with links to your best work. If you are a civil engineer, keep the style of your resume conservative and if you want to expand it into a portfolio, include links to photos of completed projects, technical skills, or performance indicators.

In short, your Web resume is a business document and it should be designed with that in mind. Not too fancy, not too plain. Get employers' attention by taking the time to create a Web resume that honors your candidacy and your profession.

Web Resume Effectiveness Checklist

To assess the effectiveness of your Web resume, check it against the following lists.

Typography

- *Fonts: Did you limit the use of fonts to one or two complementary typefaces?*
- *Type size: Is all body text all one size?*
- *Bolding: Have you limited the use of bolding to job titles, subheadings, and special emphasis?*
- *Italics: Have you reserved the use of italicized body text for special emphasis or use on book titles?*
- *Underlining: Have you completely avoided underlining text?*
- *Capitalization: Have you steered away from using all capital letters except in small doses?*
- *Contrast: Have you maximized the contrast between the page background and the body text? (Extremes of very dark and very light provide the best contrast.)*

- **Reverse type:** Have you avoided the use of reverse type (white print on a dark background), except for special design headings?

- **Print output:** When printed (ideally use both a color printer and a black and white printer for comparison), can you read the printout of your Web resume?

- **Hierarchy:** Is your body type at least 10 points in size (size 2 in HTML), and your categories one or two points larger (size 4 or 5 in HTML)?

Color

- **Graphics:** If you are in a conservative profession, is your Web resume color scheme businesslike?

- **Type:** Have you been conservative with the use of brightly colored type?

Style

- **Tie-in:** Do your graphics match your profession or have a job-related tie-in?

- **Professionalism:** Do your graphics look professional instead of cute (with the exception of professions dealing with small children)?

- **Size:** Are the graphics small enough to allow your Web resume to load in 15 seconds or less?

- **Limited use:** Do you have just one or two primary design elements?

- **Low-key graphics:** Have you avoided using a busy background graphic?

- **Style:** Does your Web resume have enough style to make it interesting?

Functionality

- **Navigation:** Is your navigation system placed strategically on the page?

- **15-second test:** Can potential employers see your best credentials immediately?

- **Download time:** Does your Web resume download in less than 15 seconds?

- **Layout size:** Is your Web page designed for smaller screens (i.e., no critical information is placed in the right margin)?

Hyperlinks

- *Placement:* Are all hyperlinks (if you have them) relevant and placed in a logical area?

- *Relevancy:* Do your hyperlinks lead to supporting data or are they just there because they can be?

- *Directed links:* Do your linked pages provide navigation that will bring the viewer back?

Copy

- *Summary:* Is your summary statement keyword-heavy? Does it immediately project you as a qualified candidate for your job target?

- *Job descriptions:* Are your job descriptions broken into smaller chunks of text and/or bulleted?

- *Proofing:* Has your resume been proofed for accuracy and consistency? Have you used a grammar checker or spell checker?

- *Strategy:* Are your links, categories, and skills listed in the most relevant order with the best stuff on top?

- *Appropriate bullets:* Have you used bullets to emphasize accomplishments and special projects, but avoided using them on each sentence?

- *Page length:* Are pages short enough to print properly?

Professionalism

- **No banners:** Have you avoided the use of banner advertising?

- **No extras:** Have you avoided extras like page counters, horoscopes, weather reports?

- **Photos:** If you are including a picture, is it professional and appropriate?

In Chapter 9 you'll be able to expand on what you've learned here as we take you step-by-step through the Web-resume creation process. Are you ready?

Web-Resume Creation: Nuts and Bolts

If you want to learn more about HTML-based resumes—if you are a "hands-on" kind of person and itching to build your own Web resume—this chapter is for you. The key issues covered in this chapter include:

- *Web page components and HTML codes*
- *Formatting strategies*
- *High-tech doodads*
- *Hands-on Web-resume creation*
- *Resources for those who want more*

The information in this chapter is not all-encompassing, but will familiarize you with the most relevant issues. By the time you have finished reading this chapter, you'll be ready to create a simple (but eye-appealing) Web resume like the one shown in Figure 9-1 at the end of this chapter.

Web Page Components

First, let's take a look at the basic components of Web page construction. As you read about these components, keep in mind that if you use an HTML editor (like the one in our sample project near the end of this chapter), you won't need to learn HTML codes. While many of you will enjoy learning about the technical aspects of HTML, others may want to skip ahead to the section "Create Your Own Web Resume" (near the end of this chapter).

Common HTML Codes

There are scores of HTML codes—used for formatting, text positioning, structure definition, hyperlinks, graphics, multimedia and JavaScript insertion, forms, tables, and so on. For this basic tutorial, we are focusing on codes that are typically used in a simple HTML document. For more detailed information, refer to the Resources section at the end of the chapter.

As you can see in Table 9-1, most HTML codes have a beginning code and an ending code (placed immediately before and after the text you want to have the desired effect).

Color

Using HTML codes, you can designate just about any color you like (for type, background, tables, etc.). While some browsers allow you

Table 9-1   HTML Codes

Common HTML Codes

Bold Type:	insert text here
Italic Type:	<i>insert text here</i>
Type Size:	<h1>insert text here</h1>
	<big>insert text here</big>
	<font size=2>insert text here</font>
Bulleted List:	<UL><LI></UL> (before each list item)
Paragraph Breaks:	 (no ending code)
Text Alignment:	<center>insert text here</center>
	<left>insert text here</left>
	<right>insert text here</right>

Adding Graphics

To add a graphic to a Web page, use the <img> tag. In its simplest form, the raw HTML code looks like this:

<img bor=0 height=120 width=160 src="picture.jpeg">

Translation: Search for a file named "picture," place it on the page with no border, and make it 120 pixels wide and 160 pixels high.

Adding Hyperlinks

To transform a string of text in an "active" hyperlink, use the <a> tag. When fully executed, the code will look something like this:

<a href="projects.html">Projects</a>

The result looks like this: <u>Projects</u>

Adding an Image Map

The HTML code for a simple image map looks like this:

<A HREF="Experience.html"><IMG SRC="Experience.gif"
Border="0" width="30" Height="15" align="bottom"></A>

In this example, a graphic named "Experience.gif" will function as a hyperlink to the HTML page called "Experience.html." The size of the button is rectangular (30 pixels wide and 15 pixels high), and it is aligned at the bottom of the frame.

Adding an Email Link

The HTML code for adding an email hyperlink is as follows:

<A href=mailto:johndoe@abc.com>johndoe@abc.com</a>

The result looks like this: <u>johndoe@abc.com</u>

to designate color by name (e.g., "red"), this method is not recognized by all Web browsers, so if you are hand-coding your text, you'll want to use the standard (216-color) Web-safe palette. Some typical color codes include the following:

Bright Red	#FF0000
Pale Yellow	#FFFFCC
Maroon	#990033
Medium Teal	#339999
Dark Blue	#000066

Web-safe color palette charts can be found in most HTML books. We encourage you to check the resource list at the end of the chapter, as it includes a hand-picked list of Web sites with color charts, tutorials, and other HTML resources.

Hyperlinks and Navigation

Hyperlinks are not rocket science, yet they are the very innovation that drives the Net's amazing growth and functionality—and this benefit extends to Web resumes as well. If you want to make your resume more flexible and interactive—or expand it beyond its one-dimensional borders—hyperlinks will take you there.

While many single-page Web resumes have no hyperlinks at all, Web portfolios need a structured navigation system to organize hyperlinks into a directory. Many long Web resumes have no navigation system, but use embedded "hot links" within the body text. Hyperlinks can be used to help your viewer navigate to different resume sections, jump to different parts of a page, access email, go to a different Web page, initiate a download, and so on.

Lost in Space?

When hyperlinks are used properly, they add a great deal of functionality to a Web page. Unfortunately, many Web resume sites have links that serve no purpose other than to take the viewer to another Web site. When the destination is nonrelevant, it tends to leave the viewer feeling rather bewildered, wondering, *why am I here?*

Hyperlinks should be included in Web resumes for the sole purpose of providing viewers with immediate access to supporting data. *Links that do not reinforce your candidacy are counterproductive.* Your goal is to keep the viewer on your Web site—not lose them in Cyberspace.

In addition, it's important to give careful thought to the order in which you place your links—especially when using a vertical navigation system. If a potential employer visited your resume site and selected only one hyperlink, which link would you want him or her to click on? *That* is the hyperlink that should be listed first on your navigation menu.

Although Web resumes don't always need navigation systems, they're a must for those who have multiple pages with major categories (i.e., Experience, Education, Projects, etc.). As has been demonstrated throughout this book, there are many ways to incorporate navigation into a Web resume. For example:

- *Left vertical: Left-sided vertical navigation (Figure 9-2) is the most popular style. When hyperlinks—or hyperlinked bars, icons, or buttons—are placed in the left margin, you can include an almost unlimited number of links. For those who want to create a multipage site, this can be a real advantage.*

- *Right vertical: Right-sided navigation must be executed carefully, because it can be a real problem for viewers who have small monitor screens. To avoid "losing" a right-sided navigation bar on a narrow screen, be sure to limit the width of your Web page to no more than 600 pixels wide. (See Figure 9-3.)*

- *Horizontal: Horizontally aligned links (across the top of a Web page) are immediately visible to the viewer when the page downloads. On the downside, there is less room for links with this method (we don't recommend stacking them more than two deep), and the links quickly scroll out of view. The resume in Figure 9-4 shows a horizontal navigation bar.*

- *Pop-up navigation bars: Pop-up navigation bars can't be depicted in a book, but they work just like they sound: They literally "pop up" as you glide your cursor over the linked text. We'll give this technology extra points for being cool, but it isn't something the average Joe or Jane needs on a resume.*

TIP

Link "destinations" (especially news articles) can be moved or deleted by the host site, so don't count on them to remain active. In some cases, a screenshot (like the figures in this book) may be a better option, as screenshots are graphic files. As such, you can control whether they are "up" or not.

- *Contextual links: Contextual links are not placed inside a bar or table, but are embedded in words or sections of resume text. The "confidential resume" example shown in Chapter 6 (Figure 6-5) shows how context-specific links (under the Key Skills category) can be used to provide "layers" of information, which allow the viewer to go to a "deeper" level if more detail is desired.*

Navigational links take many forms, including hyperlinked text, buttons, bars, bulleted lists, and linked images/image maps. However, a simple navigation system is sufficient for most Web resumes and looks terrific when properly designed.

Typography

HTML designers are limited to five "universal" type styles and four formatting options (regular, bold, italic, and underlined). If you use a type style that isn't on the list, many of your viewers will not be able to see your pages as you intended. Even worse, the wrong type style can throw your entire layout into disarray—no matter how good it looks on your monitor. Until the powers-that-be adopt more type styles, limit your use to those listed here:

Arial, Helvetica

Verdana

Georgia, Times Roman

Courier

Comic Sans

Most Web resume samples in this book were created with Arial body text. We favor its readability, and we like the way it mixes and matches with other typefaces.

If you're proficient with graphics software (like Photoshop or Paint Shop), you have another option. You can create text in any style and configuration you like, save it as a graphic, and then use it in your Web resume as an image file. Obviously, you won't be able to modify your text once it's converted into a graphic, but you will have complete control over all typography. Because of these limitations, graphic images of text should be used only when the text is unlikely to change (such as category headings or your name, for example).

Capitalization

With the exception of your name, categories, employer listings, or situations where special emphasis is required, avoid using all capital letters. Text in capital letters is not only difficult to read but it looks "blocky." In most cases, upper- and lowercase type is more attractive and easier to read.

Text Size

When body text size is set at 2 (equivalent to 10-point type in a word-processed document), category headings typically look best when they are set at size 3, 4, or 5. Experiment with different combinations to see what looks best on your document.

Type Combinations

Combining different type styles can produce interesting effects, but proceed with caution. There are several examples of mixed type in this book. For quick reference, the combinations below provide consistently good results:

- *Arial body text (HTML size 2 or 3) with Verdana category headings and name (bolded or not, in HTML size 4 or 5)*

- *Arial body text (HTML size 2 or 3) and Times Roman category headings (HTML size 4 or 5 bold—or size 6, upper- and lowercase, italicized)*

- *Arial body text (HTML size 2 or 3) with Comic Sans headings (HTML size 4 or 5, bold or not)*

Comic Sans should be used sparingly, as it has a light-hearted appearance that isn't appropriate for many resumes. Courier looks like it was created on a typewriter, so use it only if you're trying to emulate an old-fashioned "typed" look.

Instead of experimenting with mixing and matching, it's always "safe" to use one type style consistently throughout. Body text should be size 2 or 3 and major headings and names set a couple of sizes larger. (Note: When text is formatted with an HTML editor, it may use "traditional" type sizes such as 18 point for category headings and 12 point for body text.)

When Web pages are viewed on a Macintosh computer, the type appears to be smaller than when viewed on a PC.

TIP

Special Characters

While ASCII's "standard" characters fit the bill in most cases, there are times when special symbols are desired. When a nonkeyboard character is called for, you'll need to insert a specific HTML code into your text to make that character appear.

Some of the special characters you're likely to need on a Web resume are accent marks (as in résumé), round bullets (•), and em dashes (—). Refer to Table 9-2 for a list of the most common special characters and their corresponding HTML codes.

Formatting and Layout

People tend to "skim" Web pages (rather than read them), so keep this in mind as you determine your resume format and layout. After all, it takes just one quick click to exit your document and link to a competitor's resume—or to the 37 unread emails that beckon. Knowing that the Web's hypertext environment exacerbates viewers' short attention spans, you must dedicate yourself to creating pages that are inviting and engaging.

In addition to creating an attractive layout, be sure to consider text readability. This not only applies to type size and page contrast (as described in Chapter 8) but also to paragraph density. In other words, it's best to avoid large paragraphs, so break your data into small, digestible chunks. Dense blocks of text simply won't be read, so use bullets and subsections to keep your text open and inviting.

Another strategy is to build very concise job descriptions that provide more detail via embedded links. (Refer to Figure 8-2—the

Table 9-2 Common Characters and their HTML Equivalents

Character	HTML Code
é	&#233;
•	&#149:
—	&#151;
–	&#150;
#	&#35;
$	&#36;
™	&#153;
©	&#169;
®	&#174;
"	&#147;
"	&#148;

"After" resume of Dr. Jean Smythe to see how this works in an actual resume.) There is, however, one problem with this approach—employers and recruiters who print your resume won't get all the juicy details unless they print the linked pages as well.

Tables

Tables add a great deal of flexibility to the Web page creation process, as they provide a structural foundation for text, tabular information, graphics, graphic bullets, and other page elements. Tables can also be used to create simple three-dimensional borders and, with a bit of creativity, attractive graphics (see Figure 9-5). As an added bonus, table-based designs download faster than those created with graphic files.

Whether you want to add a simple navigation bar or create more sophisticated Web pages, you'll want to learn how to set up tables. Check the Resources section at the end of the chapter for Web sites that provide tutorials on HTML table creation.

Frames

Frames (commonly confused with tables) are basically "containers" for other Web pages. Unfortunately, frames have limitations that make them less than desirable for Web resumes. For example, most search engines can't index text when it resides in a framed page. Even worse, framed pages are tricky (or impossible) to print. For these reasons, we recommend that you use traditional HTML architecture.

Page Margins

One of the most common problems with Web resumes is the "Panoramic effect" achieved when Web pages span the entire width of the screen. Full-width Web pages should be avoided for two reasons. First, it is tiring to read long lines of text. Second, text on the right side of a wide page may not be viewable by viewers who have

TIP

If you're using HTML tables (to create fancy bulleted lists, categorize information, or determine the placement of page elements), take the time to plan and organize your layout before you start inserting text and graphics. This step will save a great deal of time (and grief) in the long run.

smaller screens. To avoid this problem, we recommend using tables to control page width to no more than 600 to 700 pixels.

Graphic Images and Photos

We addressed the need for restraint with graphics in Chapter 8. As you start searching for appropriate graphics, don't lose sight of the word *subtle*. It is not easy to be subtle in Cyberspace, since the great majority of Web graphics are gaudy or ostentatious.

Web graphics fall into three basic categories. The most common type of Web graphic format is GIF. GIF files are universally accepted on the Web and are created with Web-safe colors. GIF files range from simple icons to sophisticated background tiles. Animated GIFs are also readily available, but only a small percentage of them are appropriate for Web resumes.

Background images (available in both GIF and JPEG format) can add a great deal of pizzazz to Web resumes, but they must be selected carefully. For our do-it-yourself project (shown originally in Figure 9-1), we developed a page design template that can be used with any kind of tiled background. Instead of placing the background behind the text (like most resumes on the Net), we use the graphic to "frame" the page instead. The resulting resume has a more subtle design—and text which is actually readable.

Photographs (JPEG format) can be used on a Web page like any other graphic—but, as mentioned previously, they should be used with caution. First, you must decide if including a personal photo is truly in your best interest. Second, you have to consider whether you should include photos of any kind, as JPEG files can dramatically prolong downloading time. In many cases, a photograph does not add to the functionality of your site, but simply takes up valuable bandwidth.

Adding Functionality with Downloads

Every employer has different needs and preferences, so it's wise (even critical) to offer your resume in other downloadable forms.

TIP

To make it easier for our readers to complete the do-it-yourself Web resume, we've provided a nice selection of free background designs on our Web site (www.eResumeIQ.com/graphics.html). Be sure to check them out if you can't find what you need on your own.

More Web Trivia

Image maps: An image map is basically a hyperlinked picture or graphic. In Web resumes, image maps are used frequently to create a more "elegant" hyperlink. You can't "see" image maps, but when you click on one, it works like any other hyperlink.

Site maps: Site maps work like a table of contents. They vary greatly in appearance and structure, but their primary function is to provide a visual "map" of how a site is organized and linked. Large sites typically include a site map or "directory" to aid viewers who lose their way. However, unless you are creating a complex Web portfolio, a site map is not needed.

HTML, XML, and XHTML: Like HTML, XML and XHTML are markup languages. XML (standing for eXtensible Markup Language) is the foundation for the "next" generation of HTML—named XHTML.

FTP: FTP (an acronym for File Transfer Protocol) is the system used to transfer and upload Web pages from your computer to your Web host's computer. FTP protocols vary considerably, so check with your ISP or Web hosting service to get specific instructions on how to upload your page.

Java/Java Applets/JavaScript Rollovers: Java is a full-scale computer language and JavaScript is a "subset" of the Java programming language. JavaScript was developed by Netscape as an "easier" programming language. JavaScript rollovers are used to change the appearance of an image when it is selected (or approached) by the mouse cursor. Web page designers typically use JavaScript to make graphic buttons look as if they've been selected, turned off, turned on, pressed in, etc.

You can wait to see if employers request another format, but it's better to offer the option on your site, so that they can get what they need without delay.

These are the most common download formats:

- *ASCII downloads. ASCII is the most useful download option, as many employers and recruiters may need an ASCII version of your resume for database input. If you don't offer this option, you are greatly curtailing the potential effectiveness of your Web resume.*

- *PDF downloads. PDF downloads provide employers with a printable, traditionally formatted resume. Unlike a Microsoft Word version of your resume, PDF files do not carry viruses and they always print exactly as they were intended to print. They do, however, require that the viewer use a PDF reader, and this is their primary drawback (at least until everyone uses PDF technology). You can also use PDF to make a slide presentation to showcase certain types of projects.*

- *Microsoft Word downloads. Despite problems with macro viruses and compatibility, there are still some employers and recruiters who will accept or request a Microsoft Word version of your resume. MS Word is the most popular word processor in the world, so if you're going to offer a word-processed version of your resume for downloading, Microsoft Word is your best choice.*

Download Time

Statistics indicate that Web surfers will endure a wait of about 30 seconds before moving on. A highly motivated employer or recruiter may be willing to wait longer, but don't count on it.

You can "guesstimate" how long your resume will take to download by checking its size. The average download time is 1 to 2K per second, so a Web page with an 8-K background graphic takes about 4 to 8 seconds to download. If you add a 20-K photo, your download time starts moving into the "frustration" zone.

Here are a few tips that will help you minimize download time:

- *Keep the size of your page (with graphics) to no more than 35K.*

- *When selecting colors (for type or table backgrounds), use "standard" colors from the Web-safe palette. (Check the Resource section for color chart Web sites.)*

- *Always set the specific height and width setting for graphics (instead of using percentages), as this allows the page to download more quickly.*

Low-Tech Frustration

Some people who will visit your site have state-of-the-art computers, sound systems, modems, and super-speedy DSL or wired cable access. Others, though, are using "dinosaur" technology (from last year)—or even worse, from the nineties.

While it may frustrate you to be "forced" to configure your Web resume to the lowest denominator (while you wait for the rest of the world to upgrade)—that is exactly what must be done if you want your resume to be accessible to a large audience.

In addition, when planning your site, do not depend on any single high-tech venue (like video or audio) to get your primary message across, as some people in your audience won't get the message at all. Bells and whistles should be used to enhance your primary message, not deliver it.

TIP

Vincent Flanders's site, Web Pages That Suck.com, offers a free site survey to see if your graphics are bloated. Check it out at www.websitesthatsuck.com/sitesurvey.html.

- *When selecting graphics, be sure to check their size before making your final design decision. A JPEG background can be 10 times larger than a GIF background.*

Create Your Own Web Resume

To create a Web resume with the instructions that follow, you need the following:

- ***Netscape Composer:*** *Netscape Composer is an HTML editor that comes bundled with Netscape Communicator. If you don't have Netscape Communicator, you can download it free at http://home.netscape.com/download/.*

- ***Background image:*** *This graphic will be used to frame your page. We have provided free background images at eResumeIQ.com/graphics.html.*

- ***Properly prepared text:*** *You need to start with a clean ASCII file. If your text resume is not ready, refer to Chapter 3 for detailed instructions.*

Build the Page

1. Open Netscape Communicator, then select Composer from the drop-down menu on the right.

2. From the main menu at the top, click on Insert, then select Image. From the box that appears, click on Choose Location or Choose File and select your graphic file from the directory or disk where it is stored, being sure to checkmark the Use As Background option. Click OK. (When you're done with this step, the background image should cover the entire screen.)

3. Add two extra spaces at the top of the page by pressing the Enter key (on your keyboard) twice.

4. Go back to the Insert menu, but this time select the Table option. From the New Table Properties menu, select the following options:

High-Tech Doodads

Flash Resumes

If you want a resume that delivers a super-slick animated punch, you may want to consider a Flash (or Flash-enhanced) resume. Some Web resumes are created entirely in Flash, while others use Flash entry pages to introduce or "announce" a resume. Flash wins high praise for being cool, but caution must be taken to ensure that its special effects enhance the resume message, not detract from it. When a Flash resume is more "entertaining" than professional, its use is counterproductive.

Streaming Audio

If you've ever listened to a RealAudio clip, you have experienced streaming audio. Streaming audio is a relatively new technology that works like this: As the sound clip downloads it is "streaming in" at the same time. Before the advent of streaming audio, you could not listen to an audio clip until it had completely downloaded, so delays were a real problem.

However, even with the current technologies, a high-quality, 15-second video can require as much as a megabyte of space, which can slow down some computers to the point of crashing. Not a good thing!

Streaming Video

Like streaming audio, streaming video is a new technology that reduces long wait times by allowing users to view files as they are downloading. In Web resume applications, streaming video is used by job seekers to introduce themselves, describe key skills, deliver a philosophy statement, or conduct a mock interview (i.e., answer typical interview questions). Streaming video gives employers a "sneak peek" at the job seeker—which, when executed properly, can be a real plus. But when video is done poorly (as is frequently the case), a video clip can backfire and create a poor impression of the job seeker. In general, streaming video should be used when visual appearance and "performance" issues are critical—television personalities, public relations representatives, actors, and so on.

While the "mock interview" capabilities of streaming video have been touted as a "new millennium breakthrough" for long-distance job seekers (saving employers the cost of flying a candidate in for an interview), many employers and recruiters lack the high-end computers needed to capitalize on these technologies.

Number of rows:	1
Number of columns:	1
Table alignment:	Center
Border line width:	1
Cell spacing:	3
Cell padding:	25
Table width:	70% of window
Table minimum height:	100%

For the Table Background option, select Use Color, then click on the adjacent box and select White as the table color.

Click Apply (at the very bottom), then click on OK or Close to close the New Table Properties box.

When you're finished, you'll have a narrow (horizontal) white frame.

5. Cut and paste your ASCII resume file into the white frame. This creates a very basic resume (kind of a fancy ASCII resume). To eliminate extra spaces between sections of text, use a hard return (Shift + Enter) at the end of appropriate paragraphs.

Continue with the formatting instructions that follow to clean your resume up and optimize its appearance.

Jazz Up Your Resume with Formatting

- *Format your name and category headings: Highlight your name, click on Format, then select Size. Select 18. If you want to bold it, click on Format, then select Style, and from the menu, select Bold. Repeat with other categories as needed. (Alternatively, you can select formatting options from the horizontal menu bar.) If you'd like to add color to your name and category headings, simply select the text you'd like to colorize, then select a color from the drop-down menu to complement your background image.*

- *Add bullets: Highlight the text that should be bulleted, click on Format, and from the pull-down menu, select List. From the options that appear, click on Bulleted. Repeat as needed. Note: When you "bulletize" text, it will automatically be indented.*

- *Apply advanced formatting: At your discretion, you may experiment with color, type styles, border attributes, and hyperlinks. Check the Resource section at the end of the chapter for information on free Netscape Composer tutorials.*

Add Finishing Touches

Before posting your resume for all the world to see, a few finishing touches are needed:

- *Hot-link your email:* Highlight your email address, click on Link from the horizontal menu bar, and type in your email address.

- *Add meta tags:* Meta tags and keywords can be added by using the Page Properties function. (See Chapter 10 for tips on meta tags.)

- *Check for consistency:* Your goal is to maintain a consistent look and feel throughout your document. To accomplish this, check the following elements for consistency: type style (including color and size), use of color, text placement and spacing, and margins.

- *Proof it again:* In addition to proofreading it yourself, get the assistance of a trusted colleague, mentor, or significant other to view your final document. And although this can backfire (people love to criticize), it may also uncover errors or inconsistencies.

- *Save the file:* Click File, Save As. In the File Name box, type the name of your document, for instance, "lastname." Keep in mind that long file names can be cumbersome as URLs—the shorter the file name, the better.

- *Upload the file:* After saving the file, your Web resume is only available on your computer. You'll need to upload the file via your Internet Service Provider to make it available on the Web. See options in the "Need a Host?" box that follows. For more information, visit eResumeIQ.com.

- *Make sure everything works!* Your email link is especially important, but you also want to check all hyperlinks—and, of course, your telephone number!

Need a Host?

If you have your own Internet Service Provider (ISP), Web site hosting may already be available to you at no charge. So before you look at other options, contact your ISP and find out what's available. While you're at it, get instructions on how to upload your resume to your "host" site. This is typically done through a process called File Transfer Protocol (FTP). If you want to investigate other options, check out the list of resources at the end of this chapter.

Resources

The Web sites listed here provide additional information on topics related to HTML and Web page creation. However, this list is just the tip of the iceberg! If you want more information, get online, go to any search engine (we favor Google.com), and conduct a simple search for terms like *HTML, HTML training,* or *Web page design.*

HTML

- *Bare Bones Guide to HTML: http://werbach.com/bare-bones/barebones.html*
- *HTML 101: Back to Basics: www.webreference.com/html/tutorials*

Web Color Charts

- *http://lightsphere.com/colors/*
- *http://www.brobstsystems.com/colors.htm*
- *http://www.library.tudelft.nl/~avasi/colors.htm*

HTML Editors

- *http://cws.internet.com/32html.html*
- *www.html.about.com/cs/htmleditors/*
- *Netscape Composer (used to create your do-it-yourself sample) at http://home.netscape.com/download/*

Free Web Site Hosting

- *www.tracost.com/free/free-web-site-hosting.html*
- *http://www.freewebspace.net/*
- *www.free-web-site-hosting.com*

Web Graphics Optimization

- *www.infohiway.com/faster*
- *http://www.websitesthatsuck.com/sitesurvey.html*

Meta Tags

- *www.webdeveloper.com/html/html_metatag_res.html*

Streaming Audio

- *www.digitaldivas.com/zine/09-00tut/marlee_tutorial*
- *www.webdeveloper.com/multimedia/multimedia_guide_realaudio.html*

Now that you have a Web-based resume and are ready for an online job search, let's review your options for actively (or confidentially) promoting it.

Figure 9-1 Web resume created from "Build Your Own Resume" lesson.

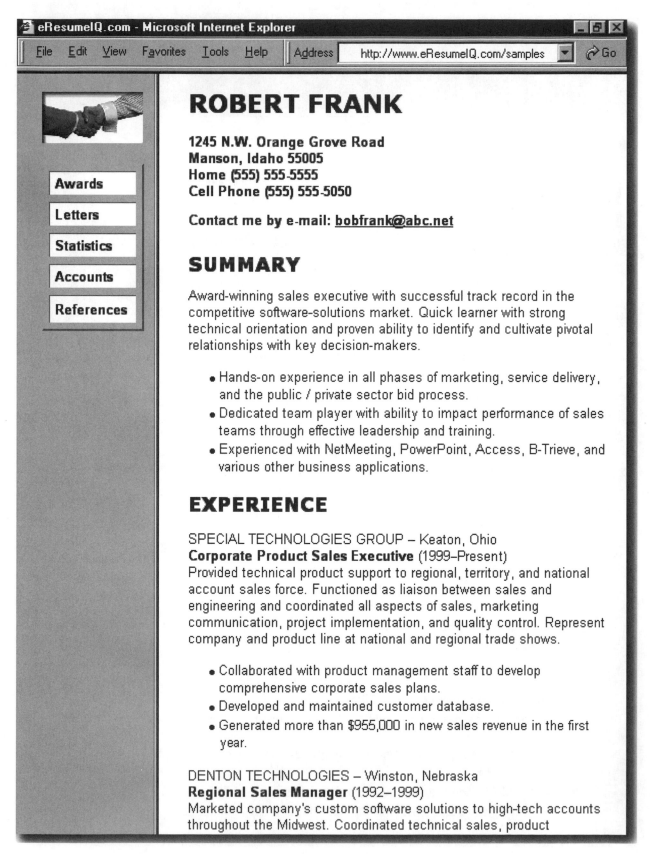

eResumeIQ.com - Microsoft Internet Explorer

File Edit View Favorites Tools Help   Address http://www.eResumeIQ.com/samples Go

Awards

Letters

Statistics

Accounts

References

ROBERT FRANK

1245 N.W. Orange Grove Road
Manson, Idaho 55005
Home (555) 555-5555
Cell Phone (555) 555-5050

Contact me by e-mail: **bobfrank@abc.net**

SUMMARY

Award-winning sales executive with successful track record in the competitive software-solutions market. Quick learner with strong technical orientation and proven ability to identify and cultivate pivotal relationships with key decision-makers.

- Hands-on experience in all phases of marketing, service delivery, and the public / private sector bid process.
- Dedicated team player with ability to impact performance of sales teams through effective leadership and training.
- Experienced with NetMeeting, PowerPoint, Access, B-Trieve, and various other business applications.

EXPERIENCE

SPECIAL TECHNOLOGIES GROUP – Keaton, Ohio
Corporate Product Sales Executive (1999–Present)
Provided technical product support to regional, territory, and national account sales force. Functioned as liaison between sales and engineering and coordinated all aspects of sales, marketing communication, project implementation, and quality control. Represent company and product line at national and regional trade shows.

- Collaborated with product management staff to develop comprehensive corporate sales plans.
- Developed and maintained customer database.
- Generated more than $955,000 in new sales revenue in the first year.

DENTON TECHNOLOGIES – Winston, Nebraska
Regional Sales Manager (1992–1999)
Marketed company's custom software solutions to high-tech accounts throughout the Midwest. Coordinated technical sales, product

Figure 9-2   Web resume displays left-sided vertical navigation bar, the most popular style for navigation.

Figure 9-3 Web resume displays right-sided navigation bar, placed far enough toward center that information isn't "lost" for those with smaller-width monitors.

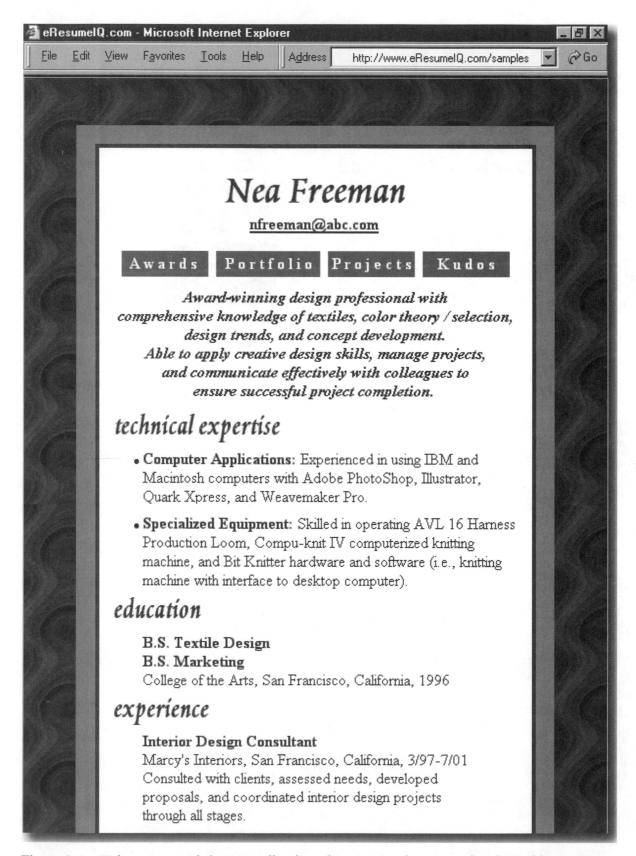

Figure 9-4   Web resume with horizontally aligned navigation bar, immediately visible to viewers when page downloads.

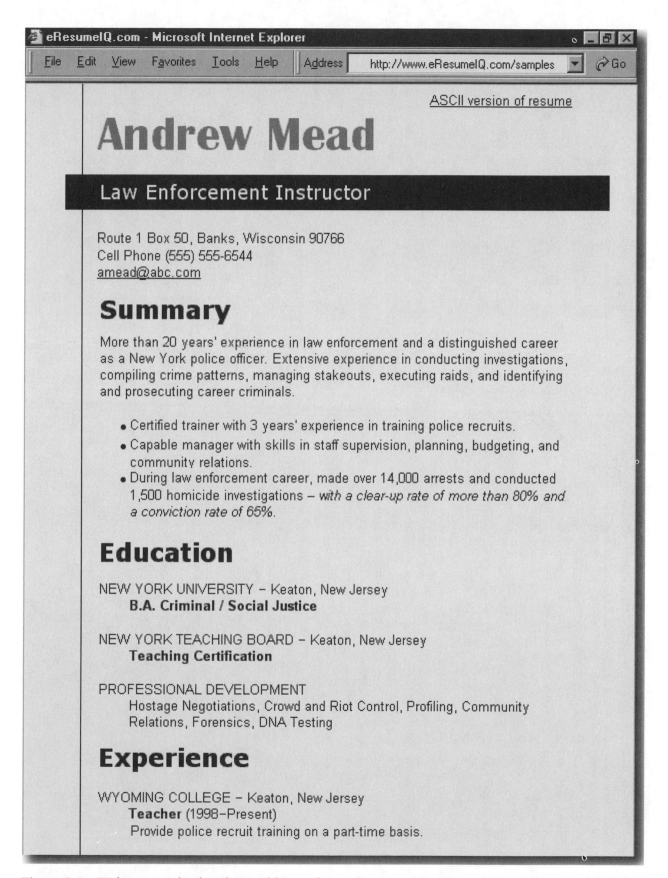

ASCII version of resume

Andrew Mead

Law Enforcement Instructor

Route 1 Box 50, Banks, Wisconsin 90766
Cell Phone (555) 555-6544
amead@abc.com

Summary

More than 20 years' experience in law enforcement and a distinguished career as a New York police officer. Extensive experience in conducting investigations, compiling crime patterns, managing stakeouts, executing raids, and identifying and prosecuting career criminals.

- Certified trainer with 3 years' experience in training police recruits.
- Capable manager with skills in staff supervision, planning, budgeting, and community relations.
- During law enforcement career, made over 14,000 arrests and conducted 1,500 homicide investigations — *with a clear-up rate of more than 80% and a conviction rate of 65%.*

Education

NEW YORK UNIVERSITY – Keaton, New Jersey
B.A. Criminal / Social Justice

NEW YORK TEACHING BOARD – Keaton, New Jersey
Teaching Certification

PROFESSIONAL DEVELOPMENT
Hostage Negotiations, Crowd and Riot Control, Profiling, Community Relations, Forensics, DNA Testing

Experience

WYOMING COLLEGE – Keaton, New Jersey
Teacher (1998–Present)
Provide police recruit training on a part-time basis.

Figure 9-5   Web resume displays how tables can be used to create simple graphics (the reverse black bar under individual's name).

Chapter 10

Getting the Word Out: Text and Web Resume Delivery Options

Whether you're conducting an active, passive, or confidential job search, there are delivery options and privacy precautions that you should be aware of to effectively promote your online resume. However, we begin this chapter with a brief review of why you should take your search online. Economics and ease of use top the list, as underscored by these statistics:

- *72 percent of hiring professionals agree that Internet resume databases are an effective hiring tool. (Source: Recruiters Network,* http://www.recruitersnetwork.com, *The Association for Internet Recruiting)*

- *The average cost per hire using a major metro newspaper is $3295 versus $377 using online sourcing. (Source: Society for Human Resource Management)*

- *82 percent of companies post job openings at their Web site. (Source: Recruiters Network, www.recruitersnetwork.com, The Association for Internet Recruiting)*

- *With Internet recruiting, the time it takes to fill jobs has decreased from more than 60 days to 30 days, and, in some cases, to as little as one or two days. (Source: RecruitSoft.com)*

- *Dollars spent on online recruiting are projected to increase from $105 million in 1998 to $1.74 billion in 2003. (Source: Forrester Research)*

- *Recruiters spend 2 to 4 hours per day, or 10 to 20 hours per week, on the large job/resume boards such as Monster.com, HotJobs.com, and Headhunter.net. (John Evans, TheShortList.com, as reported in Labor Daze)*

- *At least 10 million resumes reside on Web pages, independent of those in proprietary databases, such as Monster.com. These Web resumes can be accessed using advanced search engine tools. (Source: Glenn Gutmacher, RecruitingOnline.com)*

These statistics give you a view from the employer's side of the recruiting table. Clearly, the majority of staffing professionals use the Internet to source talent. And with good reason—it is nearly ten times more expensive to run an ad in a major newspaper than to post a job on the Internet. Recruiters are motivated to look for talent first on the Web. Don't disappoint them!

In this chapter, we'll cover the following delivery options:

- *Posting eResumes to web sites, including*
  - *General career sites*
  - *Recruiter network sites*
  - *Niche sites*
  - *Industry-related career sites*
  - *College-related sites*
  - *Regional sites*
  - *Corporate sites*
- *Using resume distribution services*
- *Registering your Web resume with search engines*

Before we discuss delivery options, let's talk a bit about privacy—one of the biggest concerns job seekers have about taking their resume online.

Keeping Your Posting Confidential

The term *confidential resume* is an oxymoron when it comes to posting your resume on the Internet. At worst, you could post your resume to a public career site and it could be seen by your boss, possibly jeopardizing your current job. Some companies actually employ sleuths to go on the Net and search for their employees' resumes.

The best answer to maintaining an active, "mostly private" online presence is to use a Web resume posted in a private database. Generally speaking, only those people who have your resume URL (along with anyone else they forward it to) will have easy access to your resume. However, search engines send out "spiders" to find and index all HTML files—whether you registered your URL or not—so when confidentiality is a critical issue, be sure to camouflage your name and other identifiers, as described in the next section.

If you want to post publicly to one of the major career sites, yet have concerns about confidentiality, consider concealing critical information on your resume. Proceed cautiously, though. Doing a good camouflage job can backfire on you. Take out too much information and you'll look evasive or omit critical keywords; leave in revealing information and you could create problems should your boss stumble across it. When posting to free sites, some of which give resume access to virtually anyone, we recommend removing your street address and other private information that you'd rather not have publicly available. To retain maximum confidentiality, consider changing the "identifiers" noted in Table 10-1.

It's unlikely that third-party recruiters would expose your search, as their reputation depends on their discretion and professionalism. To add to your own level of professionalism and protect yourself from prying eyes at work (especially those of technology professionals with access to the corporate email system), use an email address other than your employer's. The following resources provide free email accounts:

- http://www.ceoexpress.com *(use of yourname@ccocxpress.com is a nice touch for executives)*
- http://www.excite.com
- http://www.hotmail.com
- http://www.juno.com
- http://www.usa.net
- http://www.yahoo.com
- http://www.zoom.com

When signing up for these services, use a professional-sounding name. An address such as *jbrown345@yahoo.com* will put you in

Table 10-1 Making Your Resume Confidential

Item	Before—Nonconfidential Post	After—Camouflaged for Confidentiality
Email	johndoe@isp.com	candidate@myemail.net
Name	John Doe	Confidential Candidate
Address	12345 Sunnyside Lane Sun City, TX 75432	Southwest (or omit)
Company names	Pfizer Pharmaceuticals	Fortune 500 pharmaceutical leader
Dates	1998–Present	Present
Title	Division Manager	Management accountability for multistate area
Education	MBA, Duke University, 1989	MBA from top business school (omit date)
Product names	Norvasc, Zoloft, and Zithromax	Cardiovascular, antidepressant, and antibiotic products

better stead than *hockeynut@yahoo.com*. Keep in mind, however, that your identity may be determined (at sites like Yahoo) through an advanced search function. If you want total anonymity, sign up for an email address with a service that "erases" your identity, such as these:

- http://www.anonymizer.com
- http://anonymous.to/
- http://www.myemail.net
- http://www.pocamo.com/pocamomail.html
- http://www.sneakemail.com

Now that we've covered a few confidentiality precautions, let's discuss where to post your resume.

Posting eResumes to Career and Company Sites

Deciding where to post your resume can be daunting, especially when faced with tens of thousands of national, regional, and field-specific career sites on the Web. For active job seekers, we recommend a three-tiered approach to posting, which involves depositing your resume at these types of sites:

- *General career sites*
- *Niche sites/specialty career sites*
- *Company sites*

General Career Sites

General career sites serve as a one-stop shop where online job seekers can post or store resumes, apply for jobs, register for job-search agents, or conduct company research. These sites aim to serve job seekers from all functional areas and industries. When it comes to general Web sites, look for those with heavy traffic. Posting your resume where there is minimal activity is analogous to placing a billboard on an isolated back road. Traffic is measured in unique visitors or hits. Unique visitors refer to different people (email addresses), whereas hits denote the total number of times a site was visited. A site might have 1,000,000 hits a month but only 200,000 unique visitors, with each individual logging on several times in that period. Table 10-2 lists the traffic counts logged during October 2000 for the top 11 career sites.

Recruiters don't have time to search dozens of Web sites for candidates. Instead, they're apt to concentrate on a few favorites, most likely those with an abundant selection of resumes. Interestingly, the

Table 10-2 Top Career Sites as Measured by Unique Visitors

Career Site	Unique Visitors
JobsOnline.com	9.409 million
Monster.com	4.661 million
HotJobs.com	1.446 million
Headhunter.net	1.330 million
CareerPath.com	0.808 million
CareerBuilder.com	0.649 million
Jobs.com	0.593 million
FlipDog.com	0.510 million
Dice.com	0.420 million
CareerMosaic.com	0.395 million
Ajb.dni.us (America's Job Bank)	0.366 million

most visited job site, JobsOnline.com, does not offer a resume bank. That puts Monster.com on top if you are looking for optimum exposure. (And speaking of Monster.com, be sure to read "Top Five Faux Pas in Using Resume Builders" by Kim Isaacs, Monster.com Resume Expert and Director of ResumePower.com, in Chapter 4). All but one Web site in Table 10-2 are fee-based, meaning that recruiters are charged to search resumes (job seekers can post for free). America's Job Bank, brought to you in part by the U.S. Department of Labor (and employers' tax dollars), is free to recruiters.

There are other general career sites that are not listed in the top traffic list but are worthy of mention. First is Yahoo! Resumes. With parent site Yahoo! drawing more than 55 million visitors each month, it has the clout to make waves in the careers sector. Just a year after launch, Yahoo! Resumes boasted more than 380,000 resumes.

Next is the genre of recruiter networks. Posting your resume to sites such as BrilliantPeople.com (Management Recruiters International) or eKornFerry.com (Korn/Ferry International, the leader in senior-level executive search) can link you to more than 5000 search experts in offices worldwide. Networks for independently owned recruiting firms include RecruitersOnline.com and TopEchelon.com, each with some 8000 recruiters nationwide.

Table 10-3 reviews resume posting options at general career sites. You'll find information about recommended file formats, confidentiality choices, and a rating of the resume advice offered at each site.

Consider posting to both fee-based and free sites (fee or free refers to whether the recruiter pays to search the site for resumes; as a job seeker, you won't be charged to post your resume at any of the sites

Table 10-3 Review of Resume Posting Options at General Career Sites

Site	Profile Page	Format to Submit Resume	Personal Web URL	Multiple Resume Storage	Conf. Option	Quality of Resume Advice/Samples (*, **, ***)	Comments
Ajb.dni.us America's Job Bank	Yes	Text w/ Line Breaks	No	No	No	N/A	Traditional, Express, and Open Format options for resume layout. Open Format allows you to cut and paste ASCII text resume. Profile Page is based on info supplied under "Objective."
CareerBuilder.com (merged w/ CareerPath.com)	Yes	Text Only	No	Yes (5)	Yes	Advice: ** Samples: *–***	Supports "styled text." Resume samples provided by DistinctiveWeb.com are outstanding.
Dice.com	Yes	Text Only or HTML	Yes	No	Yes	N/A	Although considered a specialty site for information technology, Dice is included because of its traffic count in the top 10 career sites.
FlipDog.com	Yes	Text Only	No	No	Yes	N/A	No samples available; resume writing services advertise, most of which have samples at their sites (quality varies); those by ResumePower.com are outstanding.
Headhunter.net (merged w/ CareerMosaic.com)	No	Text w/ Line Breaks	No	Yes (20)	Yes	N/A	Click "Fixed Font" to retain control over appearance of resume.
HotJobs.com	Yes	Text Only (check Fixed Font)	Yes, but only HTML Plain-Text Style	No	Yes	Advice: ** (limited) Samples N/A	Choose Cut-and-Paste option instead of Build Your Own (latter is limited in layout). Line breaks are stripped in HotJobs version but hold in Web version. Web URL is cumbersome (http://www.hotjobs.com/cgi-bin/person-show?P_PINDEX=Q44238ZDF). Site only accepts postings from corporate recruiters, not third-party recruiters.

Site		Format			Rating	Notes
Jobs.com	No	Text only	No	Yes	Advice: ** Samples: N/A	Advice is limited. Samples are accessible only by hyperlinking and logging in to the resume-writing service Resume.com.
Monster.com	Yes (part of resume)	Text Only	No	Yes (5)	Advice: *** Samples: ***	Structured resume-builder layout prevents control over look of resume.
Yahoo! Careers	Yes	Text Only	Yes	Yes	Advice: ** Samples: N/A	Some designs are not practical for printing; no optional text download to counter this problem. Choose traditional layout options if you want employers to also be able to print. Resume advice is provided by anyone who wants to sign up as an expert. (See more info on Yahoo's Web resumes in Chapter 7.)
Brilliantpeople.com (MRI)	Yes	Text Only, RTF or HTML	No	No	Advice: ** Samples: **	Cut and paste resume or click Browse and attach a .doc or .rtf file. If you make your resume viewable to others, it is accessible only to MRI recruiters.
eKornFerry.com	Yes	Text Only	No	N/A	Advice: *** Samples: N/A	Automatically converts cut-and-pasted or typed information to XML. Produces very attractive, readable resume format. Accepts attachments in the form of .doc, .rtf, .txt, and .html. Sample resume is limited to a brief resume excerpt. Access to resume database is by Korn/Ferry consultants only.
RecruitersOnline.com (RON)	Yes	Text Only	No	Yes	Advice: N/A Samples: N/A	Doesn't allow job seeker to preview resume. Resume can be submitted to resume database or sent to specific recruiters. Resume database is accessible to RON members only.
TopEchelon.com	Yes	Text Only	No	Yes	N/A	Provides greater level of confidentiality and exclusivity because resume is posted to network database only after screening by a member recruiter. Job seeker must apply to a job posting at the site to submit resume.

Key: * = Average; ** = Good; *** = Outstanding; N/A = None Available

listed in Table 10-3). Hiring professionals use both fee-based and free sites to find candidates. In addition to America's Job Bank (ajb.dni.us), there are other smaller sites that are free to recruiters. Visit our Web site, eResumeIQ.com, for a list of more than 150 of these free sites. When posting your resume to free sites, recognize that any one who signs up to view resumes will have access to your information.

Figure 10-1 shows a resume created with Headhunter.net's resume builder; Figure 10-2 displays Monster.com's final format.

Niche/Specialty Career Sites

The second element of the three-tiered approach to posting involves posting your resume to niche career sites. Typically, these sites specialize in only three categories: position function or industry, college alumni or new graduates, and regional jobs. We'll review each category below and provide suggested sites. For a more extensive list of niche sites, visit *www.jumpstartyourjobsearch.com,* which is co-author Pat Kendall's companion site to her first book, *JumpStart Your Online Job Search in a Weekend.*

POSITION FUNCTION OR INDUSTRY SITES

Position function refers to the type of position (e.g., accountant, marketing manager, Perl programmer); *industry* refers to the type of business (e.g., investment banking, advertising, manufacturing). There are free resources that provide lists of position- and industry-specific and association sites, including these:

- *Advanced Internet Recruiting Seminar:* www.AirsDirectory.com

- *Internet Public Library's Associations on the Net:* www.ipl.org/ref/AON

- *Jump Start Your Online Job Search:* www.jumpstartyourjobsearch.com/job_search_links.html

- *Recruiter Resources:* www.RecruiterResources.com

- *Riley Guide:* www.dbm.com/jobguide

To conduct your own search for specialized sites, go to a search engine such as Google.com and type in keywords related to your industry. For instance, an HVAC engineer might use these terms: job site, HVAC industry, post resume. Once the search engine returns its results, find a site that's close to what you want, then click the link called "Similar pages" to narrow your target.

If you'd like a list of reviewed sites, invest in the latest edition of *CareerXRoads* (Jist Works, 2001), by e-recruiting experts Gerry

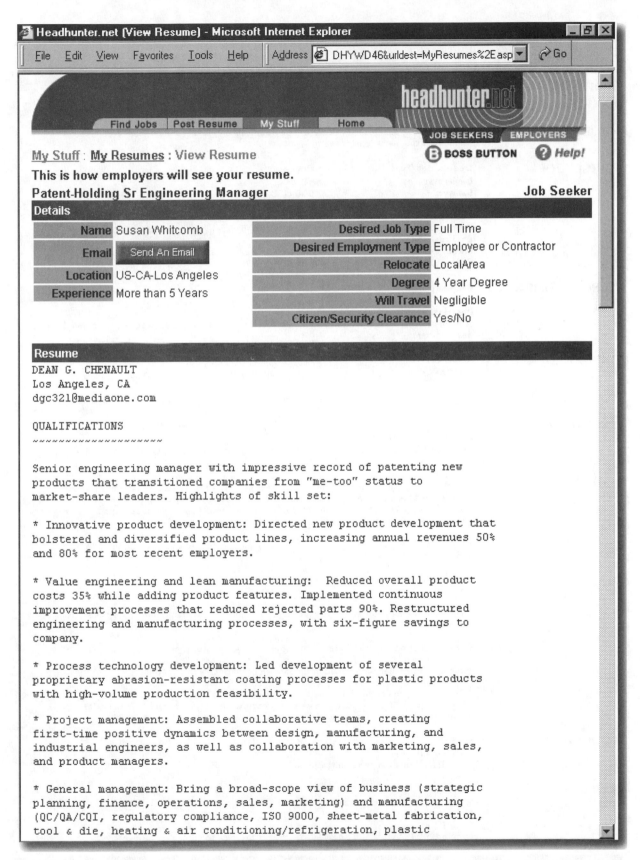

Figure 10-1   Posted resume as it appears at Headhunter.net. Appearance will vary, depending on job seeker's resume format.

Figure 10-2   Posted resume as it appears at Monster.com. Monster's resume builder generates resumes with a consistent design and layout.

Crispin and Mark Mehler. Unlike many "list" books that are massive but unwieldy—like searching for a needle in a haystack—this one narrows down its recommendations to a manageable number, giving you the crème de la crème of Web sites for specific industries. Online updates are available free at their Web site, www.careerXroads.com.

UNIVERSITY AND NEW GRADUATE SITES

Many university and college sites offer resume posting services for alumni. Your alma mater's Web site can be found by using Google.com's search engine—just type the university's name in quotes (e.g., "University of California, Los Angeles" or "UCLA").

If you're a new or soon-to-be graduate, consider posting your resume at *http://www.jobweb.com,* hosted by the National Association of Colleges and Employers (NACE). Also check out *http://www.JobDirect.com,* which was recently acquired by executive-recruiting leader Korn/Ferry International to serve its clients' needs for college graduates.

REGIONAL SITES

"I can't find a job in my home town!" This was once the cry of online job seekers in smaller cities. In the late 1990s, online opportunities for residents of New York City, Los Angeles, Chicago, and Houston were plentiful, while openings for inhabitants of the "fruited plains" were nonexistent. In the new millennium, that is no longer the case.

Some general career sites allow you to fine-tune your search to include rural areas, or alternatively, use geographic indicators as keywords. FlipDog.com excels in this; for example, it indexes job listings from the tiny mountain town of Angels Camp in California to West Boothbay Harbor in Maine. If you fail to see your town on FlipDog.com, try the regional link at MyJobSearch.com—hundreds of geographic job sites may lead you to a perfect opportunity in your neck of the woods: *http://www.myjobsearch.com/career/ regional.html*. Another nifty resource is *http://www.unicru.com,* which allows you to input your zip code and indicate how many miles you're willing to travel to work, then serves up a listing of job postings from its member companies in your travel radius.

For you urban dwellers, check into the regional sites listed in Table 10-4.

When searching job postings at any of the career sites—whether general or specialized—you can include your city (and towns in the immediate vicinity) as keywords. Doing so will return search results with job opportunities in the area of your choice.

Table 10-4   Representative Regional Career Sites

Region	Organization	Web Site URL
Midwest	Chicago Jobs	http://www.Chicagojobs.com
	Chicago Tribune Career Finder	http://www.ChicagoTribune.com/careers
	Michigan Works	http://www.Michworks.org
Northeast	Smartdog (Rochester, NY)	http://www.Smartdog.org
	Boston Works	http://www.Bostonworks.boston.com
	TriStateJobs.com	http://www.Tristatejobs.com
	WashingtonJobs.com	http://www.WashingtonPost.com/jobs
South	Carolinas CareerWeb	http://www.CarolinasCareerWeb.com
Southwest	Arizona Jobs	http://www.ArizonaJobs.com
	Houston Employment, LLC	http://www.HoustonEmployment.com
Northwest	Seattle-Jobs.com	http://www.Seattle-Jobs.com
Los Angeles	Los Angeles Times	http://www.latimes.com/class/employ
San Francisco	Craig's List	http://www.CraigsList.com

TIP

Choose from 8 million jobs!

Grassisgreener.com uses technology similar to FlipDog.com, sending out "spiders" to search employer job postings from all over the Web. Although postings are not as fresh as FlipDog.com's, they are more comprehensive. FlipDog.com claims 750,000+ listings; Grassisgreener.com shows more than 8 million, making it a great place to conduct a search for jobs specific to your locale.

Company Sites

The third element of the three-tiered approach to posting involves posting your resume on potential employers' corporate Web sites. With the profusion of general career sites on the Net, it seems that many people neglect posting to company sites. Just as you would do in a traditional job search, it's important to identify and research potential employers. Many of the general career sites listed earlier in this chapter have company research resources—Monster.com (*http://company.monster.com*) and Headhunter.net are among the best. Other helpful resources include Hoovers.com and CompaniesOnline.com.

To identify companies in your geographic area, turn to the online Yellow Pages. YellowPages.com and SuperPages.com are the equivalent of a national Yellow Pages directory, enabling you to browse by business category and city. Neither of these resources provides Web site or email addresses, but a call to the firms you identify through the site can usually yield this information.

If your target company has a job page at its Web site (most do), post your resume. If not, email it to the appropriate contact. Corporate recruiters love it when you add your resume to their proprietary databases—they save money finding you in their own backyard instead of shopping at high-priced career sites. On some corporate Web sites, you can sign up for a service that will inform you (via email) about new job openings that meet your keyword criteria.

FINDING EMAIL ADDRESSES

Finding email addresses can be one of the trickiest parts of online job searching. There are a number of email sleuth services on the Net. The Ultimates (*http://www.theultimates.com*) is a handy tool because it searches six major email-finder sites in succession (Yahoo.com, WhoWhere.com, IAF.net, Infospace.com, BigFoot.com, and Switchboard.com). The catch is that you must first know the name of the person you want to contact.

To start a name search, scour each target company's Web site—press releases, investor relations, about us, management team—for names and titles of individuals in charge of your functional area. (You can, of course, apply to the Human Resources Department, but that's not always the most effective route. You'll increase your chances of success by contacting a manager who—bowled over by your fabulous resume—will create a new job just to bring you on board!) Once you know the full name of the individual, tracking down his or her email address is a matter of determining the company's email format, which is discernable by reviewing how other company email addresses are listed on the site (e.g., *george.jones@abc.com, gjones@abc.com, george_jones@abc.com, jonesg@abc.com*, etc.).

To develop a networking contact in your target company, visit a site like Deja.com. Deja hosts a number of forums that share information. By reading the forum posts, you can identify a potential contact in your target company. All you need is the domain name of the company to get started. Let's say the company you're interested in is Sun Microsystems. Using the Power Search function at Deja.com, go to the "author" field and type *@sun.com, then click on Search to get a list of recent forum postings made by Sun employees.

Insider News!

TIP

For $29.95, you can get a monthly subscription to Hoovers.com's basic service, which provides the full name of executive-level individuals at publicly traded companies—the people with the authority to hire.

If all else fails, call the company, pray for a live voice on the other end of the phone, and ask for the email address of the appropriate hiring manager.

Resume Distribution Services

In pre-Internet days, not every job seeker could afford a direct-mail campaign. The mailing lists were expensive, production costs could run upwards of $5 per letter, and postage added up. Now, direct campaigns are affordable and commonplace, thanks to email. In fact, it's hard to find a career Web site that doesn't have resume distribution advertisements, which typically read like this: "Blast your resume!," or "Zap your resume!," or "Is your resume lost in a sea of data?" These services are very valuable to job seekers, as they cut down on hours of research time, automate the physical "mailing" process, and provide the service at a fraction of the cost of a traditional mail campaign. In most cases, distribution data is limited to executive recruiters (as opposed to employers); we found only one service that also listed high-growth companies and venture capital firms.

The major players in resume distribution are outlined in Table 10-5. When choosing a service, focus on the level of targeting available, not the total number of database contacts. You don't want to send your resume to every recruiter—just to those who specialize in your profession, industry, salary range, and geographic area. Also, be circumspect when it comes to cost—most have add-ons that can add up.

If you have a Web resume, the process of marketing requires a completely different approach.

Actively Marketing Your Web Resume

According to online recruiting gurus, the World Wide Web houses somewhere between 2 million and 15 million Web resumes—in addition to the resumes posted on job boards and career sites. Because these resumes typically belong to passive job seekers (and passive job seekers are touted as a rich untapped talent resource), the practice of using search engines to source Web resumes is becoming widespread.

To understand how the process works, let's look at it from the recruiters' perspective.

In short, the process of finding Web resumes works something like this: The recruiter goes to a favorite search engine (one that supports advanced searches) and specifies the keyword criteria by submitting a Boolean search string. For example:

Table 10-5 Review of Resume Distribution Services

Service	Level of geographic targeting available	# of contacts in database	Cost	Provides copy of data for job seeker followup	Resume bank option	Comments
ExecutiveAgent.com	State	11,000	$99 flat fee	Firm name and state only are shown prior to distributing resume (page can be printed)	Yes	Allows you to block certain firms. Accepts resumes in Word, text, or RTF. Brought to you by Kennedy Information, publishers of *The Directory of Executive Recruiters.*
ResumeBlaster.com	State	5,200+	Starts at $49	$10 extra; name and location only (address, telephone, and email omitted)	Yes	$49 for general blast to 597 recruiters; choose 3 recruiter categories for $69; 6 for $89. Gathers profile of candidate, which is then included in email to recruiters. Gives jobseeker some control over subj line. A "preview" email of resume is sent to job seeker prior to blasting. Format: recommends text only with line breaks (60-70) characters per line.
ResumEXPRESS.com	State	8,400+	Starts at $39.95	Yes, company names available on request	Yes	Founded in 1994, one of the first on the resume distribution scene. Unique targeting technology—recruiters specify resumes they'll accept by listing keywords. Offers repeat distribution at no cost. Will bring resume into formatting standards if problematic. Format: recommends text only with line breaks (60-65 characters per line).
ResumeZapper.com	State	9,100+	Starts at $49.99	$15 extra; name and location only (address, telephone, and email omitted)	No	Provides a choice of 3 recruiter categories with basic service (there are 450+ categories available); 3 add'l categories cost $19.95. No opportunity to preview resume for formatting glitches before sending. Add-ons can easily take price to $100.
YourMissingLink.com	Telephone Area Code	17,000+ *	Starts at $60	Yes; provides complete recruiter data (contact name, company, address, phone, email, Web site)	No	Clearly identifies how many recruiters will actually receive your resume. Can block any company you specify. Database is updated daily. Offers full-service or self-managed campaign. * includes recruiters, high-growth, and venture capital firms

Domain: com AND resume AND (primary keywords)

title: resume OR title: CV AND NOT "resume writers"

Boolean searches can be distinguished from "simple" searches by their use of Boolean terms such as AND, OR, AND NOT, NEAR— and a host of others such as quotes, plus signs, asterisks, and parentheses. Boolean logic incorporates various "terms" to aid in the search process and can dramatically narrow search results and eliminate nonrelevant data. Boolean searches can also be refined to source candidates with specific area codes and other geographic criteria.

Keywording Your Web Resume for Search Engines

To ensure that your Web resume can be found on the Net, you will need to pay special attention to your meta tags. Meta tags are part of your Web resume's HTML infrastructure. The proper combination of meta tags, page title, and keywords (see Table 10-6) will dictate how "findable" your resume is on the Net.

In addition, new genres of recruiting software are readily available to aid recruiters in finding both Web and ASCII resumes. These programs conduct searches on the Web, in newsgroups, and in online resume databases. The software developed by AIRS (Advanced Internet Recruiting Strategies) allows recruiters to ". . . go beyond the traditional hunting grounds of career sites and commercial resume banks and access the vast, but little known resume repositories in virtual communities and ISPs." In addition, there are full-scale search engines dedicated solely to the pursuit of Web resumes.

Search Engine Submission Tips

To register your resume with search engines, go to the search engine of your choice and follow the submission instructions (typically listed at the bottom of the page). Table 10-7 provides a list of major search engines and multiple-submission services. In some cases, search engine submission is a matter of typing in your URL and your email address; in other cases, you'll be asked to provide keywords and other information. When you have an opportunity to include keywords, give careful thought to the keywords you include and the order in which you list them.

Boolean Trivia

It's rather ironic, but "Boolean logic" was developed by nineteenth-century mathematician George Boole. Little did George know that his ideas would be widely embraced—in the twentieth century—and would play a major role in how twenty-first-century citizens research, gather, and sort information.

Table 10-6   A Closer Look at Keyword Optimization

Meta Tags: If you want your Web resume to be found on the Net (and not everyone does), optimize your meta tags. Meta tags are not visible to the human eye, but are built into your Web page's HTML infrastructure. Your objective is to include your most critical keywords—skills, industry knowledge, products, geographic criteria, certifications, and so on. When you insert keywords or keyword phrases into your meta tags, they should be separated with commas—and they should be listed and prioritized just as you do in your resume, with the most relevant information first. See Chapter 2 for more information on keywords.

Page Title: The HTML page title should include the word *resume*. This is not for employers' benefit (they know they're looking at a resume!), but is included to aid recruiters and search engines in finding your resume online. The page title also identifies the document when it's brought up as a search match (i.e., resume of Jan Johnson). You can also optimize page titles by expanding them to include keywords and skill indicators. Here are some examples:

*   Darla Henson's Resume: Marketing, B2B, Information Technology
*   Web Resume of John Granger, Technical Writer / Marcom Specialist
*   Resume of Janet Drake | Visual C++ | Active Server Pages | ASP

Avoid page titles like these:

*   Bob's resume (a bit too informal)
*   My resume
*   Rusume (a misspelled word here is extremely counterproductive)
*   Home page of Jane Doe
*   (No name)

Note: The page title is named during the creation of your Web resume. In HTML editing programs like Netscape Composer, you can add (or change) a page title by accessing the Page Properties box.

Filename: The filename (the name you give your resume when you first create it) can also function as a keyword. The best filenames are those that reflect your name (i.e., johndoe.html) or job-critical keywords (marketingmanager.html, MSCE.html, executive.html).

Content: The content or actual text of your Web resume is also searchable, of course, so be sure to incorporate keywords as described in Chapter 2.

Other Ways to Promote Your Web Resume

If confidentiality is not an issue for you, capitalize on the prestige of having a Web resume by listing your URL whenever you can—in your traditional resume, ASCII resume, job search correspondence, email signature line, personal business cards, and so on.

When confidentiality is an issue, one of the best ways to conduct a "quiet" job search is to sign up for a job agent (also known as a job notification service or personal search agent). Job agents use "push" technology to find job opportunities based on specific keyword criteria—and then send jobs directly to you via email. To use this approach, sign up for a free account at sites like Monster.com or

Table 10-7 Search Engines, Web Directories, and Submission Sites

- AltaVista.com
- Yahoo.com/Google.com
- Alltheweb.com
- HotBot.com
- InfoSeek.com
- NorthernLight.com
- Lycos.com
- Excite.com
- mmgo.com/top100.html
  (links to 100 sites that will list your site at no charge)

FlipDog.com, designate your keywords, and then sit back and wait for the results. You can respond to jobs that interest you by submitting your ASCII resume (which includes a hot link to your Web resume URL), or by sending a brief cover letter that points to your Web resume.

Online and On Top

We realize that many of you started this book feeling a little overwhelmed by the subject of online resumes. By now, we hope you're feeling on top of the technology and new rules of eResumes, confidently endowed with the knowledge to compete in the electronic job market. Whatever your situation—whether a confidential candidate equipped with an easy-to-read emailable resume or an active job seeker decked out with pasteable, postable, and Web-based resumes—we wish you much success.

Be sure to review the gallery of Web resumes that follows for more ideas on keyword content and eResume design. And, remember that some of these designs are available free at our Web site— www.eResumeIQ.com. We'll see you online!

Gallery of Web Resumes

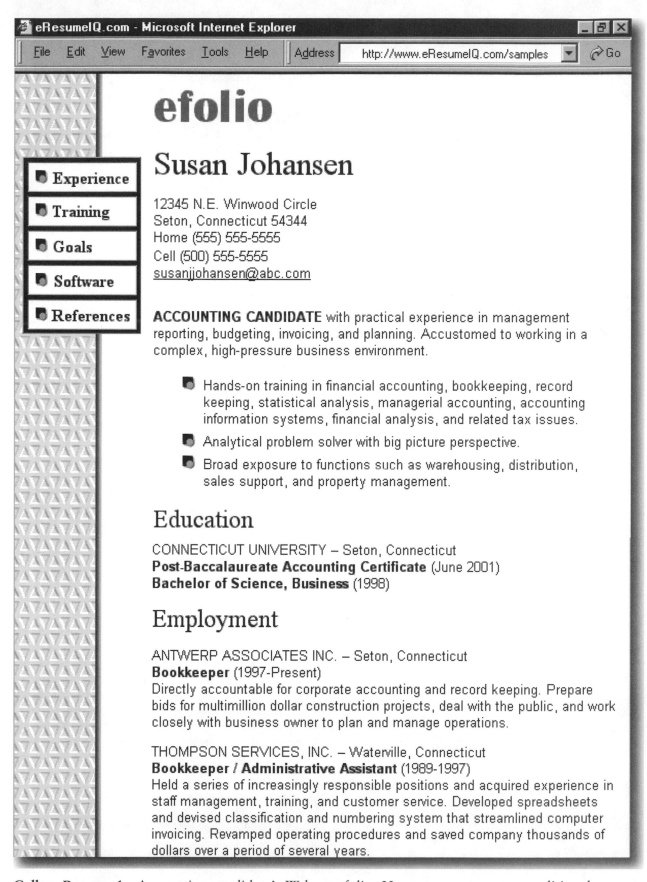

efolio

Susan Johansen

12345 N.E. Winwood Circle
Seton, Connecticut 54344
Home (555) 555-5555
Cell (500) 555-5555
susanjjohansen@abc.com

Experience

Training

Goals

Software

References

ACCOUNTING CANDIDATE with practical experience in management reporting, budgeting, invoicing, and planning. Accustomed to working in a complex, high-pressure business environment.

- Hands-on training in financial accounting, bookkeeping, record keeping, statistical analysis, managerial accounting, accounting information systems, financial analysis, and related tax issues.
- Analytical problem solver with big picture perspective.
- Broad exposure to functions such as warehousing, distribution, sales support, and property management.

Education

CONNECTICUT UNIVERSITY – Seton, Connecticut
Post-Baccalaureate Accounting Certificate (June 2001)
Bachelor of Science, Business (1998)

Employment

ANTWERP ASSOCIATES INC. – Seton, Connecticut
Bookkeeper (1997-Present)
Directly accountable for corporate accounting and record keeping. Prepare bids for multimillion dollar construction projects, deal with the public, and work closely with business owner to plan and manage operations.

THOMPSON SERVICES, INC. – Waterville, Connecticut
Bookkeeper / Administrative Assistant (1989-1997)
Held a series of increasingly responsible positions and acquired experience in staff management, training, and customer service. Developed spreadsheets and devised classification and numbering system that streamlined computer invoicing. Revamped operating procedures and saved company thousands of dollars over a period of several years.

Gallery Resume 1   Accounting candidate's Web portfolio. Home page presents a traditional resume, with navigational system providing links to details of training, goals, software experiences, and letters of reference.

File   Edit   View   Favorites   Tools   Help   Address   http://www.eResumeIQ.com/samples   Go

Marie Lefkowitz

14567 SW Oak Avenue
Portland, Oregon 97007
(555) 555-5555
mlefko@abc.com

Click here for:
ASCII Download | PDF Download

Administrative Support Expert with ten years' combined experience in office management, accounting, and executive support. Proven ability to manage multiple projects simultaneously. Certified Notary Public.

- Exceptionally organized with well-developed verbal and written communication skills.
- Experienced in using PC and Macintosh systems with Microsoft Word, Excel, PowerPoint, Access, Quicken, WordPerfect, and Lotus 1-2-3.
- Bilingual (English and Spanish).

Education

PORTLAND STATE UNIVERSITY – Portland, Oregon
Accounting Certificate (December 2000)

Course Work: Accounting Information Systems, Intermediate and Advanced Financial Accounting, Introductory and Advanced Taxation, Auditing Concepts and Practices, Management Accounting, Business Law

Experience

SUPRA MANUFACTURING – Portland, Oregon
Executive Assistant (12/97–Present)
Provide administrative support to owners and handle accounts payable for a total of 15 affiliated companies. Prepare business correspondence and reports. Reconcile checking and money market accounts and record all stock transactions for owners' trust accounts.

- Collaborated with in-house CPA to expedite financial statement output – reducing production time from five days to one day.

Gallery Resume 2   Administrative professional's Web resume. Resume features a simple sidebar, industry-specific graphic, and two download options (ASCII and PDF). Job seeker's name and category headings were created as text, with color enhancement matching the sidebar. See this resume in color at www.eResumeIQ.com.

File   Edit   View   Favorites   Tools   Help   Address   http://www.eResumeIQ.com/samples   Go

joni winston, mcse

jwinston@abc.com

ASCII Resume

Microsoft Certified Systems Engineer with broad knowledge of information systems and solid qualifications in programming, maintenance, systems analysis, and troubleshooting.

- Five years' experience in providing user support and training. Able to explain technical concepts and communicate with users and system administrators at all levels—from novices to MIS managers.
- Database specialist with three years' experience in applications development and support.
- Effective teamworker with ability to lead technical teams, manage changing priorities, and resolve problems in complex, multi-platform environments.

Technical Skills

- **Operating Systems:** DOS, Windows 95 / Windows 98 / Windows NT / Windows 2000, Novell Netware 5.0
- **Internet Protocols / Networking:** TCP / IP, Windows NT / Window 2000, Novell 5.0, Proxy Server
- **Programming Languages:** C++, Fortran, HTML
- **Applications:** Microsoft Office 2000 (Word, Excel, Access, PowerPoint) Outlook, Corel WordPerfect 7.0 Suite, Netscape Navigator, Microsoft FrontPage

Experience

BETTER HALF INTERNATIONAL, INC. – St. Louis, Missouri
Contract Computer Technician (2000-2001)

- Design and set up Microsoft Access databases at various job sites.
- Track provider information, copyright applications, and fixed asset depreciation schedules for 3,000 health care providers.
- Develop barcode generation/printing, inventory tracking, quality control, and automated counting applications.

Gallery Resume 3   ASCII download within Web resume. Reverse text is used to create name in white against a teal green background. Resume text is presented in a straightforward, no-frills manner for this technical candidate.

File   Edit   View   Favorites   Tools   Help   Address   http://www.eResumeIQ.com/samples   Go

Word ASCII

Leasing Services Executive

NATHAN NEWMAN

12345 N.W. Taylor • Tuttle River, Ohio 87654 • (555) 555-5555
nathannewman@abc.com

Dynamic, mission-oriented executive with broad background in commercial equipment financing, in-depth knowledge of the banking and credit industries, and a record of success in:

- Marketing
- Product Innovation
- Relationship Building
- Startup Management
- Business Planning
- Channel Marketing

Savvy businessperson with the vision and drive to overcome obstacles and excel in a competitive marketplace. Proven ability to lead by example, inspire loyalty, and motivate staff to exceed sales and revenue objectives. Skilled in using technology to improve efficiency and facilitate growth.

EDUCATION

MBA – University of Ohio (1996)
BS – University of Ohio (1988)

EXPERIENCE

GTO CREDIT CORP., INC. – Hermiston, Ohio
Vice President, Corporate Development (1996–2001)
Recruited to expand company presence, open new markets, and identify / develop strategic vendor alliances. Oversaw the delivery of financing and leasing products through central facility with 16-branch network and a field staff of 24.

- Negotiated exclusive multimillion sale with the Glass Products Manufacturers' Association.
- Cultivated key relationships that positioned company as

Gallery Resume 4   Corporate development executive's Web resume. Job target is listed in reverse type at top. Sidebar provides employers with choice of downloadable resume in MS Word or ASCII format. Granite sidebar gives resume a distinctive, elegant look appropriate for an executive. See this resume in color at www.eResumeIQ.com.

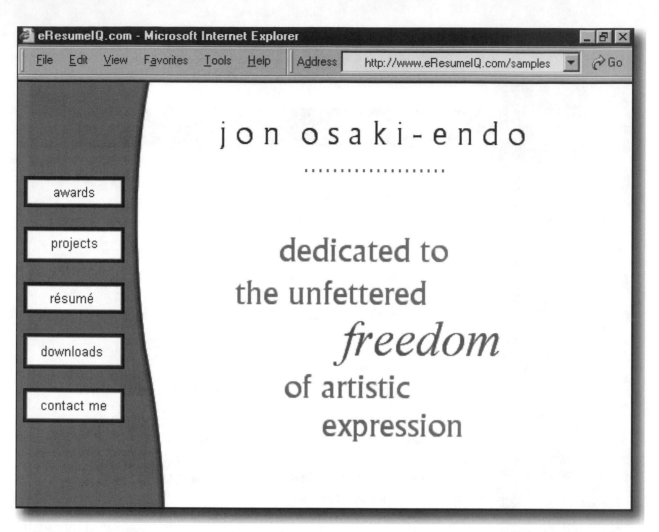

Gallery Resume 5 Creative director's home page of Web portfolio. Pages within the site include awards, projects, a chronological resume, downloads, and an email link. Graphics were created using a graphics program (Photoshop).

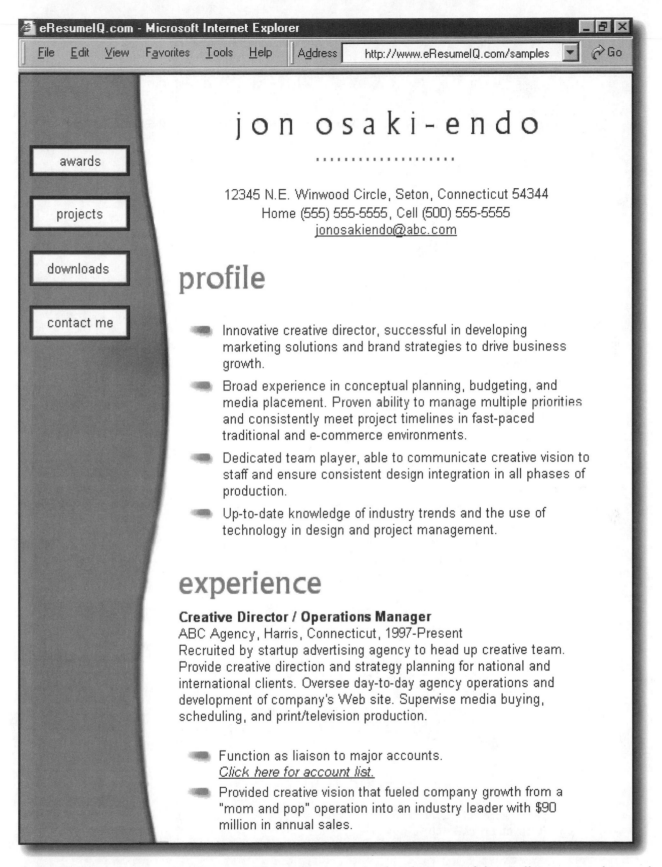

Gallery Resume 6 Creative director's Web resume contained within e-portfolio. Bullets are graphics and match the color of the curved sidebar. Text link under Experience category provides access to account list.

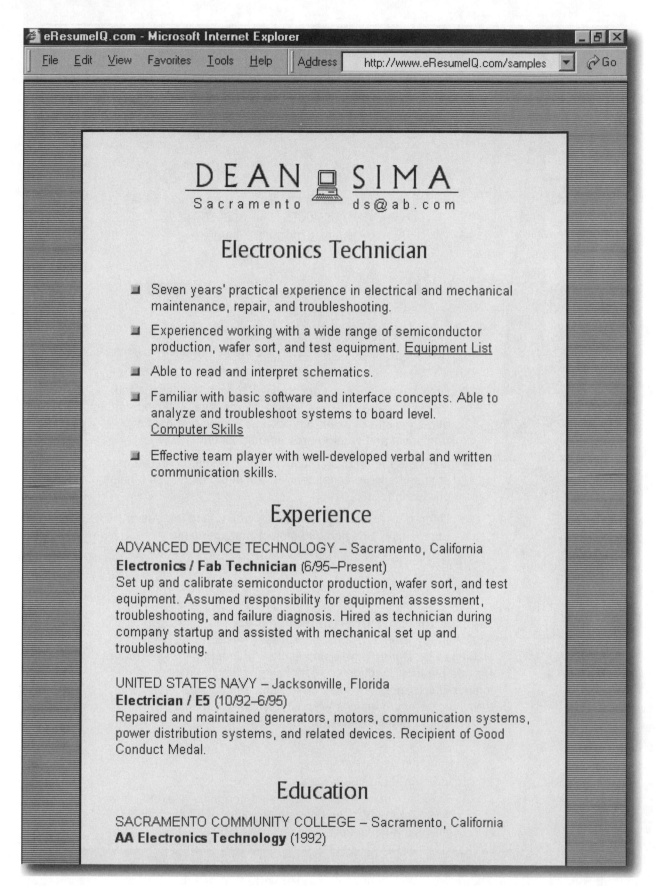

DEAN ▣ SIMA
Sacramento   ds@ab.com

Electronics Technician

- Seven years' practical experience in electrical and mechanical maintenance, repair, and troubleshooting.

- Experienced working with a wide range of semiconductor production, wafer sort, and test equipment. Equipment List

- Able to read and interpret schematics.

- Familiar with basic software and interface concepts. Able to analyze and troubleshoot systems to board level. Computer Skills

- Effective team player with well-developed verbal and written communication skills.

Experience

ADVANCED DEVICE TECHNOLOGY – Sacramento, California
Electronics / Fab Technician (6/95–Present)
Set up and calibrate semiconductor production, wafer sort, and test equipment. Assumed responsibility for equipment assessment, troubleshooting, and failure diagnosis. Hired as technician during company startup and assisted with mechanical set up and troubleshooting.

UNITED STATES NAVY – Jacksonville, Florida
Electrician / E5 (10/92–6/95)
Repaired and maintained generators, motors, communication systems, power distribution systems, and related devices. Recipient of Good Conduct Medal.

Education

SACRAMENTO COMMUNITY COLLEGE – Sacramento, California
AA Electronics Technology (1992)

Gallery Resume 7   Electronics technician's Web resume. Graphic image in heading is small (less than 1 KB) and will load quickly. In-text hyperlinks provide more detailed information on equipment experience and computer skills. A traditional border frames the resume. See this resume in color at www.eResumeIQ.com.

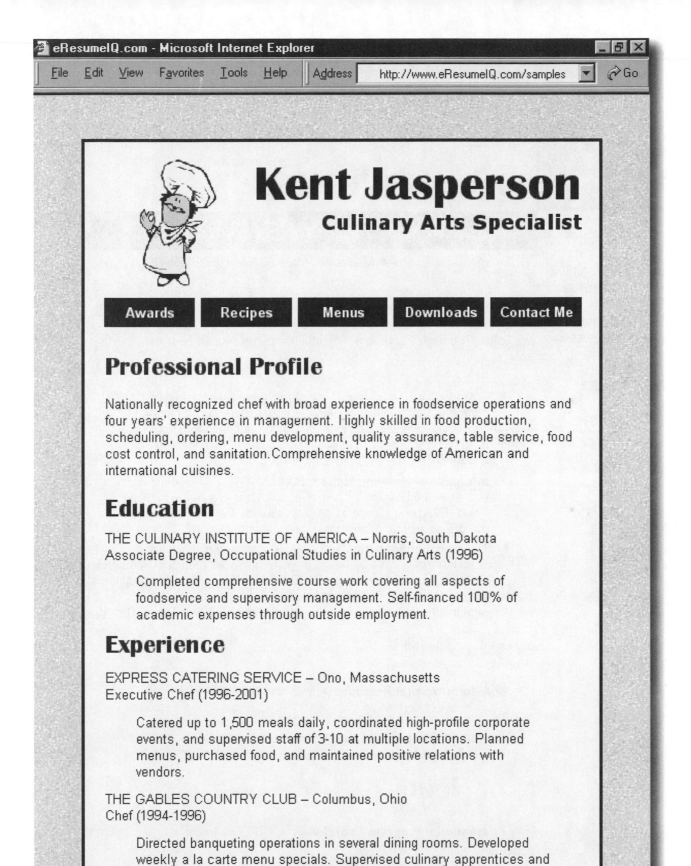

Kent Jasperson
Culinary Arts Specialist

Awards   Recipes   Menus   Downloads   Contact Me

Professional Profile

Nationally recognized chef with broad experience in foodservice operations and four years' experience in management. Highly skilled in food production, scheduling, ordering, menu development, quality assurance, table service, food cost control, and sanitation. Comprehensive knowledge of American and international cuisines.

Education

THE CULINARY INSTITUTE OF AMERICA – Norris, South Dakota
Associate Degree, Occupational Studies in Culinary Arts (1996)

> Completed comprehensive course work covering all aspects of foodservice and supervisory management. Self-financed 100% of academic expenses through outside employment.

Experience

EXPRESS CATERING SERVICE – Ono, Massachusetts
Executive Chef (1996-2001)

> Catered up to 1,500 meals daily, coordinated high-profile corporate events, and supervised staff of 3-10 at multiple locations. Planned menus, purchased food, and maintained positive relations with vendors.

THE GABLES COUNTRY CLUB – Columbus, Ohio
Chef (1994-1996)

> Directed banqueting operations in several dining rooms. Developed weekly a la carte menu specials. Supervised culinary apprentices and provided ongoing training. Hired, trained, and scheduled kitchen crew.

Gallery Resume 8 Executive chef's Web resume. Layout features an industry-specific graphic, framed border, and horizontal navigation system. Hyperlinks were created using reverse text. Links take viewers to awards, recipes with photos of food artistry, and sample menus. See this resume in color at www.eResumeIQ.com.

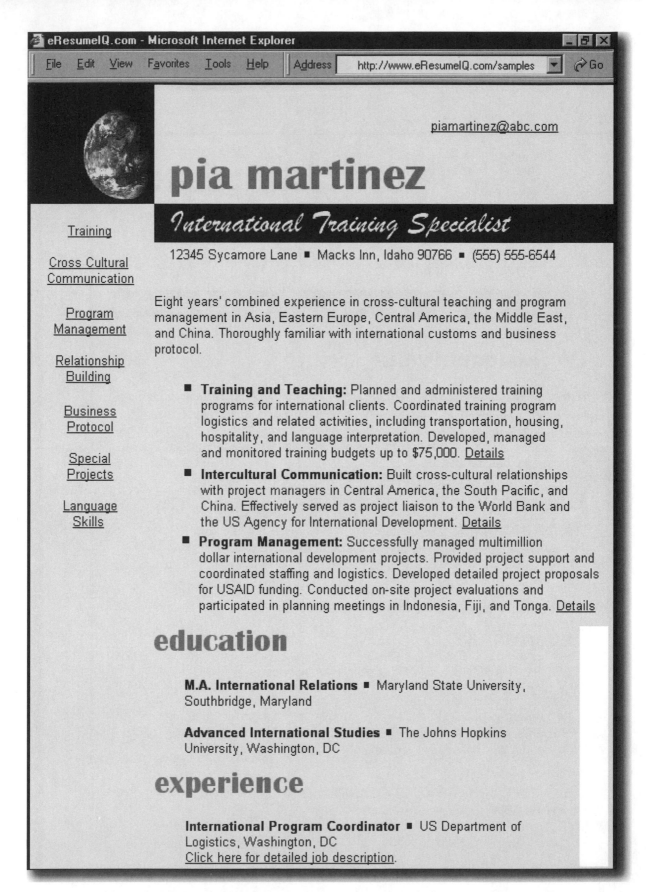

File Edit View Favorites Tools Help   Address   http://www.eResumeIQ.com/samples   Go

piamartinez@abc.com

pia martinez

International Training Specialist

12345 Sycamore Lane ▪ Macks Inn, Idaho 90766 ▪ (555) 555-6544

Training

Cross Cultural
Communication

Program
Management

Relationship
Building

Business
Protocol

Special
Projects

Language
Skills

Eight years' combined experience in cross-cultural teaching and program management in Asia, Eastern Europe, Central America, the Middle East, and China. Thoroughly familiar with international customs and business protocol.

- **Training and Teaching:** Planned and administered training programs for international clients. Coordinated training program logistics and related activities, including transportation, housing, hospitality, and language interpretation. Developed, managed and monitored training budgets up to $75,000. Details

- **Intercultural Communication:** Built cross-cultural relationships with project managers in Central America, the South Pacific, and China. Effectively served as project liaison to the World Bank and the US Agency for International Development. Details

- **Program Management:** Successfully managed multimillion dollar international development projects. Provided project support and coordinated staffing and logistics. Developed detailed project proposals for USAID funding. Conducted on-site project evaluations and participated in planning meetings in Indonesia, Fiji, and Tonga. Details

education

M.A. International Relations ▪ Maryland State University, Southbridge, Maryland

Advanced International Studies ▪ The Johns Hopkins University, Washington, DC

experience

International Program Coordinator ▪ US Department of Logistics, Washington, DC
Click here for detailed job description.

Gallery Resume 9 International training specialist's Web resume. Earth graphic emphasizes the candidate's international experiences. Use of lowercase letters in a large font give the name and category headings a unique look. In-context links provide greater detail of candidate's core skill set and job descriptions. See this resume in color at www.eResumeIQ.com.

Nancy Francisco

Sedgewick, Ohio • nanfran@abcmail.com

Career Profile

Fifteen years' experience conducting market research and translating results into effective marketing strategies, public relations messages, and advertising campaigns.

Core Competencies:

Public Opinion Research	Relationship Management
Strategic Planning	Consensus Building
Project Management	Computer Proficiency
Vendor Relations	Team Building

Click on skills above for detailed examples of representative projects.

Experience

FANSER TRANSPORTATION – Turner, Oregon
Senior Research Analyst (1998-Present)
Developed and administered public opinion research studies to identify target market segments. Managed vendor contracts, evaluated marketing and communications programs, and tracked changes in consumer behavior.

- Designed 1998 Market Segmentation study profiling customers based on attitudes, product use, geographic location, and homeowner / employment status.
- Developed a profile of Fanser's brand equity position, including market share, customer satisfaction, and brand loyalty.
- Results: Sales of Fanser products has increased steadily for more than 50 consecutive months and the new ad campaign has won several local and national awards.

Gallery Resume 10   Market research specialist's Web resume. Core competency links give viewer a strong overview of key skills, while a click-through provides in-depth supporting information in a layered format.

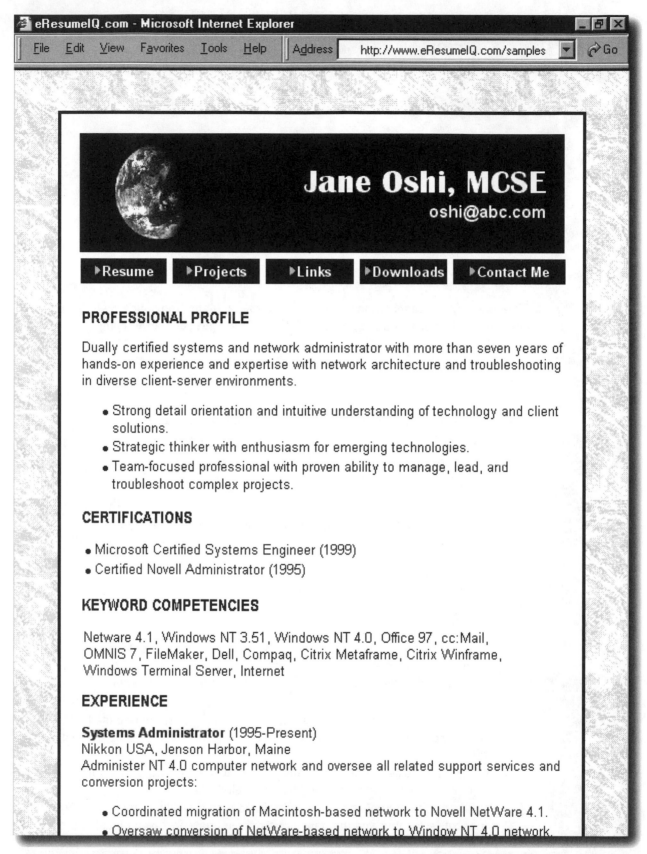

Gallery Resume 11 Microsoft Certified Systems Engineer (MCSE)'s Web resume. Heading with earth graphic and name is created using a two-column table. Resume features a horizontal navigation bar with rollover links.

ERICA JENSON

14324 SW Main
Benton, NJ 98970
555-555-5555
jenson@abc.com

Listen to
my compositions

- Music
- Awards
- Publicity
- Projects
- References

AWARD-WINNING COMPOSER

- Wrote music for the acclaimed play by Tana Alve performed at the American Theatre of Actors in Manhattan, Summer 2000
- Composed and produced experimental musical-theatre piece involving seven musicians and 13 actors at Stony Brook University, Spring 1999
- Solo for Violin selected and performed at the Oregon Bach Festival, July 1998
- Selected to participate in the SCI National Conference for students at the University of Michigan in Ann Harbor, May 1998
- Compositions performed by various instrumental and vocal ensembles (i.e., SUNY – Stony Brook, Marylhurst College, Lewis & Clark College, Warner Pacific College, Central Washington University)
- Auditor, Ernest Bloch Music Festival, Newport, Oregon, 1997

EDUCATION

Master of Arts, Music Composition (1999)
Stony Brook University, New York

Bachelor of Arts, Music Composition (1997)
Lewis & Clark College, Portland, Oregon

ACADEMIC AWARDS

Community Development Grant
Stony Brook University, New York, New York, 1999

Gallery Resume 12   Musical composer's Web resume. Lighthearted graphic is balanced by navigational system, which features a rollover menu bar. "Listen to my compositions" links viewer to MIDI files and provides audio excerpts of music compositions. A border frames the page.

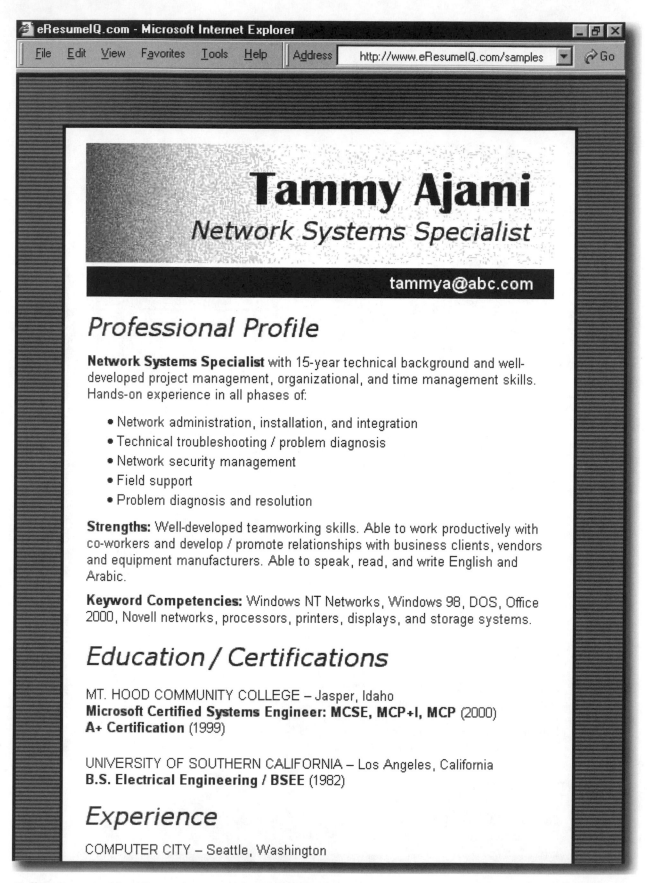

File   Edit   View   Favorites   Tools   Help   Address   http://www.eResumeIQ.com/samples   Go

Tammy Ajami
Network Systems Specialist

tammya@abc.com

Professional Profile

Network Systems Specialist with 15-year technical background and well-developed project management, organizational, and time management skills. Hands-on experience in all phases of:

- Network administration, installation, and integration
- Technical troubleshooting / problem diagnosis
- Network security management
- Field support
- Problem diagnosis and resolution

Strengths: Well-developed teamworking skills. Able to work productively with co-workers and develop / promote relationships with business clients, vendors and equipment manufacturers. Able to speak, read, and write English and Arabic.

Keyword Competencies: Windows NT Networks, Windows 98, DOS, Office 2000, Novell networks, processors, printers, displays, and storage systems.

Education / Certifications

MT. HOOD COMMUNITY COLLEGE – Jasper, Idaho
Microsoft Certified Systems Engineer: MCSE, MCP+I, MCP (2000)
A+ Certification (1999)

UNIVERSITY OF SOUTHERN CALIFORNIA – Los Angeles, California
B.S. Electrical Engineering / BSEE (1982)

Experience

COMPUTER CITY – Seattle, Washington

Gallery Resume 13   Network systems specialist's Web resume. Nested tables create the layered effect in the heading. Contact information includes email only, providing candidate with a measure of confidentiality.

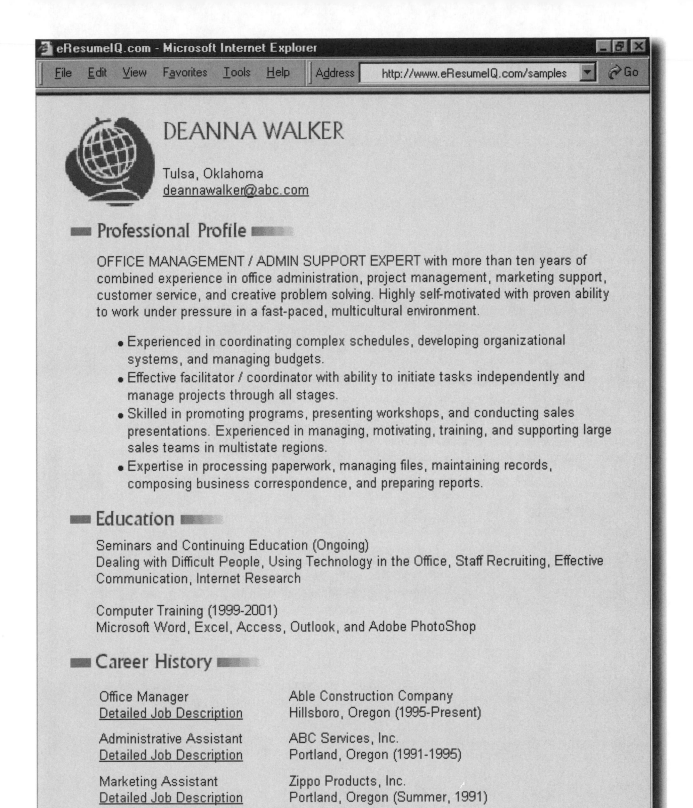

DEANNA WALKER

Tulsa, Oklahoma
deannawalker@abc.com

■ Professional Profile ■

OFFICE MANAGEMENT / ADMIN SUPPORT EXPERT with more than ten years of combined experience in office administration, project management, marketing support, customer service, and creative problem solving. Highly self-motivated with proven ability to work under pressure in a fast-paced, multicultural environment.

- Experienced in coordinating complex schedules, developing organizational systems, and managing budgets.
- Effective facilitator / coordinator with ability to initiate tasks independently and manage projects through all stages.
- Skilled in promoting programs, presenting workshops, and conducting sales presentations. Experienced in managing, motivating, training, and supporting large sales teams in multistate regions.
- Expertise in processing paperwork, managing files, maintaining records, composing business correspondence, and preparing reports.

■ Education ■

Seminars and Continuing Education (Ongoing)
Dealing with Difficult People, Using Technology in the Office, Staff Recruiting, Effective Communication, Internet Research

Computer Training (1999-2001)
Microsoft Word, Excel, Access, Outlook, and Adobe PhotoShop

■ Career History ■

Office Manager
Detailed Job Description

Able Construction Company
Hillsboro, Oregon (1995-Present)

Administrative Assistant
Detailed Job Description

ABC Services, Inc.
Portland, Oregon (1991-1995)

Marketing Assistant
Detailed Job Description

Zippo Products, Inc.
Portland, Oregon (Summer, 1991)

Leasing Consultant
Detailed Job Description

Pacific Realty
Colorado Springs, Colorado (1988-1990)

Gallery Resume 14   Office management professional's Web resume. Graphic at top left adds visual interest. Category headings were created with a three-column table. Links in Career History provide detailed job descriptions.

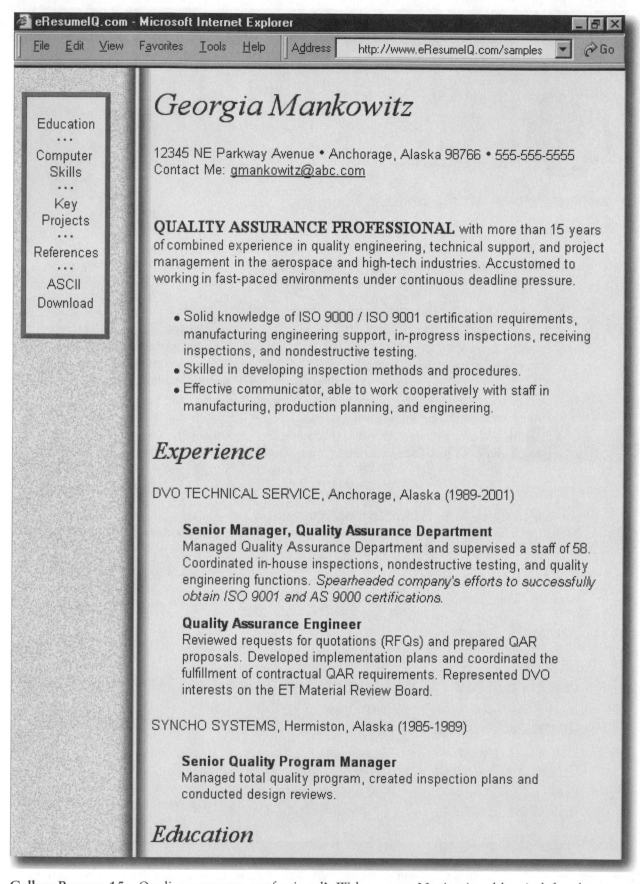

Gallery Resume 15 Quality assurance professional's Web resume. Navigational bar in left column contains rollover hyperlinks that become active with mouse-over action. An ASCII plaintext resume is provided for employer database requirements.

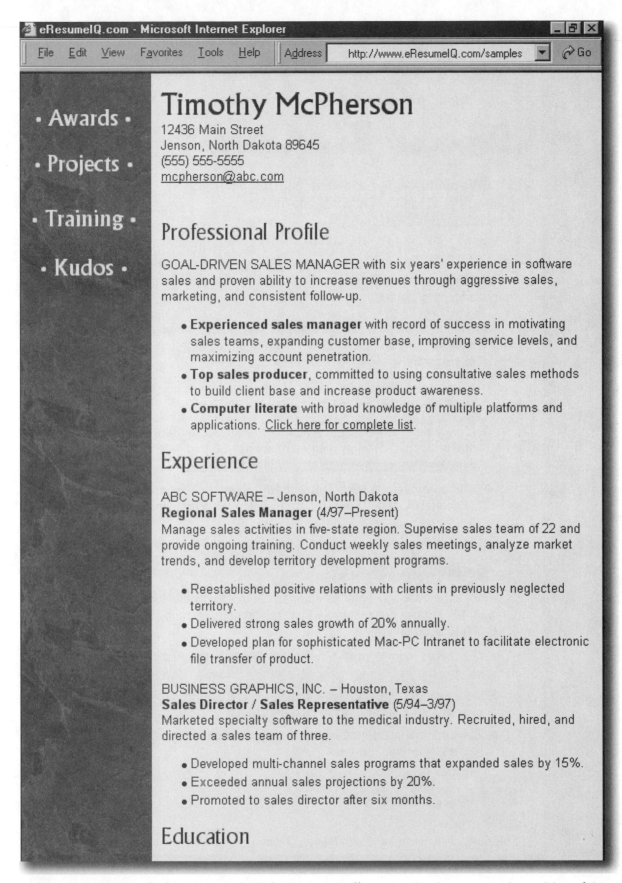

eResumeIQ.com - Microsoft Internet Explorer

File Edit View Favorites Tools Help | Address http://www.eResumeIQ.com/samples Go

- Awards -
- Projects -
- Training -
- Kudos -

Timothy McPherson

12436 Main Street
Jenson, North Dakota 89645
(555) 555-5555
mcpherson@abc.com

Professional Profile

GOAL-DRIVEN SALES MANAGER with six years' experience in software sales and proven ability to increase revenues through aggressive sales, marketing, and consistent follow-up.

- **Experienced sales manager** with record of success in motivating sales teams, expanding customer base, improving service levels, and maximizing account penetration.
- **Top sales producer**, committed to using consultative sales methods to build client base and increase product awareness.
- **Computer literate** with broad knowledge of multiple platforms and applications. Click here for complete list.

Experience

ABC SOFTWARE – Jenson, North Dakota
Regional Sales Manager (4/97–Present)
Manage sales activities in five-state region. Supervise sales team of 22 and provide ongoing training. Conduct weekly sales meetings, analyze market trends, and develop territory development programs.

- Reestablished positive relations with clients in previously neglected territory.
- Delivered strong sales growth of 20% annually.
- Developed plan for sophisticated Mac-PC Intranet to facilitate electronic file transfer of product.

BUSINESS GRAPHICS, INC. – Houston, Texas
Sales Director / Sales Representative (5/94–3/97)
Marketed specialty software to the medical industry. Recruited, hired, and directed a sales team of three.

- Developed multi-channel sales programs that expanded sales by 15%.
- Exceeded annual sales projections by 20%.
- Promoted to sales director after six months.

Education

Gallery Resume 16 Sales manager's Web resume. Rollover navigation system is positioned in a blue marble sidebar, linking to awards, projects, training, and references. In-context links provide bite-size information on computer literacy and continuing education. See this resume in color at www.eResumeIQ.com

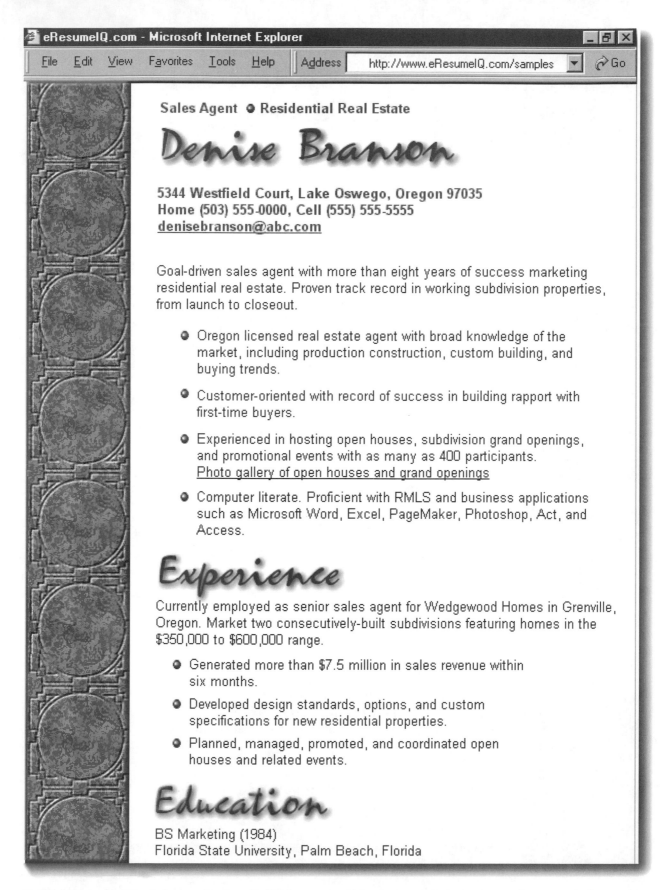

Sales Agent ● Residential Real Estate

Denise Branson

5344 Westfield Court, Lake Oswego, Oregon 97035
Home (503) 555-0000, Cell (555) 555-5555
denisebranson@abc.com

Goal-driven sales agent with more than eight years of success marketing residential real estate. Proven track record in working subdivision properties, from launch to closeout.

- Oregon licensed real estate agent with broad knowledge of the market, including production construction, custom building, and buying trends.

- Customer-oriented with record of success in building rapport with first-time buyers.

- Experienced in hosting open houses, subdivision grand openings, and promotional events with as many as 400 participants. Photo gallery of open houses and grand openings

- Computer literate. Proficient with RMLS and business applications such as Microsoft Word, Excel, PageMaker, Photoshop, Act, and Access.

Experience

Currently employed as senior sales agent for Wedgewood Homes in Grenville, Oregon. Market two consecutively-built subdivisions featuring homes in the $350,000 to $600,000 range.

- Generated more than $7.5 million in sales revenue within six months.

- Developed design standards, options, and custom specifications for new residential properties.

- Planned, managed, promoted, and coordinated open houses and related events.

Education

BS Marketing (1984)
Florida State University, Palm Beach, Florida

Gallery Resume 17 Sales professional's Web resume. Job target precedes name and contact information. Link to photo gallery of open houses provides viewers with an additional dimension of candidate's career experience. Category headings are text graphics created in Photoshop.

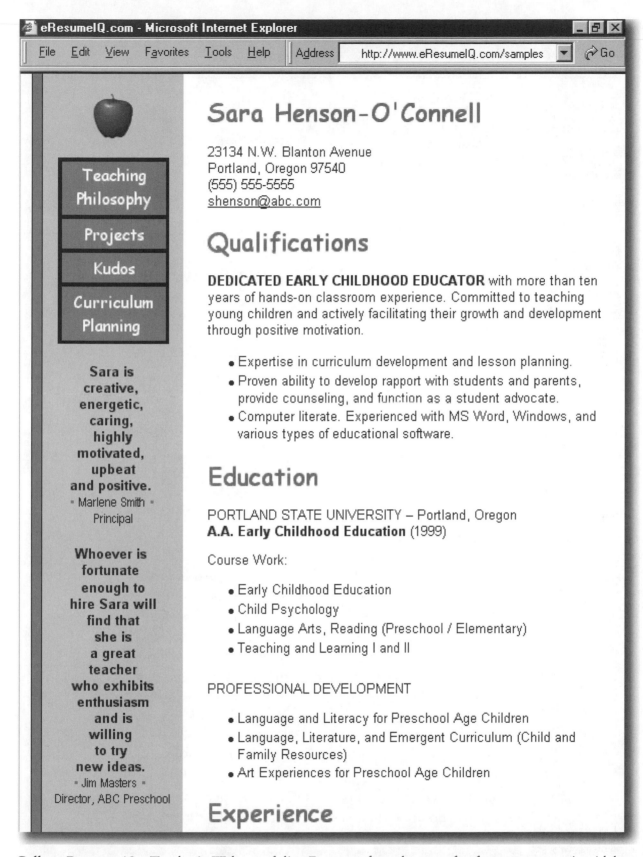

File   Edit   View   Favorites   Tools   Help   Address   http://www.eResumeIQ.com/samples   Go

Teaching
Philosophy

Projects

Kudos

Curriculum
Planning

**Sara is
creative,
energetic,
caring,
highly
motivated,
upbeat
and positive.**
▪ Marlene Smith ▪
Principal

**Whoever is
fortunate
enough to
hire Sara will
find that
she is
a great
teacher
who exhibits
enthusiasm
and is
willing
to try
new ideas.**
▪ Jim Masters ▪
Director, ABC Preschool

Sara Henson-O'Connell

23134 N.W. Blanton Avenue
Portland, Oregon 97540
(555) 555-5555
shenson@abc.com

Qualifications

DEDICATED EARLY CHILDHOOD EDUCATOR with more than ten years of hands-on classroom experience. Committed to teaching young children and actively facilitating their growth and development through positive motivation.

- Expertise in curriculum development and lesson planning.
- Proven ability to develop rapport with students and parents, provide counseling, and function as a student advocate.
- Computer literate. Experienced with MS Word, Windows, and various types of educational software.

Education

PORTLAND STATE UNIVERSITY – Portland, Oregon
A.A. Early Childhood Education (1999)

Course Work:

- Early Childhood Education
- Child Psychology
- Language Arts, Reading (Preschool / Elementary)
- Teaching and Learning I and II

PROFESSIONAL DEVELOPMENT

- Language and Literacy for Preschool Age Children
- Language, Literature, and Emergent Curriculum (Child and Family Resources)
- Art Experiences for Preschool Age Children

Experience

Gallery Resume 18   Teacher's Web portfolio. Excerpts from letters of reference appear in sidebar, giving readers an immediate glimpse of the candidate's qualifications and personality. Links to pages within the Web site include teaching philosophy, project highlights, kudos (letters of recommendation), and sample curriculum. See this e-portfolio in color at www.eResumeIQ.com.

Miri Kimball

Profile

Experience

Education

Projects

References

E-mail

4355 S.E. Grant Place
Simpson, Arkansas 65433
(555) 897-9089
trainingexpert@abc.com

TRAINING / DEVELOPMENT EXPERT with eight years' experience delivering value-added training programs in diverse business environments.

- Proven ability to develop training programs that improve productivity, customer service, and staff morale.
- Capable of developing programs that support growth, foster employee retention, and encourage leadership development.
- Computer and technology-literate. Broad knowledge of e-commerce and Web-based marketing and customer service.
- Strong project management skills and demonstrated ability to coordinate complex projects and schedules.

Experience

NUTECH ENTERTAINMENT – Simpson, Arkansas
Regional Training Manager (1996-Present)
Direct training and development functions in a 13-state region. Supervise seven store opening supervisors and oversee all store openings in region. Played a key role in facilitating and supporting company growth through staff training and development. Created and administered management development and employee training programs. Authored a 200-page training manual.

Store Opening Supervisor / Trainer (1992-1996)
Directed store openings in 14 Western states (67 locations total) and supervised up to 30 employees. Co-developed comprehensive training manual and provided training for store opening supervisors.

Gallery Resume 19 Training and development expert's Web resume. Sidebar includes a button navigational system that takes reader to points within the Web page. Email contact button is placed prominently in top right corner.

Index of Resumes

Subject Index

About the Authors

Susan Britton Whitcomb has more than sixteen years of experience as a careers writer, career coach, and specialist in resumes and portfolios for professionals. She is the author of *Resume Magic* and speaks nationally at conferences on topics such as cyber-savvy job search and resume-writing strategies. She is a Nationally Certified Resume Writer (NCRW) and Certified Career Master (CCM).

Pat Kendall is a Nationally Certified Resume Writer (NCRW) and Certified Job and Career Transition Coach (JCTC) with twenty years of experience in resume writing and job search consulting. She is the author of *Jumpstart Your Online Job Search* and president of the National Resume Writers Association.